INSIDE
CANADIAN
INTELLIGENCE

Praise for INSIDE CANADIAN INTELLIGENCE

"An engrossing and disturbing glimpse into the darker recesses of national security. Hamilton and his contributors reveal truths that should awaken a complacent country to the perils posed by growing global fanaticism."
— Alan Lofft, former editor, CBC *Current Affairs*

"Dwight Hamilton is a crisp writer whose words move like the wind. *Inside Canadian Intelligence* shows that our world doesn't work the way we would like it to. It is big, brutish, and often dangerous. And Canada's dreaming."
— Peter Carter, former senior editor, *The Financial Post*

"An overdue look at a neglected area."
— Stewart Bell, author of *Cold Terror* and *The Martyr's Oath*

"Fascinating and timely. This is a book that demanded to be written and now demands to be read. The editor and authors have done their job extremely well and we can only hope that Canadians will listen."
— Michael Coren, *Toronto Sun* columnist and broadcaster

"The authors are obviously experienced ..."
— *Intelligence Officer's Bookshelf*

A Book-of-the-Month Club Selection

"Excellent background for anyone looking to learn more about Canada's involvement in the clandestine."
— *Esprit de Corps*

INSIDE CANADIAN INTELLIGENCE

EXPOSING THE NEW REALITIES OF ESPIONAGE AND INTERNATIONAL TERRORISM

SECOND EDITION

DWIGHT HAMILTON

DUNDURN
TORONTO

Editor: Jennifer McKnight
Design: Courtney Horner
Printer: Webcom

Quotation from *A Man Called Intrepid* used with permission from Globe-Pequot Press, copyright 1976 by William Stevenson.

Library and Archives Canada Cataloguing in Publication

    Inside Canadian intelligence : exposing the new realities of espionage and international terrorism / [edited by] Dwight Hamilton. -- 2nd ed.

Includes index.
Issued also in electronic formats.
ISBN 978-1-55488-891-7

    1. Intelligence service--Canada. 2. National security--Canada. 3. Terrorism. I. Hamilton, Dwight, 1963-

JL86.I58I58 2011   327.1271   C2011-901156-5

1   2   3   4   5   15   14   13   12   11

We acknowledge the support of the **Canada Council for the Arts** and the **Ontario Arts Council** for our publishing program. We also acknowledge the financial support of the **Government of Canada** through the **Canada Book Fund** and **Livres Canada Books**, and the **Government of Ontario** through the **Ontario Book Publishing Tax Credit** and the **Ontario Media Development Corporation**.

Care has been taken to trace the ownership of copyright material used in this book. The author and the publisher welcome any information enabling them to rectify any references or credits in subsequent editions.

J. Kirk Howard, President

Printed and bound in Canada.
www.dundurn.com

Dundurn	Gazelle Book Services Limited	Dundurn
3 Church Street, Suite 500	White Cross Mills	2250 Military Road
Toronto, Ontario, Canada	High Town, Lancaster, England	Tonawanda, NY
M5E 1M2	LA1 4XS	U.S.A. 14150

*This book is dedicated to those of Canadian intelligence
services who gave their lives in the line of duty.*

"The same spirit still lives. Perhaps it only survives through struggle. It is needed now to recreate an alliance in defence of the main priorities of Western civilization. This is what we did then. This is what we can do now."

— Sir William Stephenson
A Man Called Intrepid

TABLE OF CONTENTS

PREFACE TO
THE SECOND EDITION

We were running late for the ceremony at Camp X on Remembrance Day 2010 due to the Colonel's Burmese cat. They are a bad mix with full-dress uniforms. But with eyes that appeared able to penetrate the darkness of a Rangoon night, he became impressed with the breed after an early assignment in that Far Eastern country. Shortly before, he had to pass through the famous spy school where he brushed shoulders with the likes of Sir William Stephenson (Intrepid) as well as other characters that would be best described as heroic. This was during the Second World War when many people had to do important things in a big way.

Today you don't need to fly to Burma to find a war. Before this book was originally published five years ago, Canada had not had much exposure to Islamic Jihadism, but the subsequent arrests of such terrorists in a couple of its major cities have made many Canadians realize there is a war right here at home. It is an unconventional war, and the country's intelligence and security services are some of its key participants.

I would also like to point out that any adverse mention whatsoever in this book of individual members of any political, social, ethnic, religious, or national group is not intended to insinuate that all people of that group are terrorists or their supporters. In fact, actual terrorists represent only a small minority of dedicated and often fanatical members in most such groups. It is they and their actions that are the subject of our ongoing research.

In June 2010, I was most grateful to present evidence to the Special Senate Subcommittee on Anti-terrorism, which included the Honourable Senators Hugh Segal (Chair); Serge Joyal, PC (Deputy Chair); James Cowan; George Furey; Marjory LeBreton, PC; Pierre Claude Nolin; Dennis Patterson; David Smith, PC; David Tkachuk; Mobina Jaffer; and Pamela Wallin. This new edition incorporates some of the testimony given. Again, my thanks go out to the committee for the opportunity for dialogue on this important topic. As Professor Ronald Crelinsten, a senior research associate for the Centre for Global Studies at the University of Victoria, pointed out that day, any proper counterterrorism strategy "goes well beyond an electoral horizon."

On a final note, I gratefully acknowledge the receipt of a writer's reserve grant from the Ontario Arts Council for the completion of this second edition. Please note that the information included in the main text is current to the date listed in the preface to the first edition.

Dwight Hamilton
2011

PREFACE TO
THE FIRST EDITION

You hold in your hands a remarkable book. Critics told me it would not see the light of day. Such a treatment on a subject this difficult had never been tried in the past for a reason: it was seen as too tough. After all, there are no intellectual boundaries with our topic. Intelligence. Is. Everything.

The head of the Standing Senate Committee on National Security and Defence has said that training an intelligence analyst takes about as long as training a neurosurgeon. That's about right. I was told that because of who the authors once were, the government would stop the press before the ink had dried. So why did I insist on hitting such a hard target?

First, there is an obvious and pressing need for informed debate and government action on national security *before* our city morgues begin to overflow. Canadian civilians may find the sight of scores of body bags being stacked — especially those of horribly mutilated women and children — somewhat vile. A few years before I served at CFB Toronto, a train derailment involving tanker cars with massive amounts of lethal chemicals caused the evacuation of more than two hundred thousand people from the city of Mississauga. But what is not generally known is that the emergency triggered the restriction of base personnel in faraway Downsview before the evacuation was complete. The reason given at the gate to soldiers attempting to leave? "You guys are the only ones that can deal with that many dead people," I was told they said.

On 9/11, I had to leave my desk for the trade mission of a foreign government located near the United States Consulate to help a frightened girlfriend when her offices were being evacuated. "If an unruly place like Afghanistan can result in havoc in your own streets, then you have to act," co-author John Thompson told the *Globe and Mail* the next day. When beginning work on this book I was asked by a senior member of the media, "Do you think we will be hit?"

Yes, I do.

Second, errors of fact and interpretation, disinformation, and shallow or misleading commentary are rife in the field. This should hardly come as a surprise in a world where leading civil servants routinely classify everything that they can, creating a culture of secrecy not so much for the national interest as for their own careers and self-image. In addition, academics, journalists, and others often draw conclusions from incredibly incomplete records and sometimes have an agenda of their own that is not in the best interests of the average Canadian citizen.

Some guardians of the public's right to know do it for the all right reasons and are staunch professionals, but some are driven by white-hot vocational ego, or the political dictates of their employers, or the mandates of other interested parties. And some may be just inexperienced, reckless, or undereducated. This may be hard to believe, but I know of a highly successful editor who was (and perhaps still is) utterly ignorant of secondary school-level Canadian history.

To muddy the waters for the both the competent and incompetent messengers, all governments can lie to conceal intent or information or to placate voters. And if serving spooks cannot talk about their work, the public is left in the dark.

Intelligence personnel cannot fear the dark; they often do their best work in it. The authors possess unique insight into the subject matter for the simple reason that they have been in special circumstances. Because of our experiences, we also have access to information that may not be known to others but that is considered unclassified and therefore printable. When questioned about his abilities in *A Case of Identity*, Sherlock Holmes replied, "It is my business to know things."

A word is required concerning the chapter on the Security Intelligence Review Committee (SIRC) written by *Globe and Mail* national correspondent Robert Matas. His contribution provides an invaluable editorial balance to what would have been a work written exclusively by former intelligence men. I asked for his personal assessment on the matters he covers, and that is what you will read. In addition, no one likely knows more unclassified information about the Air India case than he does, having covered it for so long for a major broadsheet. He raises some very serious questions.

In Canada, control of the security of the state ultimately rests with the prime minister. Key intelligence policy issues are given direction by him or her. The prime minister is supported by the Privy Council Office (PCO), which has a senior official whose mandate is to coordinate the activities of the intelligence sector. The office also houses the Intelligence Assessment Secretariat, whose job is to assess political, economic, strategic, and security intelligence for use by the prime minister, the Cabinet, and other senior officials. The highest forum at the officials' level for the regular consideration of intelligence matters is the Interdepartmental Committee on Security and Intelligence. It is the main body that reviews proposals and ministerial submissions. Myriad committees and working groups too numerous to list here exist to provide advice and support.

Much has been made in the wake of 9/11 of the new department calling itself Public Safety and Emergency Preparedness Canada (PSEPC). As you will read in the following chapters, a good number of our national security entities now report through PSEPC, whereas in the past their concerns were represented by the solicitor general. After examining the issue at some length, however, it is unclear that substantial improvement has been made that will translate into a safer environment for the average Canadian. Anyone hoping that the national security reporting and decision-making mechanisms are superior now should bear in mind that this is the same department that operates the routinely ridiculed federal firearms' registry, which is widely seen as ineffective from a security standpoint and negligent from a taxpayer's perspective.

The information contained herein is current to February 1, 2006. Any conclusions based upon that information are therefore time-sensitive as well. Four appendices are also included to provide the reader with a more in-depth understanding of the national security sector. Appendix II is the Security of Information Act, which replaced the long-standing Official Secrets Act (by which Rimsa, Thompson, and I are sometimes still bound). Only reading this act will provide the true scope of what is, and what is not, permissible under Canadian law in the areas that we discuss. Although it is a public document, to the best of our knowledge it has not appeared in any other book on this topic.

Appendix III is a section of the Canadian Criminal Code that outlines offences deemed by the government to be "terrorism." For the record, here are the new rules of war, some of which are a direct result of the 9/11 attacks in the United States. Unless you want to mess with the Mounties, do not try any of these at home.

Appendix IV is a copy of Bill C-409, which was a proposal for the federal government to create a formal civilian entity to engage in the field of international security intelligence gathering. This function is currently outside the mandate of the Canadian Security Intelligence Service (CSIS).

For comparison, in Great Britain, the Secret Intelligence Service (SIS, or MI-6) spies, MI-5 catches enemy spies, and Scotland Yard (which is now to be folded into a larger organization) makes arrests if required. In case you are wondering, the prefixes stand for "military intelligence," although both agencies are under civilian control and have spheres of operations that encompass more than national defence issues. The moniker is historical in nature. In the U.S., the Central Intelligence Agency (CIA) is both spy and spy catcher, and the Federal Bureau of Investigation (FBI) helps catch spies and makes the arrests. Back here at home, Bill C-409 died on the table, and it is unclear if the debate over its necessity will reach that stage again.

The authors are now members of the public. We received no government funding for, and no official co-operation, with our work. Any views expressed are solely those of the authors or quoted sources and are in no way intended to represent an official or unofficial government policy or position on any matter. Finally, no intelligence agency attempted to influence the contents of this book. Four contributors backed out of their assignments, however, which is no surprise. The authors feel that perhaps persons of interest will launch credibility/character assassination attempts or issue death threats.

Dwight Hamilton
2006

CHAPTER 1

KNOW YOUR ENEMY
by Dwight Hamilton

"The fifth most important Christian country to be targeted."

As an intelligence operative I had to read a lot of disturbing documents in my day, but none were as alarming as an al Qaeda Jihad training manual, which I recently obtained years after leaving the section at headquarters. And since the first rule I was taught by my superiors was to "know your enemy," the document is worth quoting at length here. *Declaration of Jihad Against the Country's Tyrants*, which when translated from the original Arabic runs nearly two hundred pages, will give you an idea of what the Western security services are up against in the War on Terror.

Given the document's strong religious overtones, it should be pointed out that its authors' views and prescriptions in no way represent those of the vast majority of Muslims. But Islam has very violent roots, and its initial spread in the seventh to tenth centuries was entirely through conquest. This surge eventually subsided until the eighteenth century Wahhabi revival on the Arabian Peninsula harkened back to this violent legacy.

Islam is an innately conservative social religion, and many of its societies have had considerable difficulty in adjusting to the modern world, despite the oil wealth of the Persian Gulf. In the 1970s, wealthy Saudi Wahhabists funded a militant revival that, combined with the Islamic revolution inside Iran and the Soviet invasion of Afghanistan, generated a potent Jihad (or Holy War) movement. The Jihadists have destabilized several Islamic countries, ignited many regional conflicts, and launched significant terrorist attacks against the West.

But to the authors of this version of the Jihad manual, the watershed event that defines their cause occurred on March 3, 1924, when they feel a godless West imposed itself upon Islam. Shortly before, the Grand National Assembly of Turkey had declared that country a republic and Mustafa Kemal was elected as its first president, thus bringing the Ottoman Empire to a close. On March 3 the Khalifate (an Islamic natural state wherein religious principles dictate its organization and behaviour) was abolished in Turkey and the ruling Ottoman family was deported. Sharia law offices were closed and religious education was banned from the public school system. The manual states that in the republican aftermath the new rulers "aimed at producing a wasted generation that pursued everything that is Western." But "young men who were raised by [the new rulers] woke up from their sleep and returned to Allah, regretting and repenting."

The text indicates that the Jihadists are prepared to rectify with violence what they consider to be a major historical injustice that was brought upon them. This is one of the hallmarks of a new type of terrorism. In the past, terrorist groups that targeted the West were seeking revolutionary change exclusively, but with Islamic extremists retribution is as equally important. Their actions are designed to punish target nations without distinction between their political, military, and economic sectors and without worrying about the effects on their civilian populations.

The manual reads:

> These young men realized that an Islamic government would never be established except by the bomb and rifle. Islam does not coincide or make a truce with unbelief, but rather confronts it. The confrontation that Islam calls for with these godless and apostate regimes does not know Socratic debates, Platonic ideals nor Aristotelian diplomacy. But it knows the dialogue of bullets, the ideals of assassination, bombing and destruction, and the diplomacy of the cannon and machine gun.

The young came to prepare themselves for Jihad commanded by the majestic Allah's order in the holy Koran. Islamic governments have never and will never be established through peaceful solutions and cooperative councils. They are established as they always have been: by pen and gun; by word and bullet; by tongue and teeth. The main mission for which the military organization is responsible for is the overthrow of the godless regimes and their replacement with an Islamic regime.

These opening pages raise a few points. Contrary to what some have suggested, the threat posed by al Qaeda and its affiliates will not evaporate with a few regional political changes, such as the creation of a new Palestine peacefully co-existing with Israel or the removal of American influence from Saudi Arabia. The Jihadists are aiming for a worldwide Khalifate. "Operations against enemy individuals" are considered short-term goals; the establishment of an Islamic state is the ultimate one. It is fitting that the manual's cover emblem shows a sword cutting through the globe.

Other factors that distinguish the Jihadists from older terrorist groups include their lack of regard for bad press in the world's media and a similar disregard for the fact that their sponsor states (such as Afghanistan under the Taliban) will suffer from the West's reprisals. While power vacuums like Somalia are still valuable to terrorists, al Qaeda is truly a global entity, and national support is not as crucial as it once was.

In addition, there is no room for negotiation in their Holy War. In the past, ideologies of terrorist groups that opposed the West were political, which usually meant they were either Communist or Fascist. But they never matched the suicidal zeal of al Qaeda. Communists are atheists and don't expect thirty virgins upon their arrival at the Pearly Gates. "It is necessary that all Adam's children obey," the manual states. It doesn't matter that not all of Adam's children bow toward Mecca. Al Qaeda's message is convert or die.

Turning to practical matters, the manual's first lesson outlines eight tasks for Islamic Jihadists:

1. gathering information about the enemy, the land, the installations, and the neighbours;
2. kidnapping enemy personnel, documents, secrets, and arms;
3. assassinating enemy personnel as well as foreign tourists;
4. freeing the brothers who are captured by the enemy;
5. spreading rumours and writing statements that instigate people against the enemy;
6. blasting and destroying the places of amusement, immorality, and sin; not a vital target;
7. blasting and destroying the embassies and attacking vital economic centres; and
8. blasting and destroying bridges leading into and out of the cities.

In addition to lessons on using small arms and explosives, the manual features detailed instructions on using counterfeit currency and forged documents to infiltrate target nations. Also covered are secret writing, ciphers and codes, kidnapping and assassination techniques, and guidelines for beating and killing hostages. Not much is missed; examples in espionage are given from Roman times to the present. Attention is given to finding secure apartments and hiding places in target nations as well as employing means of transportation and clandestine methods of communication. Recipes for complex poisons like ricin and abrin are given along with a simply made, toxic vegetable soup based on a bowel movement.

What characteristics should someone have to carry out al Qaeda's work? Patience and discipline are paramount for a Jihadist, as well as a bizarre peace of mind. "The member should have a calm personality that allows him to endure psychological traumas such as those involving bloodshed, murder, arrest, imprisonment and reverse psychological traumas such as killing one or all of his organization's comrades," the manual's authors write. Perhaps the Jihadists would label someone who can murder their own comrades as calm, but mental health professionals would call it psychotic.

Psychological operations or "hearts and minds" campaigns have been a vital part of warfare for ages. As the Nazis' minister of propaganda, Goebbels elevated it to a fine art. With the Jihadists, their campaign of terror fulfills ten PsyOps objectives outlined in the manual:

- Boosting Islamic morale and lowering that of the Enemy
- Preparing and training new members for future tasks
- [Inflicting on the West] a form of necessary punishment
- Mocking the regime's admiration among the population
- Removing the personalities that stand in the way of the Da'wa [Islamic call]
- Agitating [the population] regarding publicized matters
- Rejecting compliance with, and submission to, the regime's practices
- Giving legitimacy to the Jama'a [Islamic group]
- Spreading fear and terror through the regime's ranks
- Bringing new members to the Organization's ranks

But is all of this just fear mongering? There is a prevailing feeling among a complacent Canadian public that "it can't happen here." In security circles it is known as the "peaceable kingdom" theory. According to one survey conducted a year after 9/11, an alarming 77 percent of Canadians think a terrorist attack could not occur here. While that is a comforting thought, it is also false — spies are everywhere, including right next door. Here is a case that, for me anyway, hit too close to home.

In the summer of 1994 I had just moved into an apartment in Toronto on the south side of Roehampton Avenue, a couple of blocks east of Yonge Street. When she wasn't appearing in the television series *Road to Avonlea*, actress Sarah Polley also lived there at the time.

That October I got more new neighbours who would appear on television, although not in a series as wholesome as one about a little girl from Prince Edward Island. Just a few buildings to the west on the same side of the street, Ian and Laurie Lambert moved in. Ian would later attend the same classes at the same college of the same university I had. To top it off, we even had adjacent room numbers in our respective buildings: 601 and 602.

The only trouble with my new neighbours was that Ian and Laurie were actually Dmitry Olshevsky and Yelena Olshevskaya of the Russian Foreign Intelligence Service (SVR), which replaced the KGB after the collapse of the Soviet Union.

It was like a classic KGB Directorate S operation: the Lamberts were "sleepers," covert agents who can wait for years before beginning their espionage activities. The couple received short-wave radio messages from SVR headquarters in Moscow as well as from a Line N officer working under Russian diplomatic cover in Ottawa. After a lengthy CSIS investigation code-named Operation Stanley Cup, the Royal Canadian Mounted Police (RCMP) eventually arrested the pair on May 22, 1996. Afterward, the incident received widespread attention in newspapers, on television, and even in a book.

If it weren't for that publicity, however, I would have never known a thing. So if Russian spies can sleep on my street, then al Qaeda operatives certainly can too. The manual emphasizes learning Western customs: agents are to gather information from the open media and pay special attention to the opinions, comments, and jokes of common people to assimilate. Traditional male Muslim traits such as wearing beards, chewing toothpicks, and wearing long shirts with little Korans in their pockets are also discouraged in operational zones.

The Lambert case also illustrates the second major threat facing Canada's national security today: the theft of high technology through economic or corporate intelligence. Keep in mind that the Cold War had already ended by the time the "Centre" in Moscow made the decision to embark on a very risky, costly, and time-consuming "illegal resident" caper in Canada. But to the Russians, it was worth it. We are one of the most technologically advanced countries in the world. Russia, despite its espionage efforts, is still many years behind. But with folks like the Lamberts working for you, it's possible to catch up much more quickly.

International terrorists have been playing catch-up in the last decade too. Some scholars have dubbed the new threat "high/low terrorism." Attacks produce extremely high casualties from the relatively low technology used and the low cost involved in mounting operations. The idea is not that new, however — the first classified briefing I attended raised the possibility of weapons of mass destruction falling into the hands of terrorists. But today their use is imminent. "The spectre of nuclear or bio-terrorism brings to the fore major destruction of urban infrastructure and loss of life. Such a threat envisages much more devastation in life and property than most terrorist attacks have effected to date with the exception of 9/11," says retired intelligence officer David Rubin, QC. "Unfortunately, the cost of nuclear and bio-weapons is dramatically falling leaving non-state actors with potential access to them, and thereby fundamentally altering military strategy from that of state to state conflict to that of state to non-state. Nuclear or bio-weapon terrorism poses a much greater threat to civilization than the traditional terrorism carried out to date," he adds. "Democracies must devote the maximum effort to control the markets and availability of such weapons to terrorist groups. Even more so, we must develop a military strategy, in conjunction with a political and economic strategy, to minimize any local popular support toward them."

This is truly a time when war is on our doorstep. "We have incredibly close business relations with the United States, are territorially adjacent, and in the final analysis we are a democratic nation with values that are anathema to many of these groups of terrorists," Rubin says.

It is the economic aspect that may be the most important. How many shocks like 9/11 can the United States withstand without collapsing? It's estimated that the direct cost of that strike was about $40 billion and caused a 3 percent drop in GDP over two years. In contrast, it cost al Qaeda about $500,000 to plan and execute. It's well-known that Canada and the U.S. have the largest bilateral trade flow in the world, pegged at $400 billion annually. Disruption of just a few of our interdependencies would be devastating. Take the St. Lawrence Seaway, for example. Each year, ships using the Welland Canal carry grain, iron ore, coal, and steel worth $7 billion, and nearly two hundred thousand jobs depend on it. How about border crossings? When security was tightened at the

Ambassador Bridge between Detroit and Windsor in the first weeks following 9/11, tractor trailers were backed up for six miles. If enough attacks on these types of targets are successful, al Qaeda's Jihad could bankrupt America.

Do Canadians have what it will take to win the War on Terror? Those who are in uniform risking their lives on a daily basis likely know what it will take. But during my service Canada had a military over eighty thousand strong. Today we have only fifty-two thousand "peacekeepers," as post-Pearsonian politicians like to refer to them. They are the dwindling few following a proud heritage of duty. I knew that I had to measure up to the example set by my grandfather. In October of 1916, he was among the men of the Fourth Canadian Infantry Battalion tasked to take Regina Trench, a network of muddy German dugouts near the Somme River in France.

The First World War was characterized by some of the most sustained bloodshed in military history, and the day he received shrapnel in his left knee and wrist was no exception. John Marteinson writes in *We Stand On Guard*, "Entire companies were wiped out crossing No-Man's Land, others were slaughtered by torrents of machine-gun fire when they came upon the uncut barbed-wire belts. A few greatly reduced companies did get into Regina Trench, only to be driven off or in some cases overpowered by incessant German counterattacks. The day ended with over half of the attacking force dead or wounded, and with no gain at all."

Yet despite this slaughter the historian noted, "In all of these engagements, large and small, the soldiers showed remarkable determination and great personal bravery, most unreported and unrewarded." This is no surprise. Canadians were known then as the shock troops of the Triple Entente, and German military intelligence assumed an attack was imminent if Canadian units were spotted near the front.

But the War on Terror cannot be won in five or six years like the twentieth century's major conflicts. Can Canadians cope with what will likely be a thirty-year campaign? "Psychologically this presents a tremendous burden but such must be met if we are to survive. We are confronted with a life or death situation, which, although quiet today, may become significantly more devastating than at any time since 9/11.

At present, Canada's efforts against all types of terrorism have been modest. Preparation, vigilance, and anticipation must become part of our lives," says Rubin. "We must not be complacent and must treat the issue with the highest level of importance and be prepared to spend countless more in order to achieve sufficient protection. It is unrealistic for Canada's governments, public, and military to do otherwise."

It may in fact be suicidal. To use Churchill's term, we are the "soft underbelly" of the United States. So it should not come as a shock that al Qaeda has already stated we are "the fifth most important Christian country to be targeted." The U.S., Great Britain, Spain, and Australia have already been hit.

Who's next?

CHAPTER 2

FRIENDS IN HIGH PLACES
by John Thompson

*"If I have a different view of the world from many of my contemporaries,
it's because I know a lot more about it than they do."*

The first time I visited Cheyenne Mountain in Colorado, Canadian
and American personnel managing the key operations centre for the
North American Aerospace Defence Command (NORAD) were busy
tracking a Soviet Bear bomber by radar as it passed down the east coast
of the U.S. and watching the Iraqis and Iranians fire short-range ballistic
missiles at each other through the take from their satellites. The second
time, the same mixed crew was using OHTB radar to track an illicit drug
flight off the west coast of North America — one that probably imagined
it was well out of radar range.

Fortunately, I visited the mountain both times as a civilian. While
in the military, there was lots of sensitive material coming over my
desk that had been generated by our allies and was being shared with
us. These included clandestine photos of emerging Soviet helicopter
designs, an analysis of North Korea's extensive belt of fortified
marshalling jump-off points for an invasion of the South, and a candid
review of the performance of France's Exocet anti-ship missiles in the
Falklands War. This last was marked for "AUS/CAN/UK/US EYES
ONLY" — an example of the close co-operation that occurs between
what some of our other allies refer to, half jokingly, as the "Anglo-
Saxon Mafia."

If I have a different view of the world from many of my contemporaries, it's because I know a lot more about it than they do. Awareness of military realities is rare in Canada, particularly in our government. Worse still, too many Canadians entertain some notions of "soft power" or a supposed legacy as peacekeepers to give much thought as to why a sovereign nation must retain arms. To understand the role our military plays in developing intelligence for Canada, a review of Defence Policy 101 might be useful.

First, the world is a dangerous place. For those who forget, in the last century Canadian military personnel fought in the Boer War, the First and Second World Wars, Korea, the 1991 Gulf War, and the Kosovo air campaign. Canadian troops were often actively engaged in combat on peacekeeping missions, particularly in Cyprus, the Congo, and Bosnia and Croatia, while our personnel were often killed by hostile actions elsewhere. The many exertions required in the Cold War cannot be dismissed, nor can our major deployments of troops for internal security in 1970 and 1990 during the Front de libération du Québec (FLQ) and Oka crises. In this century, Canada is confronted with the War on Terror, and our troops were deployed to Afghanistan soon after 9/11. Predictions of "peace in our time" are as useful as the similar mad optimism about a stable international order in the years before both world wars.

Second, Canada is huge, owning the second-largest mass of territory on earth, but we have a small population mostly stretched out in a long, narrow, settled strip on our southern edge. This dispersal means significant hindrances in time and distance confront us whenever we try to concentrate resources for any purpose — a fact realized on many occasions during the violent episodes of our history in the eighteenth and nineteenth centuries, and one that underscored the importance of building our national railway in the 1880s.

Third, on our spherical world, the shortest distance between two points is frequently not a straight line but a curve, and a number of the shortest curves between, oh, China and Russia and the U.S. travel straight over Canada. Forget the usual Mercator projection, try looking at a globe from different angles sometime.

Because of this, Canada has always needed help to guarantee our sovereignty and protect our interests. Our first partner was Great Britain, followed by the U.S. after the Ogdensburg Agreement. Before 1940,

Britain was one of the strongest nations in the world and had the most powerful navy afloat. But since then the U.S. has been in pole position. To avoid the appearance of total dependence on these nations, we used to furnish a disproportionate contribution to major endeavours, as in both world wars, but also actively encouraged the development of a larger defence network, such as the North Atlantic Treaty Organization (NATO). Previously, neither the British nor the Americans expected much of us, but Uncle Sam is growing tired of someone whose defence spending is disproportionately light compared to that of his other friends.

Reliance on allies, particularly our necessary partnership with a major power, has several drawbacks. Regarding intelligence, they don't need to tell us everything and seldom do so. Security is, like many other things, about national self-interest, and pure altruism is not a reliable commodity between nations. So if we want to find out what is really going in some particular spheres of activity, we need to be involved there. In short, if you want to sit in on a particular game, you have to put some chips on the table.

Militaries thrive on intelligence. Besides the political intelligence that everyone wants, they need technical intelligence, data on the capabilities and organization of other militaries, detailed knowledge of local conditions, and much else. The Department of National Defence (DND) has to keep the government informed, and Cabinet is supposed to be briefed at least once a week. The Canadian Forces are also partnered with other government agencies and police forces in the War on Terror and for other problems, particularly in emergency preparedness and with the new Integrated National Security Enforcement Teams (INSETS).

The Canadian Forces' appetite for information is enormous and continuous, and like so much else with our military, we usually can't meet this need with our own resources. Canada is tied into collective defence with the U.S. and our other allies through hundreds of treaties and agreements. With the Americans alone we have some 190 in force as of the time of this writing, fifty-eight of which have a direct bearing on our defence relationships with them, including some of the world's longest-standing peace treaties, and twenty-seven of which have mixed military/civilian applications. We also have hundreds more informal ties, contracts, and agreements between components of both militaries.

Canada's security relationships are also expressed through NATO, wherein we have dozens more agreements in force, and through the American, British, Canadian, Australian, and New Zealand Armies' Program (ABCA), which has led to agreements on standardization of practices and equipment and the sharing of intelligence. Our policy is also affected by our participation in the United Nations, the Organization of American States and its Inter-American Defense Board, the Commonwealth, and the Francophonie. All of these provide forums for security co-operation and for the flow of information from other sources. Some of these organizations generate intelligence and distribute it among their member states. We receive extensive intelligence from NATO and from ABCA, and we share much of what is developed by the Canadian military with them. Less material comes from the other associations.

Some agreements are, if not exactly secret, at least seldom mentioned in any public forum. The particulars of many others have been left out of public documents altogether. Canada's involvement in research in underwater acoustics, electronic warfare, and chemical and biological defence are referred to in various places, but the specific details would not be made available outside of forums where the Security of Information Act could apply (see Appendix II). Yet all of these programs generate information that is of use to our military and to our Cabinet — even if it seldom listens to the details, or understands them.

When our government declines to get involved in a particular program, such as the American ballistic missile defence or Northern Command (NORTHCOM), the U.S. military headquarters for coordinating continental defence, we run the risk of losing access to information as well as the chance to participate in matters of importance for our own protection. As for NORTHCOM, the Americans understood that our participation would be vital and let in Canadian liaison officers and observers, some of whom were empowered to commit us to planning, joint operations, intelligence, and joint logistics arrangements anyway. After the rejection of participation in missile defence by the previous Liberal government, it remains to be seen if the Americans will be quite so generous about future access to information in this field.

The North American Air Defense Command was established in 1958 and has been a centrepiece of Canada's security arrangements ever since. Renamed the North American Aerospace Defense Command in 1981, NORAD is headquartered in Colorado and is charged with aerospace defence and control of North American airspace. Although first configured to provide integrated air defence against Soviet bombers, it also provides early warning of missile launches and monitors traffic in space, keeping track of tens of thousands of objects in orbit so that space shuttles and the International Space Station can safely operate. NORAD also looks out for illicit drug flights and other unauthorized intrusions or departures from flight plans in North American airspace.

Canadians have always occupied a number of its key positions, including some within Cheyenne Mountain itself. The senior watch officer during 9/11 was a Canadian, and our air force officers have always either chaired or been the vice-chair of the threat assessment team that would have determined whether North America was being attacked with ballistic missiles. Throughout much of the Cold War, part of the "finger on the button" was Canadian, a degree of involvement in American strategic response afforded to no other ally.

NORAD receives data from several radar chains, including the formidable OHTB radar that can monitor flights hundreds of kilometres away from the shores of the continent. Vital information, particularly on ballistic missile launches anywhere in the world, first comes into NORAD via the feed from infrared satellites parked in geosynchronous orbit. These automatically spot the heat plume of any launched ballistic missile and can track it through the boost stage, giving instant data on its trajectory, bearing, and range. Participation within the organization has significantly enhanced Canada's security for years, giving us the opportunity to see everything going on around the edges of our airspace and letting us automatically know about ballistic missile tests and attacks around the world in real time.

With the government's refusal to participate in ballistic missile defence, despite it now being a high priority for all of NATO, not just the Americans, it remains to be seen whether this latter function will remain with NORAD or whether the U.S. will seek to create an American-only anti–ballistic missile function without Canadian eyes and ears present.

To complement the organization, Airborne Warning and Air Control Systems aircraft (AWACS) are deployed, which are essentially flying battle management centres for fighter aircraft that mount powerful radars. When up about ten thousand metres in the air they can see considerably further than equivalent radar embedded on a hilltop; they were originally designed to handle the massive air battles that would have resulted from a Soviet invasion of Western Europe. The E-3 family of American-designed AWACS that were built around the old Boeing 707s are formidable assets, and a fleet of eighteen was purchased for NATO, while others were earmarked for the air defence of North America. Our personnel serve on both fleets.

Because AWACS see for long distances, they tend to be sent off to cover other problem areas in the post–Cold War environment. NATO's fleet has been sent at various times to cover the Balkans, northern Iraq, north-western Iran, airspace over Libya's coast, and the frontier between NATO nations and the Russian hegemony. The planes develop intelligence on the performance of aircraft, radar frequencies and surface-to-air missile batteries, as well as the general condition of potentially hostile air forces. AWACS in American service have been active in much of the world, and when assigned to NATO they also cover the Caribbean airspace to the south of the U.S., including Cuba. Much of the information these two fleets amass is shared with Canada.

Notwithstanding the pictures of the Royal Navy's Lord Nelson and its long history in our navy's wardrooms, the real heritage of Canada's ships and sailors comes from almost a century of sub-hunting. Between the U-boat peril of both world wars and the frequent appearance of Soviet submarines off our coasts during the Cold War, the Canadian Navy has more experience hunting submarines with surface ships than almost any other. It is no accident that our underwater acoustic technologies are some of the most advanced in the world.

But submarines are meant to be stealth weapons, and even our two closest allies tend to be very guarded about the full extent of their technology and operations, especially with respect to those armed with nuclear-tipped ballistic missiles. It is usually in the best interests of the American and Royal navies to share information with us about submarines from non-NATO/allied members, but the fullest disclosure comes only when they know that we have ears in the water too. This is one of the unmentioned reasons why it is important for the Canadian Navy to operate submarines of its own.

In the 1950s, the U.S. began to develop a vast network of underwater microphones on cables called the SOSUS Array. These were deployed throughout many of the world's oceans with bases on land to receive the take from the arrays. One was in Argentia, Newfoundland. The system functioned as a strategic "burglar alarm" for Soviet submarines as they entered the Atlantic, and it often reliably guided naval assets to areas where Soviet subs were lurking. It was of immense strategic value, but the U.S. manned the system itself and shared data with Canada and other allies only when it was necessary.

Argentia was highly secure and the object of several very specific agreements between the Americans and ourselves. It also was a prime target for Soviet spies, and one was arrested and convicted following a U.S. sting operation. Stephen Joseph Ratkai was a Canadian short-order cook who made frequent trips back to Hungary; he was used by the Soviets to react to the dangling bait of a seemingly disaffected U.S. Navy officer from Argentia. He was subsequently arrested by Canadian authorities, convicted, and sentenced to nine years' imprisonment by the Newfoundland Superior Court.

SOSUS became less useful as the last generation of Soviet submarines came on line in the 1980s, but it is now paying dividends to civilian oceanographers and marine biologists who can use some of the arrays to listen to marine life. In its place is the new SURTASS system, one that has joint Canadian and American involvement. This passive system is being fitted to Canadian and U.S. warships now, but the new low-frequency active version has ecologists in an uproar over allegations that its powerful acoustic transmissions can harm marine life. In any event, the ships are supposed to be crewed by civilians. In 1994, Canada and the U.S. agreed on the establishment of a new jointly staffed undersea surveillance facility in Halifax. Details are unavailable as the memorandum of understanding is quite unspecific, but this presumably gives Canada greater access to intelligence about submarine traffic in its waters than ever before.

A major part of the American strategic deterrent also rests with the Trident missile submarines operating out of Puget Sound, Washington, which must reach their hidden patrol regions out in the great reaches of the Pacific via the Juan de Fuca Strait off Victoria, British Columbia. While the U.S. Navy is especially guarded about the movements of these subs, it is not unknown for elements of our Pacific fleet to be keeping a presence off the ends of the straits every now and then, particularly if some Russian- or Chinese-flagged vessel is lingering in the area with no clear purpose.

As is the case with the army and air force, operational deployments by the navy also result in the receipt of intelligence generated by allied forces. Canadian warships have been involved in co-operative exercises with allied navies and in the Standing Force Atlantic (SFATLANT) for decades. Additionally, the U.S. Navy admires Canada's new patrol frigates, particularly for their strong anti-submarine warfare capabilities; and has often asked for one to accompany various task forces and carrier groups in far-off waters. The deployment of Canadian warships into the Indian Ocean and Persian Gulf with the War on Terror has also resulted in the receipt and generation of specific intelligence about the region as well as about al Qaeda.

Sailors and airmen tend to operate in an environment that is absolutely dominated by advanced technology and strategic concerns. Soldiers tend to have more prosaic concerns: What are the roads like? How bad is the weather on average? If we go there, who might shoot at us, and with what?

Most headquarters with any grouping over company size include a combat-arms officer who has been assigned an intelligence function, if not a cell of trained and dedicated military intelligence personnel. They play vital roles in the planning and deployment of any force, but especially in robust humanitarian operations, nation building, armed interventions, and other potentially dangerous functions that most Canadians think of as "peacekeeping."

Throughout the Cold War, the major function of posted intelligence personnel within our army was working on Soviet/Warsaw Pact orders of battle and familiarization with their equipment, tactics, and doctrines. Their tasks have become far more varied since then. Operations in the former Yugoslavia, Somalia, Rwanda, and Afghanistan have demanded the ability to rapidly develop accurate knowledge on all local factions and their capabilities and probable intentions, as well as to continually keep that knowledge current. This is one of the few areas within the army where close attention has been paid to providing new resources and capabilities. The new Coyote reconnaissance vehicles, run by armoured corps troops, and the growing unmanned drone inventory are therefore very necessary.

In recent years, the U.S. Marines, with some consultation with the Canadian military, started developing a new doctrine for handling themselves in what is characterized as a three-block war. In one block troops engage in humanitarian relief, in the next they work on restoring civil authority, and in the third they engage in deadly combat with local actors. The same activities can be taking place in the same community concurrently, and the group that you feed or support one hour might be shooting at you the next. Environments like these do exist, and various Western armies, including Canada's, have had to confront them. The demand for accurate and timely intelligence is overwhelming under these circumstances.

Another phrase that the Marines are looking at again is "small wars," describing complex situations where a military finds itself confronting non-military problems and threats. The small war doesn't seem to be much in the lexicography of the Canadian Army, but the British and French recognize the term, having used it often in the nineteenth century to describe the same sort of things that modern peacekeepers often do. In these, the gathering of intelligence is critical.

In contrast to naval and air environments, an army relies much more heavily on the human aspects of operations. Individual leadership and peer respect, while important everywhere in the military, are vital in this environment, and army units tend to place particular value on human contact and social relations for unit cohesion and in the development of intelligence.

Direct liaison, particularly with local figures and militia leaders, is extremely valuable when an army is deployed to trouble spots, and most commanders value officers and NCOs who have a talent for this. One cultural problem that led to trouble for some officers in the former Yugoslavia was that many local people, particularly the Serbs, seldom discussed anything unless it was over several drinks. Some Canadian units then assigned designated drinkers to handle negotiations and develop local contacts. This happened to be in violation of very strict (and one might argue anal-retentive) anti-alcohol policies from National Defence Headquarters in far-off Ottawa.

Canada participates in numerous military exchange programs wherein personnel might be slotted into positions with allied forces that are similar to the ones they usually hold. A fighter pilot might be dropped into a Luftwaffe or Royal Air Force squadron to see how they do things and to carry back new insights and ideas to their own branch of service. The army places even more value on this, particularly since there are so many capabilities in allied army and marine units that Canada has never developed or has lost.

Canadian army officers on exchange fought in U.S. and British units in the first Gulf War, and again in the 2003 invasion of Iraq. While our personnel were involved in the liberation of Afghanistan, a few participated while on exchange to American units. At least one Canadian was also active with British troops who recaptured the Falkland Islands in 1982. These personnel brought back valuable experiences and considerable insight into the actual conduct of operations and the reality of local conditions.

The Canadian military is somewhat over-officered, having had at several times in recent years more captains than corporals on call. One way to keep part of the surplus actively employed is to send them to overseas headquarters with NATO, on peacekeeping and similar missions, or to the U.S. military. Personnel contributions to various HQs are usually subject to agreed limits, but the officers sent to NORAD in Colorado, SFATLANT in Norfolk, NATO in Brussels, CENTCOM in Florida, and a host of other places have undertaken valuable work and bring back considerable experience that we would not otherwise have accessed.

Special operations forces per se first appeared in the Second World War, usually as elite troops for raiding and reconnaissance under difficult circumstances. Canada made an early joint entry into this field by participating in the 1st Special Service Force with the U.S., the famed "Devils' Brigade." As a new component in the war, special operations forces were often misused, considered elite troops for conventional battlefield tasks, and the Devils' Brigade took heavy casualties before being broken up. Oddly, America's "Green Berets" see themselves as directly descended from this unit, while the Canadian survivors were lumped back in with the 1st Canadian Parachute Battalion.

Since the Second World War, many of the forces that appeared in other nations continued to find new roles, particularly in the small wars that attended the breakup of the British and French colonial systems. The British Special Air Service (SAS) and Royal Marine Commandos hunted guerrillas in Malaysia and Borneo, while the Green Berets trained anti-guerrilla forces from Greece to Vietnam. At other times, special operations forces were tasked with creating guerrillas to bedevil other countries.

Given the need to inhibit direct confrontations between the nuclear-armed superpowers, some special operations forces also became increasingly tasked with discreet reconnaissance tasks. This was particularly true of the Soviet Spetsnaz (special operations forces). When terrorism lurched back into view in the 1960s and 1970s, many countries looked to these troops to provide a response to aircraft hijackings and hostage incidents. Some of them also developed expertise in protecting VIPs and critical personnel from assassination.

Special operations forces often operate at some place where intelligence, strategy, psychological warfare, and clandestine soldiering all come together. But Canada sat aside from most of this evolution as the United States, Australia, Britain, France, Germany, and even tiny New Zealand developed their own capabilities during the Cold War.

The usual entry route is to first belong to an elite conventional unit such as a parachute regiment or the U.S. Army Rangers. But the world's most celebrated unit, the SAS, is willing to attempt to train any volunteer who survives its ferocious selection course. During this time, it was not unknown for particularly gifted Canadians to occasionally get a shot at an exchange tour with such units of other armies, and the Canadian Airborne Regiment occasionally rubbed elbows with the Green Berets and the SAS on training exercises. The Americans, British, and French also used to sometimes give regular Canadian infantry, who were widely seen for many years as being of exceptional quality, slots on their elite training courses.

At its heart, their world is a strange one and initiates go to odd places and do unusual things, many of which are directly connected to the intelligence world. Examples include clandestinely crossing into a hostile country to bring out a dissident or spy, lying for days in a covert observation post in Beirut in the trunk of a derelict car, or doing some quasi-anonymous demolition work. Canadian troops were left out of this world, although they could hear some of the quietly told stories from time to time. Thankfully, this has changed with the creation of Joint Task Force 2 (JTF-2), Canada's first foray into the special operations world. JTF-2 has been active, from painting targets in the former Yugoslavia with lasers for smart bombs to monitoring violent Aboriginal militants to fighting against al Qaeda in Afghanistan. They also have provided armed escorts for Canadian commanders and other figures in many trouble spots and allegedly have undertaken covert reconnaissance for the government.

If Canada is to continue to be truly aware of what is going on in the world, it needs to continue to send its military out to participate in alliance activities. This is something it can only do if it has capable units and trained personnel available to demonstrate our commitment to collective security. Fighter controllers need to work with real fighter squadrons before they can be slotted into AWACS aircraft. We need capable warships and submarines to buy access to the maritime world and to hear what goes on underneath the surface of our own coastal waters. Our army needs to be able to sustain viable combat-ready formations for deployment elsewhere.

It has been argued that a military is like an insurance policy — pay your premiums and you'll have the help you need when in trouble. Miss payments or look for a cheap policy and you'll get what you deserve. But a military is also like an entertainment package that allows access to Internet sites and pay-per-view channels that are invaluable. You can't learn what's there unless you keep your payments up. Otherwise, it will be too late.

CHAPTER 3

SPY CATCHERS
by Kostas Rimsa

"On three separate occasions in a ten-year period, I was offered the chance to buy or broker nuclear materials ..."

It was a cold evening in Vilnius in fall 1991. I sat in a dark blue Lada with one hand on an AKSU automatic, conducting a protective surveillance with a group of Lithuanian Secret Service watchers that I had just finished training. A warning had been received threatening to hit the new U.S. Embassy and living annex with a terrorist rocket-propelled grenade attack. The Counter Assault Team, which included snipers, was off on another operation. No one else was available to do the job properly. Fleetingly, I mused about the Canadian Security Intelligence Service and its watchers.

"The watchers" is the old nickname for the civilian surveillance operatives that worked for the RCMP Security Service. The original organization came into being back in 1955, and by the end of the 1950s units were located in all major Canadian cities. It still exists today. The mission of the branch is to support the surveillance of suspects or targets through physical surveillance by foot, by vehicle, or from a fixed location, in either rural or urban terrain. These operatives are true human intelligence (HUMINT) sources of CSIS. Highly skilled in counter-surveillance, the targets are often suspected terrorists or foreign intelligence service operatives conducting economic, scientific, or technological espionage. No fewer than three cars are used with two operatives in each, and six cars with three people in each is often the norm. The number is determined by the counter-surveillance ability of the target, their consequence, and, most importantly, the availability of personnel and material. In fact, this number is not outrageous depending on the situation.

As long ago as 1999, Canada's top intelligence official bluntly warned Parliament that his service was investigating fifty terrorist organizations and about 350 individuals, numbers that no doubt have grown since then. The report was based on a confidential CSIS document, *Exploitation of Canada's Immigration System: An Overview of Security Intelligence Concerns.* Another CSIS report released in 2004 said that terrorism in Canada was quickly evolving from fundraising "to actually planning and preparing terrorist acts from Canadian territory."

To better perceive the current situation in CSIS, you must be aware that the agency's budget was cut, along with that of every other government department, by about 20 percent in the ten years prior to 9/11. CSIS's staffing fell to 2,200 from an estimated high of 2,700. If it had not been for 9/11, the agency would have been emasculated in the shadows, as were the Canadian Forces.

CSIS was created by an act of Parliament in 1984. The act established it as a domestic service fulfilling a purely defensive role as a counterintelligence agency investigating threats to Canada's national security. CSIS also provides security assessments to all federal departments and agencies, with the exception of the RCMP and some Department of National Defence personnel. The agency also provides advance warning to government departments and agencies about activities that may constitute threats. Other government departments and agencies have the responsibility to take direct action to counter them. CSIS does not have law enforcement powers; only police do.

The Counter Intelligence Branch monitors threats stemming from the espionage activities of other national governments' intelligence operations. It is divided into the Economic Security and Information, Security Information Operations, Trans-national Crime, and Foreign Influenced Activity sections.

In the past few years, CSIS has assigned more of its resources to investigate the activities of foreign governments conducting economic espionage here. The efforts of foreign governments to appropriate proprietary information and technology covertly are a growing challenge. And traditional espionage and foreign interference continue to take place in Canada: many apprehended agents in the past have been declared personae non grata without fanfare. The Branch provides the government with advice about emerging threats of serious violence that could affect national security and also conducts investigations into terrorist links of individuals and organizations.

The Counter Intelligence Branch also provides security screening to all federal government departments (with the exception of the RCMP and DND, which conduct their own). Checks are made on applicants for positions requiring clearance and for immigration and citizenship. Much of the increased budget of subsequent years has been earmarked for both government and immigration screening programs. CSIS's checks fall into three main program categories: Government Screening, Foreign Screening, and Immigration and Citizenship Screening. A fourth program, Front End Screening, has recently been added that attempts to vet select refugees as soon as possible. Foreign Screening is conducted at the request of allied governments.

There are three main levels of clearance as defined by the government's security policy: Confidential, Secret, and Top Secret. The level required is determined by the need for access to classified information or assets in the performance of duties associated with an individual's employment. The lower two levels are done by computer.

CSIS created the Counter Proliferation Branch in July 2002, bringing together proliferation-related investigations that the Counter Terrorism and Counter Intelligence branches handle. CSIS has also more resources investigating the activities of foreign governments that try to procure Canadian technology that can be used for the development of weapons of mass destruction. Canada sells its CANDU nuclear reactors around the world and is a leading nation in nuclear technology.

On three separate occasions in a ten-year period, I was offered the chance to buy or broker nuclear materials from the former Soviet Union. All of the different types offered could have been used to manufacture a "dirty bomb." Sometimes the offers are scams and sometimes part of entrapment schemes by the authorities that would allow them to remove you from the economic or political scene. The authorities or others may also then be in a position to blackmail you. As many overseas countries do not have anti-entrapment laws, as do Canada and the U.S., it is perfectly legal to set you up with an illegal offer of business and then jail you. By the way, the last offer for nuclear material was made to me just days before 9/11.

The Research, Analysis and Production Branch underwent a major reorganization in 1996–97 to improve the coordination of intelligence production with the Privy Council Office's Intelligence Assessment Secretariat. It also enhances the intelligence support to the main consumers of its product inside CSIS including the operational desks, the executive, security liaison officers, and other sections. This branch adopted a new structure with four divisions: Counter Intelligence, Foreign Intelligence, Counter-terrorism, and Distribution (which prepares documents such as the public annual report and the classified annual report to the Solicitor General).

Only in January 2004 did the government establish the National Risk Assessment Centre, which manages and coordinates the national and international watch lists on an around-the-clock basis. It acts as a focal point and an interface between offices at the international, national, and local levels. The centre has increased Canada's ability to detect and interdict the movement of high-risk people and goods by analyzing information and sharing it with front-line staff and international partners.

CSIS co-operates with Canadian law enforcement agencies and intelligence units of all federal departments, as well as with all levels of local and provincial government. It also maintains roughly 250 co-operative relationships with more than 125 countries. The CSIS Act prevents the agency from confirming or denying the existence of specific operations. To disclose would impede its investigative capabilities and harm national security. But compared to other foreign intelligence agencies, it is anything but secretive. CSIS personnel are accountable to the director, who in turn reports to the solicitor general, who in turn reports to the head of Public Safety and Emergency Preparedness Canada.

All methods of investigation used by CSIS are subject to several levels of approval before they are deployed. Intrusive methods such as electronic surveillance, mail opening, and covert searches all require a warrant issued by a judge of the federal court of Canada. The Security Intelligence Review Committee, an independent agency, is responsible for overseeing CSIS.

The initial manpower for CSIS when it was first created came from the RCMP Security Service, with limited recruitment of civilians and soldiers. Many of the Security Service personnel either retired over the next five years or returned to the RCMP. Following this, recruitment concentrated on members of local or provincial civilian police, eventually returning to a more civilian base. As the Public Service imposed its mentality and bureaucratic procedures, the selection of new recruits is said to have suffered. Training, which is conducted internally, also became civilian in its nature. Unlike the Mounties, CSIS agents do not carry guns under most circumstances. I would categorize the individuals in CSIS into three groups: those who still remain from the old days, those who were trained in the field by the "old boys," and the public servants. To many of those selected and only partially indoctrinated, being an Intelligence Officer (IO) has become just another job, but with the limited mystique of being a "spy"; they are not as regimented as the members of the military and of the paramilitary RCMP. Many inside and outside question the selection and, more importantly, the training and indoctrination of CSIS personnel. Here, the opinions of the British as well as the different American agencies could play a vital role in raising morale and enhancing the abilities of its membership.

Before I raise the next point I should explain that I am a Québécois. My family has inter-married with the French of Quebec. Learning a second language is a valuable asset in intelligence. It is almost mandatory to speak more than one language, especially in a country like Canada. I am fluent in two languages and can get along in several others, including French. When operating overseas, if I could not speak the language, I travelled with an interpreter. But the following are some concerns of many CSIS personnel, not just my own opinions.

The first problem lies in getting the most competent people into positions of authority. This has not been happening in our federal government because of its French language policy. Being best doesn't matter if you don't speak French. The second problem is that we are a land of immigrants, and it is not uncommon for many who become Canadian citizens to speak several languages. My father was fluent in eight. The rub is that French is not one of the languages often spoken by our new immigrants. Canadian language policy is grossly unfair, considering that 40 percent of Canada's citizens are new immigrants or from immigrant families. What will the government do in about ten years when there will be more Chinese than French speakers here? I can see a World Court ruling being required. Unfortunately, it seems more important to speak French in CSIS than to speak the language of the targeted enemy and the community they hide in.

Then there's the problem of just numbers. The KGB once had more than eighty operatives conducting foot surveillance on one target in the old town of a certain Baltic city. Surveillance must often be active 24/7. On a high-threat target the personnel and equipment required might be eighteen cars and fifty-four operatives on three shifts of eight hours for a five-day period. The cost involved in following only one target can be enormous. If you have thirty suspects in a given city with ties to a terrorist organization, you would require six to eighteen operatives for each. A total of 180 would be a minimum, but you would really want 540 to do a good job. The realities for CSIS are different from what should be.

The KGB trained their top surveillance operatives for eleven weeks, and our regimen is even more comprehensive. This gives you a glimmer of perspective on the situation here with fifty known terrorist organizations and 350 terrorist-associated individuals. This is in addition to certain foreign embassies, in which up to 30 percent of the staff are currently espionage agents. There are also the "illegals" and the "sleepers," who sometimes inadvertently expose themselves. And what about the Canadians or foreign nationals who are providing these operatives with information? The need for more trained watchers is evident. In addition, a reserve should be developed. These could be former watchers utilized on a part-time or as needed basis. Another solution would be to pass on certain duties to specially vetted contracted private investigation companies that would handle lower-end details.

Within CSIS, the Intelligence Officer category is responsible for the collection, analysis, and production of intelligence. IOs conduct both overt and covert operations and can be compared to a police officer or private investigator. They collect information (which when processed becomes intelligence) regarding possible offences regarding national security, verify accusations, assist in carrying out searches, and testify in court. One of the key functions of an IO in counter-terrorism investigations is conducting community interviews. These allow residents to voice their opinions and concerns and also aid CSIS with threat assessments against domestic extremist groups, international terrorists, and fronts. They are also conducted in regards to security screening and espionage activity, political or economic. Such interviews are easier if the IO is of the same ethnic group, or a related group, as the community or if he or she speaks its language. Trust is the true basis of the collection of information from anyone. To conduct such interviews and weed out the terrorists and spies that live among us, an IO must be also well-schooled and practised in interviewing techniques, and Kinesic lie detection.

Proper application of the techniques learned takes several years, and junior IOs spend time in the company of a senior IO who shows them how to apply what they have learned. IOs often use the buddy system during interviews and much of the tradecraft taught requires two to participate. This gives an insight into the manpower required to conduct thousands of interviews or assessments each year.

Only someone with no understanding of CSIS would claim that CSIS operates with prejudice and uses profiling in a negative sense. If this were the case, there would be no information forthcoming from the Canadian ethnic communities on which CSIS depends. In short, the lifeblood of CSIS would be drained. It must be also understood that its investigations are primarily focused on gathering information, not collecting evidence. This fact still does not appear to be understood by the media or the public. Only if the results of an investigation show that an offence has been committed does the IO in charge take the necessary legal steps to involve the RCMP. The agency is a defensive, domestic counter-intelligence service restricted to investigating threats to its country's national security. It is not a foreign intelligence service that conducts offensive operations for its government in other countries.

Because it takes time to develop IOs, it is important that the strategic direction of collection be identified several years in advance before any given threat materializes, in order to recruit, train, and develop the required personnel. But our political leaders prefer to wait until the threat actually appears, and by then it is too late to counter it. Two examples of this would be the rise of Russian organized crime in Canada and the new wave of terrorism. Both were identified early on by CSIS and were reported to the government. No money to counter them was immediately allotted, though, and by the time it was, it was too little to curtail the first threat. It is quite questionable whether enough money is being allocated to the threat of terrorism.

CSIS prepares reports, studies, and briefs on various issues for policy-makers. Analysis occurs at the operational and strategic levels. Operational analysis combines intelligence gathered by the service with information from other sources. The final product gives context to or further explains the significance of the original information. Strategic analysis aims to create in-depth and policy-relevant intelligence assessments. Failure occurs any time the chain is broken, and this can happen during the intelligence collection or analysis phases. Important information may be readily available, but it is useless without successful interpretation and analysis. Possible causes include unintelligent analysis, misinterpretation, and preconceived conclusions. Because of CSIS's procedures, however, failure is rare. The true problem lies not with the analysts but with those who receive their reports.

All intelligence analysts are taught to be cold and unemotional and to restrain any prejudice they may have in order to provide an objective analysis of any given threat or situation. To assist analysts in remaining objective, CSIS uses a series of standard operating procedures (SOPs). The final product is reviewed by a series of more senior analysts. It is important to know that there are different types of analysts. Some work on academic projects utilizing unclassified and/or classified material, producing strategic analysis. Others assist in the direction of field staff, producing products that are operational or tactical. In both cases, the preferred analyst will have practical field experience.

In operational analysis, direction comes in the form of recommendations for information required, which will be collected by investigators. An analyst with field experience knows with what difficulty and by what means the required information will be obtained and will also have insight into the material that a purely academic analyst will not. Both insight and academic knowledge are required — if you have one without the other, you are not complete. To train in the formats and techniques required by SOPs takes only a few weeks, but to gain insight takes many years. Unfortunately, the combination of academic training and experienced insight is disappearing in the system. If any mistakes occur on the analysis side, it will be because of this.

Regional Analysts are required to have at least five years' experience in the research and analysis of socio-political, economic, and foreign policy developments, as well as a sound cultural understanding of regions such as Asia, the Middle East, or Russia. Knowledge based on travel throughout the area is considered desirable; in fact, first-hand knowledge should be realized to be vital. In some countries showing a fist is a sign of support and not anger, just as shooting into the air is an act of celebration and not warning. It is important to know such details. As important are the differences in their decision-making processes when compared to ours.

To become a CSIS analyst you need a minimum of a Master's degree in an applicable field, with five years of related experience. The candidate must have demonstrated expertise in research and analysis of the field, preferably accompanied by an extensive publication record. In short, candidates for analyst positions are purely academics. But a mix of backgrounds is a vital thing at the strategic level, and at the operational level pure academics are a hindrance. All analysts should be selected from IOs at this level: With fifteen to twenty years of cross-training in different areas, and having dealt with a multitude of ethnic communities, they could only be outdone by those who have served as true spies involved in overseas operations.

What keeps the future in focus for CSIS are the National Threat Intelligence Estimates, which reflect the emerging dangers for the next fifteen years. Unfortunately, the federal government does not pay attention to them. The economic threat of China is a good example. Here, I suspect that the politicians who favour corporations doing business with China will never budget funds to prepare for such a threat. It is not in their self-interest, or perhaps they are employing the psychological defence mechanism of denial. Here again, I must interject that there is no prejudice in my statements. I have worked in Hong Kong, where I have Chinese relatives. As an intelligence analyst, one of the first things that I was taught is that there is no room for prejudice and that it is the government of the nation that is the threat, not its citizens. A good analyst knows and has experienced, through travel and interaction, many cultures. And China can't be ignored.

Economic espionage is the use or facilitation of illegal, clandestine, coercive, or deceptive means by a foreign government or its surrogates to acquire economic intelligence. Economic espionage activity exposes Canadian companies to unfair disadvantages, jeopardizing our jobs, our competitiveness, and our R&D investment levels. CSIS does not investigate company-to-company industrial espionage. But it investigates the activities of foreign governments and the theft of new technology. Canada is a good place to steal American know-how because of our close manufacturing ties with American industry and a lax domestic attitude to security. Among the largest offenders are the intelligence agencies of Russia and China, which is Canada's second-largest trading partner after the U.S. and also our fastest growing export market. Chinese companies have already purchased shares in Canadian energy firms (opening the oil sands to them) as well as in a pipeline to the West Coast that will bring oil to port and then by sea to the Asian mainland.

Although known mostly for its patience in its collection of unclassified information using professors and exchange students, China conducts espionage using the same techniques as the Russians. When I was working in Eastern Europe it was common to see Russian intelligence services arrange for the bankruptcy of a targeted company and then bail its owner out, thereby gaining control of it, and then using "front" agents under the guise of doing business. The other technique was for the Russian SVR to approach a large international Russian firm, say in oil or mining, and persuade the oligarch to allow an intelligence residency (a group of up to fifty intelligence officers) to operate in an affiliate office in a foreign country. It is not wise for the oligarch to refuse, and, as can be seen by events with Yukos Oil over the last year or so, it does not help if the oligarch gets into trouble with the Russian government leadership.

China uses the same tactic at times. Business fronts, some of them even chains of Chinese restaurants, have been used in France and other countries. A problem not taken into consideration by our government is that in this age of globalization the sale of Canadian steel and oil companies to Russian or state-owned Chinese interests may yield short-term profits, but it will also result in the expansion of economic espionage activity, costing Canadian citizens their long-term livelihoods. An expansion of CSIS will also be required. Based on my figures of possible agents and the manpower requirements to counter a threat from only one company, the financial outlay to the federal government would be considerable. Technology theft and economic espionage is a growth area, and Canada will often be a preferred objective when we are compared to the "hard target" of the U.S.

This is one argument for the creation of a true Canadian foreign intelligence service, one that aggressively seeks out information of economic use to be shared with Canadian companies. Note that an agency limited to this goal need not be overt. The work could be conducted surreptitiously without even our own companies being aware of it. Another suggestion would be to form a centre that collects "open source" information and processes it to classified product. Some may say that such organizations exist even within the government, but the keys to this operation would be selecting collectors and analysts and having healthy government financing. Such an institute could even operate from a foreign country. The Russians, for example, had such a facility operating from one of the Baltic states, conducting operations using the cover of a local import-export business. As well, our intelligence agencies often have classified economic and technological information that would be of use to Canadian companies. In some cases, declassification of certain material is possible, and corporations that had been specially vetted could then share it. Note that all of these recommendations have practical and moral considerations that have not been addressed.

Within one year after 9/11 there seemed to appear a dozen new organizations (or, as some academics wrongly stated, "new intelligence agencies") in Canada. But we did not create 180,000 new jobs in the sector, as happened in the U.S. with the formation of the Department of

Homeland Security. Instead, we shuffled everyone around and hired very few new staff at a very low level. It was simply a reorganization of existing resources. Some of the changes had been recommended thirty years before by the McDonald Commission, not to mention in different Senate reports leading up to 9/11. But that's the show business of Canadian politics over the past decade and more. What the public doesn't realize is that even the need for several dozen competent intelligence analysts is a critical shortage in a country our size.

There also continue to be questions about Canada's foreign activities due to problems of the CSIS Act's wording and the changing nature of CSIS operations abroad. Section 12 of the act sets its primary mandate as collecting information and intelligence related to "threats to the security of Canada." Note that CSIS is not restricted by geographic area and can and does collect intelligence abroad, but only in regards to Canada's security. In addition to overt liaison activity, foreign covert activities have been expanded and changed recently. In the mid-1990s this often meant co-operating with a sister service from another country and establishing joint operations to obtain information of mutual concern. But since the late 1990s (always subject to resource considerations and a careful risk assessment) CSIS has increased its covert foreign operations. This has been due to the changing nature of threats facing Canada, but it was also a logical development of its growing experience in these operations and of our country's often unique access to sources able to provide information about our security.

As expertise has grown, CSIS's foreign operations have expanded to tasking human sources to travel abroad, recruit foreign sources, and meet them in third countries. Even SIRC recommended that the agency's policy for approving investigative activities outside Canada be amended to include collecting certain information. But CSIS is severely limited by funding for foreign operations and by law cannot collect non-threat-related intelligence or target foreign government agencies. Moreover, internal shuffling of personnel every few years to be cross-trained takes away from developing the professionalism required for true espionage. At any rate, the functions of intelligence and counter-intelligence would have to be separated into two agencies as they are in all democracies.

One of the strongest arguments against the creation of a foreign intelligence agency has been constantly put forth by Foreign Affairs Canada. They argue that the world would view Canadians as potential spies, and this could have dire consequences. It's as if the department has no one travelling overseas, let alone working abroad. I have news for their staff: I personally have had dealings with many foreign intelligence services, including members of the Russian FSB and SVR and "retired" KGB members. Not one believed me when I said that Canada did not have a foreign intelligence agency. They all believed that I was from such an agency. "Just because we cannot prove that such an agency exists doesn't mean there isn't one. It's just very good at what it does," they told me.

Foreign Affairs can forget about preserving the image of Canada as an innocent virgin; that smokescreen is reserved purely for internal consumption by the average Canadian citizen. But it is Foreign Affairs that sets the direction for policy. When policies are finally determined, it passes them to the Treasury Department to prepare the proper directives and other paperwork, which are then passed to the ministries to put into actual play. Canadian reality is usually whatever Foreign Affairs believes to be true.

Another argument used is that CSIS already conducts foreign intelligence operations. But as you've seen, their scope is severely limited. Russian counter-intelligence can do much more to defend its own country than can CSIS. It is permitted to operate overseas, but it is also responsible for infiltration of foreign agencies for the purpose of counter-intelligence. In short, it could target CSIS to determine if it is spying on Russia. CSIS cannot do the same, yet its act permits it to have foreign operations to defend Canada against foreign threats. In short, CSIS is handcuffed in defending the government and its citizens, even itself.

CSIS is a perpetually evolving organization adapting as necessary to changes in the global environment. Canadians should also realize that it is accountable to independent oversight and must work by the principle of the rule of law, while terrorists respect no borders, international or moral. CSIS does everything in its power to protect Canadian citizens at home and abroad. This is done to such an extent that even warnings of assassination threats for ordinary civilians working overseas are dispensed on an individual basis. This I know for a fact. But like many of our intelligence agencies, bureaucracy, politically motivated government policies, and resource constraints due to budget restrictions have greatly affected CSIS. This is alarming. There is no more important role for government than ensuring the security of its citizens. We, as Canadians, must never lose sight of this.

CHAPTER 4

THE HORSEMEN
by Kostas Rimsa

"Former KGB members told me the RCMP was always a very professional foe to be reckoned with."

He was six feet, four inches with an appearance more like a CEO than an experienced counter-intelligence officer from the RCMP Security Service. I was sitting in a hotel lobby in downtown Toronto when we first met. His partner was just a bit smaller, also dressed in a suit. Both were fit and well-educated, with the ability to quickly grasp the matters at hand. They understood that Canada is and has been at war with different foreign intelligence agencies for years, just as we are at war with terrorism today. The men of the old Security Service were true hunters. They were men you could trust with your life. Today, many of them still serve as members of the RCMP's National Security Investigations Section (NSIS) and participate in joint task force operations.

The Mounties are organized under the authority of a federal act and headed by a commissioner who, under the direction of the minister of Public Safety, controls the force of more than twenty-two thousand officers. The RCMP provides policing in all provinces and territories except Ontario and Quebec and maintains eight crime detection laboratories, the Canadian Police Information Centre (a computerized intelligence database created in the 1970s and still in use today) in Ottawa, and other support entities. The force is divided into four regions and fifteen operational divisions with headquarters located in Ottawa and detachments in all provinces and territories. The RCMP is responsible for both criminal investigations and those involving national security.

Protection of national security became a serious concern only during the Second World War. RCMP headquarters employed only three members and two stenographers in 1939, with field units in the larger cities investigating threats. After the war, the defection of Soviet cipher clerk Igor Gouzenko removed any thoughts the government might have had about reducing the security intelligence function to pre-war levels. RCMP security operations expanded and evolved under several names: Special Branch in the 1950s, the Directorate of Security and Intelligence in the 1960s, and the Security Service in the 1970s. In that decade the RCMP also expanded into new areas such as airport policing and VIP security.

The creation of the Canadian Security Intelligence Service took place in 1984 after the RCMP lost responsibility for security intelligence investigations but retained its duties collecting evidence and arresting suspects. National security investigations are now conducted by NSIS, which is dispersed regionally, with members often operating as part of joint task forces. CSIS does not have the right to arrest and interrogate, but NSIS does and is responsible for collecting evidence needed in court, with the assistance of CSIS. The recent inclusion of terrorist-related offences into the Canadian Criminal Code (see Appendix III) has narrowed the gap between security and criminal intelligence as well as between CSIS and the RCMP.

Since 9/11, the national security activities of the RCMP have expanded significantly. As a result of the Anti-terrorism Act and amendments to the Criminal Code and other legislation, virtually all actions relating to terrorism have now been criminalized and are within the force's mandate. It has also been given extraordinary powers in connection with national security, including the power to conduct preventive detentions, to convene investigative hearings, and to carry out electronic surveillance in respect of such crimes. These powers are subject to approval by the solicitor general and to judicial control.

The Criminal Intelligence Directorate is where the majority of national security information and intelligence is analyzed and disseminated internally and externally. Most is stored on the top-secret

Secure Criminal Investigations System database. Accessed on a strict "need-to-know" basis, information on this database is also given to other agencies, both domestic and foreign. Headquarters coordinates formal requests, but more informal exchanges at the field officer level also take place.

RCMP analysts are responsible for the preparation of threat assessments and specific projects such as the Canadian Air Carrier Protective Program, which places RCMP officers on certain flights, and for providing support for listing Terrorist Entities under the Criminal Code. At the divisional level, operational functions are carried out by NSIS and, since 9/11, by Integrated National Security Enforcement Teams located in Toronto, Ottawa, Vancouver, and Montreal.

Approximately 285 RCMP members were engaged in national security functions at headquarters and with the INSETs in 2004. Other groups relevant to national security that include the RCMP are Integrated Border Enforcement Teams (IBETs) and Integrated Immigration Enforcement Teams (IIETs). Both groups carry out investigations, the former those related to border security and the latter those related to enforcing certain provisions of the Immigration and Refugee Protection Act and the Citizenship Act.

Discussions continue regarding the creation of IBETs, which will be conducting focused investigations between ports under the lead of the RCMP. These teams will harmonize information and intelligence gathering, coordinate cross-border enforcement activities, and work closely with American counterparts. The responsibility for customs laws at the border is shared. The Canada Customs and Revenue Agency (CCRA) concentrated its activities at ports of entry, while the responsibility between ports of entry rests with the RCMP. In 2003 the CCRA was reorganized into the Canada Revenue Agency (CRA) and the Canada Border Services Agency (CBSA), which amalgamated Canada Customs from the CCRA with border personnel.

The focus of the RCMP's counter-terrorism strategy is on "preventing, detecting, and deterring terrorist activity in Canada and abroad" using an intelligence-led and integrated approach with security teams. NSIS has the full support of the RCMP, making it a formidable force in countering criminal, foreign government, and terrorist threats to national security.

Even with the creation of CSIS, the Mounties maintained a significant intelligence-gathering capability. The continued involvement arose out of a new approach to law enforcement known as intelligence-led policing, which was adopted by the RCMP in the late 1980s after many members returned to the force after leaving CSIS. This new approach is guided by information about potential crimes and criminals before any breach of the law has necessarily occurred. To effectively carry out its crime prevention mandate, the RCMP gathers information about the capabilities, vulnerabilities, and intentions of criminals and their organizations. The sharing of such with other domestic and foreign agencies by the RCMP is part of the process.

In national security operations, the purpose for which the RCMP and other police gather intelligence is different from that of CSIS. The Mounties gather intelligence to support their crime-prevention and criminal-apprehension responsibilities, while CSIS collects information in order to advise the government on threats to Canada. The RCMP and CSIS were from the outset intended to have a symbiotic relationship as outlined in legislation and in a memorandum of understanding, and the force is also required to provide CSIS with operational support in certain circumstances. The Mounties are also key to the Integrated Threat Assessment Centre situated at CSIS HQ. Its mandate is to create assessments of all potential threats to Canada and distribute them as required. It is supported by, and staffed with, representatives of a number of departments including Public Safety and Emergency Preparedness Canada, the Communications Security Establishment (CSE), and the Department of National Defence.

"We should not forget that several hundred Muslims were among those killed on September 11, 2001, in the World Trade Center. Crime has no colour, it has no language or religion. How we enforce the law should not be influenced in any way by any of these issues," said RCMP Commissioner Giuliano Zaccardelli in 2004 at a conference named "Reviving the Islamic Spirit." He was commenting on accusations of inappropriate racial profiling by Canadian security services in the wake of 9/11. But the force's critics miss a crucial point. Notwithstanding that the RCMP has had years of community policing and race relations experience, today there are six hundred thousand Muslims living legally in Canada. This would be a large number of people, mostly citizens, to ostracize by inappropriate behaviour, including the use of profiling. It must also be remembered that some of the Muslims caught participating in the terrorist Jihad have been Caucasian. Add some false documentation that can be easily obtained by most terrorist networks and visual profiling can be misleading. Investigators from NSIS are very aware of this.

Both NSIS and CSIS officers work closely with analysts, who use "indicators." There are strong indicators and weaker ones. Being a Muslim is an extremely weak indicator of being an Islamic terrorist: most of the members of the Muslim community in Canada — and, for that matter, in the world — are innocent. It is a matter of logic that even if a suspect is a Muslim of very strong faith, it does not make him or her a terrorist. A strong indicator would be receiving information from an allied country's intelligence service indicating a person is a terrorist or a suspect. Another would be proof of travel to a known terrorist base or knowledge of actual training. An even stronger indicator would be the interception of phone, computer, or fax communications that indicate veiled speech. Yet another would be association with known terrorists, since many of the current Islamic organizations recruit close friends or family members.

There has to be a significant cluster of strong indicators before a person is classified as a terrorist suspect. In addition, a suspect can be of different categories. They may be involved in obtaining money for the cause; acting as a community agitator; or being an actual *Mujahideen*. These different categories automatically imply different types of indicators as proof of possible terrorist group involvement. In addition, indicators are not necessarily in themselves proof of conscious involvement in a terrorist organization.

NSIS investigators are aware that there are naive people who participate in terrorist fronts, not realizing that they have been duped by terrorist supporters into actions that support the cause. These are called "false flag operations," where a cover story is presented and members are recruited thinking that they are working for some noble cause. Organizations that collect money for the victims of government action, such as wives or children of those in jail, are common. The

Irish Republican Army used NORAID in both Canada and the U.S. for many years, funnelling the money collected by its duped volunteers to finance terrorist operations. The collection of monies for legal funds in defence of suspected terrorists is also widespread. Other fronts apply political pressure on governments from within. False flag operations can also be used for the purpose of careful recruitment by identifying possible future Jihadists. No one is born a terrorist; they are made through careful long-term indoctrination, often manipulated by the terrorist groups themselves. This is why every physical terrorist action is considered a form of propaganda for the purpose of bringing new recruits to the cause.

Strong indicators and/or proof have been used in the detention of all the terrorist suspects now in Canadian jails. Some have been identified by known captured terrorists, others by name, and still others by photograph. One could say that a captured terrorist, even a highly placed leader of a terrorist organization, may want for various reasons to ingratiate himself to his captors and therefore is not a credible witness. But neither NSIS nor CSIS officers are as incompetent as some fronts would have Canadians believe.

What they don't tell you in the movies is that when an apprehended terrorist is presented with a series of photographs for identification, a high proportion are not of terrorist suspects at all but of known innocent people. By using such a method with a terrorist who is only beginning to co-operate with the authorities, NSIS investigators quickly determine if they are attempting to deceive or if they are prepared to work with them. Such control photographs, though perhaps not as many as initially, are used throughout the interrogation process to ensure truthful participation. As well as such tests, other tradecraft is applied by NSIS investigators that must remain classified.

In addition, interrogators are well aware that the pressure can be so great that a psychologically weak individual will confess even though he or she is not guilty. This type of suspect is a great concern. It must be understood that an interrogator, whether working for a police force or an intelligence agency, is schooled in a primary principle of discovering the truth, so all acts admitted to by the subject have to be proven independently.

Apprehended terrorists held at Guantanamo Bay, Cuba, have directly fingered some of those currently in jail here; it is highly unlikely that a mistake has been made and that innocent men have been sitting behind bars for several years without recourse. Yet front groups, whether terrorist controlled or not, continue to protest their innocence and allege cruel and unusual detention. Their statements are meant for both the government and the public, but more importantly, they frighten members of the Canadian Muslim community. NSIS also does not have the time or manpower to waste on fishing expeditions or following the wrong track with indiscriminate profiling of innocent Canadian Muslims. People who believe otherwise are misguided or ill-informed. Some who protest do so out of principle, from fear of mistakes occurring — not that there is clear evidence that any have been actually made. Others know exactly what they are doing and have a nefarious purpose.

NSIS also knows that criminals of any type — common, organized, or terrorist — are taught to one degree or another to lie to investigators and interrogators. Terrorists from associated groups of al Qaeda are even taught how to resist interrogation tactics. To understand criminals and terrorists better, Canadians should remember some words of TV icon Bart Simpson, who in his simplistic way reveals the tactic when he says, "I didn't do it. I wasn't there. No one saw me. You can't prove it." But some of the current NSIS investigators are from the ranks of the old Security Service, with decades of experience in this area. As former members of the KGB have told me personally, "The RCMP Security Service was always a very professional foe to be reckoned with."

In May 2003, two men were arrested for immigration violations, and by August there were nineteen Pakistani men in custody with rumours that some or all were part of a Canadian-based al Qaeda cell. They were rounded up by a joint task force of the RCMP and Citizenship and Immigration Canada (CIC) working on Project Thread; Security Certificates were used to arrest and detain them as potential threats to national security. It was another month before it was verified that the individuals involved were not terrorists but involved in "just" immigration fraud. The men were then deported. As in other cases that become public, instead of hailing the task force members as heroes for apprehending these criminals, even though they weren't terrorists, there was sharp criticism in the press of the task force's action and why Security Certificates were used.

To put things in perspective, it must be remembered that Canada is on the al Qaeda hit list and is the only country not to have been targeted yet. The RCMP is also now a proactive force, not just a reactive one as it was before 1988. It is intelligence-driven and does not want a 9/11 on our soil. Moreover, investigations are time-consuming and manpower-intensive, and time is a precious commodity when dealing in counter-terrorism. It was quickly obvious in the previously cited case that the task force had run across something out of the ordinary. Nineteen individuals, as in 9/11, were tied together by a common bond of region and nationality, all were of the same age group as those who participated in 9/11, and all came from a country that is known to still harbour al Qaeda in its cities and hinterlands. All suspects were identified as using student visas as a cover for other activities, as did the 9/11 terrorists, and some of the suspects were involved in the manufacture and distribution of false documentation, as is often the norm in an active terrorist cell structure.

There were other indicators of possible terrorist activity as well. With such a large group of suspects already in place in Toronto, the major city of Canada, time to investigate more thoroughly could not be given before taking action. The RCMP and other Canadian agencies know full well that even if agreements for exchanging information between countries are in place, requests for information, even though honoured eventually, may take too long because of disparities between technology, methods, and other factors. In addition, filed requests may not necessarily be accurate (sometimes on purpose); the infiltration of intelligence and police agencies is a common tactic of al Qaeda–associated terrorist groups.

It appears that the authorities who signed the appropriate warrants and Security Certificates were also in agreement with the investigators about the need to act immediately, from both a legal and common sense point of view. The fact that those arrested were in the end proven to be illegal aliens who were returned to their homeland at taxpayer expense should not take away from the preventative actions taken by the CIC and the RCMP. Perhaps next time it will not be "just" illegal immigrants.

Two other incidents involving the Mounties and national security have recently received widespread media attention and should be mentioned as well. On January 2004, the federal government ordered the Commission of Inquiry into the Actions of Canadian Officials in Relation to Maher Arar. According to its report, the RCMP was not faulted for sharing any information with U.S. authorities. The commission did point out that there was a limited number of formal policies and guidelines governing the intake and dissemination of such information, however. One exception is a November 2003 Ministerial Directive that requires the Public Safety Minister to approve of formal or informal agreements and other forms of co-operation between the force and foreign agencies like the FBI and CIA. It must be remembered that the Mounties have been sharing information with such organizations, especially American ones, for decades without problems or public attention.

The Arar case is a very isolated one, an aberration of sorts. The pertinent issue was the legal right of the U.S. under international law to detain and then deport Arar via Jordan to Syria, where he alleges he was tortured. The problem was a political one for the government when this act of "rendition," as the Americans call it, affected a dual citizen of Canada and the matter came to the public's eye. Because of political ramifications, rendition is not used by the U.S. without good reason, especially when it involves a Canadian citizen. What those reasons are, only the Americans know.

The media were quick to lay blame, however, seeing a great emotional story with public appeal. Both the RCMP and CSIS were quickly faulted for the resulting torture, which is a typical poor exercise in logic. And as usual, our federal government allowed the agencies to take the heat without playing interference.

The second incident involves the Arar affair as well. In 2004, the group Reporters Without Borders released its list of the most dangerous places for journalists. Canada was ranked eighteenth out of 167 countries because of RCMP raids on an *Ottawa Citizen* reporter's home and on the offices of the newspaper itself in connection to leaked secret government documents involving the Arar case. The purpose of the raid was to learn how the reporter obtained the documents. She faced possible criminal charges under the new Security of Information Act (see Appendix II);

the raid is the first instance of police acting on this act. Enthusiastic Canadian journalists should take note of Section 4 (1) of the act, which states, "Every person is guilty of an offence under this Act who, having in his possession or control any secret official code word, password, sketch, plan, model, article, note, document or information that relates to or is used in a prohibited place, or that has been made or obtained in contravention of this Act, or that has been entrusted in confidence to him by any person holding office under Her Majesty."

The press is not exempt from this. A report in the *Citizen* on November 8, 2003, stated that "security officials leaked allegations" about Arar "in the weeks leading to his return to Canada." While that is a serious internal security matter, what is of greater concern is the attitude of the press and of certain groups among the Canadian public.

Journalists around the world will always claim that the people have the right to know virtually everything. They also believe that receiving classified information is normal and their right. It isn't. It is like being a fence (a buyer and seller of stolen goods). Being in possession of classified material without the appropriate level of clearance and a need to know is a criminal offence.

Information released from such documents can get informants or agents working for our side killed. This was the case back in the late 1970s when the names of a series of CIA operatives overseas were released by the "underground" magazine *Covert Action*. Over a dozen were murdered, many working counter-terrorism in Latin America. The response from the magazine was that the American people have the right to know. Even though this case is extreme, information from classified documents can be detrimental to operations, to the personnel working on them, and in some cases to the diplomatic and economic relationships of countries involved. While the information may not appear to be overly damaging to a reporter, they have not been trained to evaluate such matters. To a highly trained terrorist, this may not be the case at all. The information may just provide their organization with the missing piece of a puzzle involving internal security. Canadian journalists watch too much American TV. They make the mistake of thinking that our constitution gives them the same strong case for freedom of the press as does the American one. It does not.

Some "experts" have stated that Muslims in the Western democracies, including Canada, would be reluctant to join an intelligence service or police force. This is not true. Many Muslims believe that the actions of terrorist groups are an affront to Islam because of the tactics that they use. They may join as a form of their own personal Jihad to counter the spread of an indecent perception of Islam to the world. Or they may desire revenge against the terrorists, as hundreds of Muslims died in the 9/11 attacks and most people killed since then in terrorist incidents have been of that faith. In 2004, the number of Muslim deaths due to terrorist action was so high that al Qaeda changed its tactics in Saudi Arabia; they had lost support from the local population because of "the deaths of so many believers." Recruitment of Canadian citizens of Muslim backgrounds must be a priority for the RCMP as well as for all our police and intelligence agencies. They know the culture, the languages, and the terrain, and they fit in where required. It would take special efforts by the RCMP in regards to counter-intelligence, but dividends would pay off enormously.

Another priority for the force should be the formation of a unit similar to the FBI's Critical Incident Response Group (CIRG), which is on call for operations overseas wherever a terrorist incident strikes U.S. property or its citizens. Even an incident involving one American can initiate a mobile response. Geared to deploy by aircraft, CIRG advises foreign governments and conducts its own investigations when permitted by foreign hosts. The unit includes FBI hostage negotiators who can monitor or conduct hostage/kidnap situations, forensic specialists complete with mobile labs, bomb-disposal technicians that can conduct investigations after a blast, interrogators, analysts, and specialists in communications and surveillance technology.

The Americans will extradite and put on trial anyone who has committed a criminal act against U.S. property or citizens overseas, and CIRG collects evidence suitable for American courts. Most importantly, every American can be assured that if he or she is in harm's way anywhere in the world, the U.S. government will be in the country of the incident within hours, working on his or her behalf or determining what happened and making the appropriate arrangements. By contrast, if you are a Canadian, perhaps someone from one of our embassies or consulates in another country, different from the one where the incident took place, will pick up a phone and attempt to determine what has happened. If you are a Canadian in trouble overseas, this difference gives the words "left behind" a totally different meaning. I know.

An international role like the one played by CIRG would be ideal for the Mounties as the force already has a formidable reputation abroad. In spring 2001, I was with the minister of Internal Affairs of one of the Baltic countries discussing the need for greater security controls due to the corruption of that country's national police. As I later walked through the government building's maze-like hallways that were specially built for possible coup attempts and urban warfare, one of the minister's advisors was blunt. The RCMP had an image of incorruptibility and iron discipline, he said. This was earned in the former Soviet Union not only because of the force's ability to "get their man" but also because in the some sixty years that the KGB and its associates operated in Canada, they were able to compromise the force only once.

CHAPTER 5

OTHER COPS
by John Thompson

"This is an investigation with no end, the threads keep going everywhere."

It was the Mountie's clumsy hand-off signal that first got my attention. One of the results of being trained in observation is that one begins to notice that life on even the most familiar streets is suddenly much more interesting and complicated than one thought. This is why I noticed the classic three-man tail pattern around a short, well-dressed, middle-aged Mediterranean man going through Toronto's Yorkville shopping district.

They weren't in red tunics and Stetsons, but they might as well have been. All three were tall, fit men in early middle age with moustaches who stood out as products of the old Regina Barracks moulding press the RCMP seem to have lost in recent years. All three were also carrying attaché cases and folded copies of the *Globe and Mail*. One trailed their target, one flanked him on the opposite side of the street, and the third was leading him by about fifty metres. Their target must have been aware of them too, for he started to dawdle and window shop (a seemingly innocuous activity, but also a good way of using reflections in the window to look around you). I was fascinated and followed the whole show for a few blocks.

The Mounties have learned a lot since that tail in 1982, and it's also possible that I was watching a training exercise — the Litton bombing terrorists who were arrested by one of their teams disguised as British

Columbian road workers in 1983 were completely taken by surprise. In that same year, I also watched a pair of Toronto cops in the "old clothes" squad pop right out of a normal street background to arrest a belligerent drunk, and neither one would have rated a second look otherwise.

Over the years since, I've had occasional glimpses of police doing intelligence work: a uniformed cop with a video camera lodged in a cedar hedge, filming a store front in Vancouver; sundry undercover types filming a Liberation Tamil Tigers of Eelam rally in front of the Ontario Legislature (and being photographed by Tiger front men in turn); or officers using my office for the hasty wiring of an informer going off to transact a drug deal. I was interviewed by members of a police intelligence unit after receiving a mail bomb from an Animal Liberation Front (ALF) terrorist in 1995, and have interviewed them in turn about their own jobs.

Despite the cachet normally associated with intelligence gathering, it is really a prosaic task for a working day. The police who undertake these tasks are usually down-to-earth, tremendously practical, and have a relaxed attitude about human behaviour (they've seen most of it at one point or another).

Canadian police have come a long way since the days of wooden truncheons and tin rattles; they've had to cope with an increasingly sophisticated criminal environment and severe technological challenges. It was clear that a revolution was brewing in the field in the 1990s, but the sweeping changes now underway were accelerated by 9/11. Few people understand the vital role of the police in generating and using intelligence in modern Canada, nor do they comprehend that a minor revolution has occurred.

Most of Canada's older police forces appeared in the 1830s and 1840s. The officers were often selected on the basis of size and physical presence and were sent out into their communities with a nightstick for troublesome miscreants and a rattle or whistle for signalling purposes. The contemporary serial killer, organized terrorist group, urban street gang, or transnational criminal society had yet to appear in Canada, and they were far from common elsewhere.

By 1900, the police might be equipped with revolvers (although this was by no means universal) and perhaps had a telephone call box to make reports during rounds. They were just starting to learn about some new phenomena. One of America's first serial killers had slain and buried two children in Toronto in the early 1890s, and the Fenians had killed Thomas D'Arcy McGee in 1869 in Canada's first political assassination. Urban street gangs had crossed the Atlantic into the U.S., though they seemed absent for the time being in Canada. The Sicilian Black Hand (the forerunner to the Mafia) and the Chinese Triads had established their first bridgeheads here, but these two early transnational criminal societies largely confined their attentions to their own communities.

By 1950, the typical Canadian cop was now likely to be making his way around in a radio-equipped patrol car and was almost invariably armed with a revolver. Although two world wars had put a dent in the crime rate, serial and sexual killers were not entirely unknown, nor was terrorism, although it seems innocuous enough by our current standards. Urban street gangs were rare, as were transnational criminal societies, but they had made inroads here through alien smuggling into the U.S. and a tiny narcotics industry. Canada had also experienced an earlier flirtation with Prohibition, and gangs of Canadian criminals had aped the American examples that combined cars and firearms for bank robberies and other activities.

Canadian police had to respond to new challenges, and many larger municipal forces had created specialist sub-units. Detective squads, an innovation in about 1900, were much more common in 1950. Some cities had vice and homicide squads, and some cars might also be detailed for hold-up responses. These developments mark the beginning of police intelligence work in Canada.

Police work is naturally reactive — something occurs and they respond. If a crime appears to have been committed, they conduct an investigation to determine what actually happened, and hopefully this leads them to a suspect who can be charged and, again hopefully, convicted. Developing intelligence is something altogether different: police start to become proactive. They gather information that can lead them to predict where Madame Suzie is likely to re-establish her brothel next time around. Thus, officers can be positioned to shut down the establishment and arrest Madame Suzie within hours of its opening, rather than waiting for complaints to come in from the neighbours over several weeks.

But many officers had some difficulty coping with the concept of developing and using intelligence for one simple yet profound reason: intelligence-grade material is not evidence-grade material. Intelligence lets officers see a pattern and understand the general picture about a specific group or activity, but this is not the same as securing sufficient evidence to warrant laying charges. It took some time for the utility of intelligence gathering to be accepted by various forces.

Intelligence activities let police make better use of their resources, identify priorities, and work to deter crime rather than react to it. Police work, particularly against gangs, criminal societies, or terrorist groups, depends on informants. One of the great strengths of intelligence squads is that they allow police to identify likely informants early in an investigation and recruit them. Intelligence can be used to find weak points in criminal enterprises, and it lets police focus their efforts in a way that causes the most harm.

By 1975, specialist squads to handle high-risk situations had formed in several cities, armed with rifles, shotguns, and sometimes automatic weapons. Special investigation units were much more common, particularly as a result of the skyrocketing narcotics industry. Terrorist groups and transnational criminal societies were firmly established in Canada, although without the diversity that we know so well today. Urban street gangs were well-established and already linking up with the more established criminal underworld, particularly in Montreal. Serial killers and sexual predators had also become far more common.

Canadian cops had to cope with a tougher environment than any of their predecessors had known, and they had to develop institutions and procedures to deal with it. But the situation often changed faster than they could respond to it. Criminal societies are informal and usually lack a strict structural hierarchy; even outlaw motorcycle gangs and the Italian Mafia tend to operate informally for everyday activities. Also, it is much easier for criminals to begin a new enterprise than it is for police to investigate it and gather sufficient information to lay charges with confidence: A money laundering conduit can sometimes be established by criminals in a few hours, while it takes police months to develop information on it and shut it down. No matter what police do, criminals tend to be more adaptable and flexible.

As well, Canadian society, while never homogeneous, has become much more diverse over the past thirty years. Most criminal societies and terrorist groups tend to recruit along narrow ethnic lines, and this forces police to learn new languages and cultural skills to cope. Hiring new members from within recently arrived ethnic groups is not a complete solution either, as it takes years for an officer to become seasoned.

A political establishment that is nervous about being seen to be going after members of a particular ethnic group doesn't help matters much either. Jamaican Posses, Tamil Tigers, Mohawk Warriors, and South Chinese gangs have all learned that having a political front-person scream "racism" can be very handy in handicapping police investigations.

Another problem sometimes lies with police culture itself. By the nature of their jobs and their perspectives, police officers tend to isolate themselves within their communities. Police see the rest of us as civilians, and as they spend their careers dealing primarily with people in trouble, drunks, or stupid or malevolent members of society, there is a tendency to socialize with the only other people who truly understand what the job entails — other cops. An "us versus them" attitude can also develop toward other police forces.

Much police work depends on developing informants and carefully cultivating these often touchy or understandably nervous sources of information. If intelligence is to be shared with other forces, they might want to interview an officer's informants, thus endangering a relationship that is fragile at the best of times. One force might discount evidence they didn't gather themselves or may seem careless about protecting it. Or they might just operate differently from one's own force. This has tended to militate against close working relationships in the past.

Municipal police forces in Quebec and Ontario might resent their provincial colleagues, and both might resent the RCMP. Some officers might also discount the worth of employees of other agencies such as Transport Canada, CSIS, the Canadian Forces, or private security companies. These self-defeating attitudes still appear from time to time, but increasingly seem most prevalent in more junior officers, in much the same way that the most "regimental" soldiers tend to be the youngest ones.

Yet today's police officers — with their body armour, semiautomatic handguns, plastic batons, pepper spray, miniature radios, and computer terminals — have learned to overcome many of these handicaps. They are the cutting edge of a series of networks reaching through our entire society, and they are far more likely to engage in predictive policing, getting ahead of problems before they manifest themselves. How did they get here?

One of the maxims that emerged from the War on Terror is, "It takes a network to fight a network." Most modern terrorist groups and criminal societies evolved into networks years ago; loose cells might be cluttered around a specific locality or activity, and the group relies on shared backgrounds and common ethnic or cultural identities for socialization between these nodes. Traditional police and security approaches can tackle only one node at a time, and seldom with decisive or lasting effect.

In the early 1960s, some people were already beginning to recognize the limitations of conventional approaches in tackling criminal societies. At a meeting of Attorneys General from the federal and provincial governments in 1966, creating a central clearinghouse for information on organized crime was proposed. By 1970 this had manifested itself in the Criminal Intelligence Service of Canada (CISC) with a central bureau in Ottawa and nine provincial ones. The CISC has grown slowly, with every sign of the usual cautious reticence about public involvement that is typical of Canadian civil servants and senior police officers. Yet even as early as 1976, it led to the creation of the Automated Criminal Intelligence Information System, one of the world's first police computer networks. The CISC gathers raw data and specific intelligence and pools it for further refinement and analysis.

Currently there are some 380 agencies and entities that contribute to and make use of the CISC, and most senior police officers agree that it is a very useful organization. The Automated Criminal Intelligence Information System, somewhat updated since 1976, is still a vital resource maintained by the service. The RCMP's commissioner heads the organization, and twenty-two representatives from other police forces with permanent intelligence units meet twice a year to steer the group. These biannual meetings serve to share new concerns and direct new priorities. Most of the funding and staff come from the RCMP, but personnel are also seconded there from other police and security-related agencies.

Starting in the mid-1990s, the CISC also began to release a declassified annual report on the organized crime picture in Canada. While it tends to be brief and contain few specific details, it is a practical public reference, providing an *ex cathedra* view of major problems. The main focus of the CISC is on criminal societies and major criminal activities. Counterterrorism is not a part of its usual brief or mandate, but there are many ways around this. The report for 2004 highlights the leaky security at Canada's ports and airports, a situation that organized crime already capitalizes on, but also one that represents a severe risk from opportunistic terrorists. A central role for Canada in North American security also revolves around the Smart Border Initiative along the Canada–U.S. border, and the CISC is expressing concerns about organized criminal activities on the border and the role of the new IBETs in countering them.

Concerns about criminal threats to the security of Canadian consumers and their credit/debit cards also have ramifications in the fight against terrorism, as the basic training course for al Qaeda members in Afghanistan included a section on supporting yourself through this activity. Counterfeiting is also a money maker for the supporters of the Tamil Tigers in Canada.

There are a lot of misleading notions about just what it is that a police intelligence service does, and visions of Czarist or Parisian *agents provocateurs* spring to mind. One long-time member of the agitprop rent-a-mob in Toronto, who entertains the notion that he is a dangerous radical with a thick police file, might be acutely disappointed to find that no file exists and that the officers from the downtown division who have had to drag him away from sundry protest marches view him as a harmless pest.

Some police intelligence units are large formal organizations and have grown to mirror the CISC in their own right. The Criminal Intelligence Service of Ontario (CISO) is largely run by the Ontario Provincial Police (OPP) but has representation from several municipal and regional police forces. Others face complex jurisdictional environments in their localities. Halifax and Vancouver police have to contend with major rail and port facilities within their cities, which are often administered by federal laws and once had their own specialist agencies. Vancouver, like Montreal and Toronto, has also seen large suburbs evolve into cities in their own respect, leading to a need to coordinate more closely with nearby municipal police forces than might be the case for Saskatoon, Saint John, or Yellowknife.

The initial role of police intelligence services, particularly in cities, is to collect and collate data concerning criminal activities that occur on an ongoing basis. One of the usual functions of these groups, particularly after the formation of the CISC, was to liaise with other forces to facilitate the sharing of information. Most members were long-time detectives or specialist investigators recruited from vice, narcotics, and homicide squads. They also facilitated the internal transfer of information between such squads, which sometimes was not easy.

While the RCMP Security Service was concerned with foreign spies and members of hostile political groups within Canada (such as the Communist Party of Canada or the Ku Klux Klan), provincial and municipal police forces had no mandate to investigate these issues. Outside of Quebec, where local police forces had to respond to a series of FLQ bombs through the 1960s, terrorism was barely on the mental horizon of most police forces. This situation changed in the 1970s.

While preparing for the 1976 Olympic Games in Montreal, the memories of the massacre of Israeli athletes in Munich in 1972 loomed large. The RCMP was aware that Black September and other Palestinian groups were trying to stick their toes into Canadian waters as early as 1972. Police in our major cities were also coping with increased political violence from émigré communities and had learned from the European and American experience with radical leftist terrorists to keep a loose watch on Canadian anarchists.

It still took a long time for the awareness of potential terrorist threats in Canada to properly sink in. Even in the mid-1980s, many police were entirely unaware of the significance of the circled A graffiti that was occasionally spray-painted on their cars by anarchists, and if the intelligence squads were passing off some of the more disquieting remarks from blurry copies of the *Bulldozer* and *Friends of Durruti* newsletters, awareness of this community certainly was not growing. The work of the Litton bombers changed this only slightly.

But the 1985 Air India bombing and the takeover of the Turkish embassy in Ottawa proved instructive, and more forces started to devote intelligence resources to potential sources of terrorism. An additional spur came from the growing activities of the ALF, particularly in southern Ontario, where a spree of vandalism was underway at research centres and meat packers.

But while free to investigate a terrorist attack and treat it purely as a criminal matter, collecting material on anarchists, ALF supporters, or activists for the Khalsa movement or the Tamil Tigers was only incidental for most police forces. Without the authority and the legal tool kit to act against terrorist groups, most could only collect material for background purposes. But like many intelligence officers in other organizations, they were often privately fascinated by the bizarre worldviews they encountered, and wanted to read more out of curiosity.

Regardless, there were clear signs even in the early 1990s that many police forces still really didn't know what to do with their intelligence units. In Toronto they turned out in body armour with submachine guns and assault rifles to provide security at the trial of some Trinidadian Islamic terrorists who had planned a spree of attacks there. They also turned out in the same gear to augment security around several foreign leaders. This was important work, certainly, but it could have been undertaken by other officers without calling most of the squad out for several days. But a revolution in Canadian policing was about to begin, and it would carry the intelligence units along.

Another development in police intelligence emerged from investigations into high-profile serial offenders in the 1980s and 1990s. Police were slowly learning the benefit of using multiple professional perspectives, particularly from the forensics side, in trying to uncover the habits of serial killers to learn more about their behaviours and future patterns. Vital pioneering work in this field came out of the geographical profiling methodology developed in British Columbia in the mid-1990s by Simon Fraser University's School of Criminology in co-operation with the Vancouver Police Department and the RCMP. This is one of several tools in suspect prioritization and data management that have emerged within the last decade in Canada, the U.S., and Great Britain.

Another technique that emerged from organized crime and street gang investigations in the U.S. has become widely accepted. Police intelligence agencies now start to map out the organization by taking known gang members or mobsters and then charting out all of their movements and their social contacts. Eventually sufficient data enables analytical models to provide a picture of the larger network and to identify pivotal figures who might otherwise have escaped the notice of the police. If three or four gang members keep visiting the same dry cleaning store every day, then there might be grounds to suppose it is used for laundering drug money. The bank executive who eats lunch three times a week in the same restaurant that two senior mobsters frequent might be doing the same thing. This lets police develop new angles of investigation and chart out the organization of a group even before arresting any of its members.

The creation of the Canadian Security Intelligence Service was the result of a long and painful inquiry into the RCMP's Security Service, its long-time intelligence branch. The whole tale of the service has been recounted elsewhere, and someday they might actually get the plaudits that they often deserved, but it was clear that the federal government wanted to make a new start.

Since its inception in 1984, the agency has managed to mature as a security service. Between mishandling the Air India investigation and facing jurisdictional issues, there were numerous press reports about infighting between CSIS and the RCMP, even though both organizations reported to the same boss, the solicitor general. But the seeds of a fruitful co-operation with police were planted with the Canadian Security Intelligence Service Act, which mandated the creation of the organization and defined its powers. The act allows CSIS to enter into joint activities with Canadian police forces with the oversight of the Security Intelligence Review Committee and the various provincial ministers of police. It took a few years for the police and CSIS to warm up to each other, especially since both tended to remain protective of their sources and many of the new and inexperienced CSIS officers were exceptionally guarded about sharing information.

In the early 1990s, local police were starting to recognize the worth of networking through the CISC and other satellite organizations and were getting used to occasional input from CSIS. At the same time, though, Canada's transnational criminal societies and the presence of supporters of terrorist organizations grew. For the criminals, the main engine of growth was the black market in cigarettes, although the overall size of this industry at its height in 1993 was a fraction of that of the ongoing market in narcotics and illegal drugs. But the tobacco smuggling conduit across the Canada–U.S. border was also leading to a flood of illegal small arms inside Canada, most of which were ending up in the hands of criminals on our streets. Cops are invariably the first to recognize a new problem, and the flood of firearms triggered Project Gun-Runner, a collaborative investigation between five Ontario forces that ran between 1992 and 1994.

The startling findings from Gun-Runner led to the creation of Ontario's Provincial Weapons Enforcement Unit to tackle the problem. The unit was created as a subset of CISO and became a task force with involvement from the RCMP, OPP, and numerous metropolitan or regional forces in the province. The growing diversity of Canada's criminal scene was also noted in the early 1990s. Besides the traditional Mafia, outlaw bike gangs, and the Franco-Irish Montreal underworld, new and exceptionally violent players had appeared on the scene: new Chinese Triads such as the Big Circle Boys in partnership with Vietnamese gangs, the Russian Mafiya, Haitians in Montreal, the Jamaican Posses in Ontario, violent Sikhs in the aftermath of the Babbar Khalsa insurgency, and the newly arriving Tamil Tiger supporters from Sri Lanka.

This also led to a proliferation of police task forces, oriented toward particular problems. Expertise, especially with municipal police in some major cities and long-serving detachment commanders with the RCMP, led to increased appreciation between various police. The task forces were also holding seats open for representatives from Transport Canada, Revenue Canada, Citizenship and Immigration Canada — although this department was often subjected to major limitations in its effectiveness — and occasional liaison police officers from the United States.

The rapidly accumulating experience in joint task forces would soon stand Canada in good stead. In the aftermath of 9/11, it became manifestly clear to our government that we simply cannot afford a prolonged shutdown of the Canada–U.S. border. Moreover, al Qaeda has directly threatened Canada at least twice and members of the group have been identified here. There was also an intimation of coming trouble following the arrest of Ahmed Ressam in December 1999; as one officer assigned told me in 2003, "This is an investigation with no end, the threads keep going everywhere."

With the passage of Bill C-36 and a set of tough new anti-terrorism laws in early 2002 (see Appendix III), Canadian police had the go-ahead for even closer work with CSIS and could start to directly develop intelligence on terrorism. Moreover, new orders for increased border security were about to make additional demands.

One early spinoff was the creation of Integrated National Security Enforcement Teams. These combine police with assets from Transport Canada, CIC (which shows many signs of being more co-operative), DND, CSIS, and Revenue Canada. INSETs have been created in several Canadian provinces, particularly for work in major ports and other areas with complex jurisdictional environments.

Ontario has also seen the creation of the first Joint Force Operation (JFO), which also combines municipal, provincial, and federal police with CSIS, along with input from other federal and provincial agencies. CSIS is also pressing the JFO to do more work on hate crimes (perhaps to clear this work from their own overloaded agendas). The JFO is mandated to undertake strategic intelligence work and is developing its own human sources to facilitate its investigations. In Ontario, both the JFO and the CISO have also established regional task forces, and a similar process is at work in other provinces.

PATS is another new acronym on the Canadian policing scene: Provincial Anti-Terrorism Sections. Most provinces have created them to work with their INSETs and IBETs. These preceded work on the new Smart Border Initiative between Canada and the United States, but they combine a variety of Canadian and American agencies working as joint forces around critical border areas. The successes of the smuggling industry in the early 1990s are not likely to be repeated.

The result of this alphabet soup of acronyms is that Canadian police intelligence has been extensively reorganized in the last five years. Most major municipal and regional police have now arranged their intelligence services to reflect the multi-agency task force concept, and this is seen at international airports, key border crossing areas, and major port facilities. Some major Canadian municipal police forces also have liaison officers from larger American cities, and vice versa. Toronto and New York are now linked this way. These networks of interlaced agencies at the federal, provincial, regional, municipal, and local levels work in loose conjunction. The organized criminal and the terrorist security networks operate loosely in tandem to add an extra dimension to their capabilities.

Canada's police intelligence agencies at every level of government have become node points in overlapping networks that share information and intelligence data on a timely basis and can work on joint investigations without any of the time consuming delays and obstructions that occurred so often in the past. As a network-oriented structure they can be more flexible and responsive. Another effect, depending on your perspective, is either sinister or beneficial. A number of criminals have cultivated political contacts or even created their own sources inside the criminal justice system in several provinces. These have resulted in interference and obstruction for police investigations. But now a biker in Montreal or a Triad leader in Vancouver might not be sure just what force is looking into their affairs, and calling a sympathetic politician or compromised clerk in the Crown Attorney's office might afford no protection at all. To fight networked problems, the police have finally developed networks of their own.

The evolving analytical tools that have arisen to handle organized crime and serial killers are also being embraced in the War on Terror, and no Canadian police force underestimates this threat anymore. These new arrangements will make today's constables far more effective agents for security than they ever were before.

CHAPTER 6

FOLLOW THEIR MONEY
by Dwight Hamilton

"It is as if this banking did not take place."

T he Iranian businessman still didn't know what Gabriel Marion did for a living. For several months now, Marion had been giving the man high-end retail shopping bags full of well-worn Canadian $20, $50, and $100 bills, up to $100,000 at a time. Sometimes he dropped them off at the Iranian's Toronto office; on other occasions he would wait in hotel lobbies where a courier would pick up the bulky parcels. With minimal conversation, a sort of brief eye contact, and a nervous nod, the courier would be gone with the money. And once the Iranian knocked off 5 percent for his troubles, Marion got crisp, American $100 notes in return the very same day.

With this track record, maybe the Iranian didn't need to worry. Marion was always decked out in impeccable, made-to-measure suits and an out-of-season suntan. He was extremely calm and collected, even when not smoking a DuMaurier. He also appeared awash in cash, occasionally phoning the Iranian in Toronto with his orders from Europe, Asia, and even Hawaii. He had even put a tail on Marion in an attempt to confirm his bona fides and check if he was a cop. He seemed clean. Still, it would be better business to know what Marion's business was, he reckoned.

As they sat opposite each other in the restaurant of Toronto's posh Park Plaza Hotel, the waiter placed large, white napkins on both men's laps. Not too many restaurants do that these days. The Iranian waited for

him to disappear and pressed Marion again about his lucrative business.
"It's better that I not say," Marion said softly.

"I can be trusted. We've done a lot of business. About $800,000 so far, am I correct?"

Leaning over the table, Marion put his mouth and right hand within an inch of the Iranian's ear and whispered, "Heroin. But I don't touch the stuff."

Unconcerned, the Iranian replied, "This conversation did not take place."

But conversations between the two after that included a proposed introduction to the largest heroin exporter in Turkey. There was nothing to fear, insisted the Iranian, as a top-ranking Turkish cop had been turned and could offer protection for the pipeline. Perhaps more importantly, moving money around the world would not be a problem. He could exchange Marion's money in Canada and U.S. dollars could be picked up in Frankfurt, Germany, or other European cities. A simple telephone call to a contact there providing a name and code word was all it took. At the end of the month or another agreed-upon time, the Iranian and his Frankfurt counterpart would reconcile their ledgers and, if need be, transfer funds by courier or use front companies to transfer the money. That way there would be no bank records to trace the financial transactions or link them together in a conspiracy.

What the Iranian didn't know was that Marion *was* a high-level undercover cop. He was working for the RCMP's O Division, Proceeds of Crime Unit, which specialized in tracing and seizing financial assets derived from criminal organizations. Before budget cutbacks forced the RCMP to abandon a Toronto presence, Marion was stationed at the Mounties' old Jarvis Street headquarters. Officers went into undercover stings unarmed, as they were usually patted down by their prey, and had to rely on their sharp wits when situations went sour.

The periphery of what Marion had infiltrated is known as *hawallah* in India, *hundi* in Pakistan, or *fei qian* in China: ancient underground banking systems based on trust, which are nearly paperless and so leave no audit trail. The Somali Al Barakaat actually operated with storefronts until it was shut down in the U.S. Authorities there are still trying to prove it was linked to terrorist financing. *Hawallahs* were not established to facilitate criminal activity but to simplify the exchange of funds within cloistered communities. Even today, many people in certain cultures have little understanding of, or confidence in, conventional banking, and remittance agents enjoy widespread acceptance and usage in South Asia and the Middle East. The vast majority of remittances are routine, but authorities estimate as much as 60 percent of Burma's drug money passes through such a payment system and between $2 billion to $5 billion clears through Pakistan each year, much more than its total of above-board foreign transfers.

It's also the banking method of choice for international terrorists. One can approach a goldsmith, currency trader, or travel agency, which are found in every major bazaar in New Delhi, for example, and deposit money to be remitted to an associate in Bangkok. The depositor receives a chit, which can be as common as a specially marked movie ticket or a low-value rupee bill, and mails it to Bangkok. Once there, it's presented to an associate who can withdraw in Thai baht. Veiled in secrecy, performed via personal contacts and with a mostly deliberate absence of record keeping, it is as if this banking did not take place.

The Financial Transactions and Reports Analysis Centre (FINTRAC) was created in 2000 and reports to Parliament via the finance minister. Originally set up to combat money laundering by organized crime and the booming middle-class offshore tax-evasion market, its mandate was enlarged after 9/11 to include terrorist financing, receiving at least an extra $35 million so far for that additional tasking.

The agency receives millions of transaction reports each year from banks, accountants, real estate brokers, foreign exchange dealers, stockbrokers, life insurance agents, Canada Post, the Canada Border Services Agency, and casinos among others. All cash transactions and international transfers over $10,000 are reported along with any others that are too suspicious for financial entities to ignore. Individuals must also report large amounts of cash they take across borders, as one eighty-four-year-old woman found out when customs caught her with $13,000 at Toronto's Pearson International Airport. FINTRAC also conducts compliance examinations and hosts awareness seminars to those who report. If an examination reveals deficiencies, a letter is sent recommending best practices and sometimes a time limit to put them in effect.

Using transaction reports, FINTRAC then develops intelligence by grouping related transactions, establishing identification if accounts are numbered, and mining databases of similar foreign agencies. If the director is convinced by a disclosure committee that there is likely a case of money laundering or terrorist financing, a case disclosure is given to law enforcement or CSIS to aid in a potential investigation. The CBSA, the CRA, and CIC may also be notified.

With a yearly budget of over $35 million, the centre is the government's point man in its national initiative against money laundering and funding terrorism. In fiscal 2003–04, the agency made 160 new disclosures with a total value of under $700 million. Of these, 149 were of suspected money laundering, forty-four were of suspected terrorist activity, and four involved both pursuits. The transaction dollar value of national security threats the agency dealt with was about $70 million. But to date there have been no arrests or convictions resulting from FINTRAC's information. One assumes that the investigations into three individuals and five businesses in 2003–04 on the grounds of national security are still ongoing.

Headquartered in Ottawa, the agency employs about two hundred personnel with backgrounds in forensic accounting, law, national security, banking, and securities. As far as government pay rates go, it's not too bad. The former manager of the Quebec regional office, who was fired for having an affair with a fellow employee, made $91,000 in 2003. That year the centre hosted thirty-five international delegations and workshops, and its employees attended more in foreign jurisdictions. Membership has its privileges.

But there are some big problems with FINTRAC's ability to aid in the country's security, not least that it needs an audit trail of some sort to follow. It would have been totally useless in Marion's heroin case. But according to critics, one of the biggest legislative hurdles is Canada's anti-Orwellian Privacy Act. "Protecting the personal information under its control guides every aspect of the Centre's operations," the agency's 2004 annual report stated. Consequently, it operates at arm's length from all police and other intelligence units. Even access to the databases of its American counterpart, FinCEN, is severely limited due to the act. Thankfully, the RCMP and the CBSA have established liaison.

Accountants and real estate agents must report only when carrying out certain activities for their clients. "Possession or control of terrorist-owned property" is required to be reported only if it is known, not suspected. And in an incredible omission from Canada's security laws, one group that doesn't have to file any reports to FINTRAC is Canada's law profession. It is argued that it could violate attorney-client privilege if defence lawyers were forced to testify against their own clients, which is true. The same argument was tried in the United States, however, and its courts have so far told the American Bar Association to forget it. Lawyers must report. In the old days here in Canada, a lawyer's discretion dictated any disclosure to police; today they are prohibited by law from talking.

"Solicitor-client privilege is a fundamental right in a democracy, but there needs to be some form of checks and balances in place. Such rules should include clear conflicts of interest where counsel is receiving large sums of cash from a client who has no means to account or support these funds," says Marion. "A money launderer's goal is depositing cash in financial institutions through solicitor's bank accounts. Serious money launderers, in order to conceal their source of funds, almost invariably depend on a chartered accountant and a lawyer to assist them in the process," he continues. "This could include providing letters of references, setting up sham companies and providing fraudulent accounting statements. A name of a lawyer and accountant goes a long way in getting banks to accept money from individuals who alone would not 'pass the smell test.'"

Another glitch in the system is that FINTRAC decides what should be investigated, not the police. Law enforcement must establish reasonable grounds before applying to a judge to obtain permission for a designated disclosure. They cannot ask what information exists on an individual but must know exactly what they're looking for, despite the fact that most investigations involve some sort of exploration. It's what doesn't appear on an investigator's radar screen that could be the *sine qua non* of success. FINTRAC can basically furnish name, rank, and serial number, but not why it looked into the individual in the first place or what analysis was done to decide to release a disclosure. Internal information sharing among echelons is also bumpy, and despite numerous memoranda of understanding with foreign financial intelligence units, FINTRAC's reach rarely extends beyond Canada's borders, where some of the most incriminating activity occurs.

The centre boasts, "Canada has become recognized internationally as a leader in the fight against money laundering and terrorist financing." This is a surprising change. In 2003, the Auditor General admitted, "Canada was one of the last industrialized countries to introduce a system of mandatory reporting of suspicious transactions."

In terms of North American banks having a presence in offshore tax havens before 9/11, only New York's Citibank beat our own Bank of Nova Scotia. One source told me he couldn't walk a block in downtown Nassau without seeing a Scotiabank sign. Likely its only Caribbean branch that hasn't seen dubious financial activity in recent years is the long-defunct one I once passed in Havana. Could be a regime thing. Grey-uniformed police are ubiquitous in that part of town, and they can carry nifty mini-shotguns with pistol grips. It pays to behave in Cuba. "Be like Ché."

Some other Canadian banks aren't lily white either when it comes to "global private banking"; you can check out their annual reports to see how much of their revenue comes from offshore activities, all of which are perfectly legal, of course.

It would be hard to find a more damning indictment of FINTRAC than the Auditor General's 2004 report entitled *Implementation of the National Initiative to Combat Money Laundering.* After gleaning the opinions of several financial and police officers, the audit paints a disturbing picture of a paper tiger. The most important conclusion I draw from the report is that FINTRAC does not produce intelligence at all but merely furnishes information, much like a database. The centre also has no set of written criteria to guide its analysts in determining when a disclosure threshold has been satisfied. Guess they just wing it. Moreover, the data isn't even timely, which is a key aspect in any investigation. As a result, the audit noted that law enforcement does not "give much weight" to the centre's disclosures.

In other countries, the links between the police and agencies like FINTRAC are much closer and information is exchanged more easily. Regarding the centre's obsession with privacy, the audit asked an obvious question: "Should disclosure of information on what makes an activity suspect also be prohibited?" It is in Canada.

Regarding compliance, the centre doesn't have enough resources to monitor those who should be reporting. As for the money exchange businesses that can be found in corner stores and gas stations, they aren't registered, so there's no way of keeping track of them anyway. And if you choose not to report, the penalties are more lenient than in the U.S. So what about tax dodgers, the original target for FINTRAC? As of March 2004, the centre had fingered two. With a wild understatement, the audit found this to be "unusually low."

Money laundering takes place in several stages. The placement phase is the actual entry of criminal proceeds into the financial system by deposits, cash purchase of bank drafts or cashier's cheques, or wire transfers abroad. When funds reach the integration stage it is almost impossible to tell them apart from legitimate money.

Two laundering techniques are commingling and layering. A case of commingling could involve a cash-intensive business depositing way over its expected cash flow in mainly $20 bills as opposed to regularly clearing the till with notes of various denominations. It could be an effort to blend the proceeds from illicit drug sales with those of the small business. Layering could entail someone receiving frequent international wire transfers and buying bank drafts or cashier's cheques made out to another party, which are then deposited at a different bank. If at the same time they pay a mortgage in cash and also make large cash deposits, it's a slam dunk for investigators. Unlike drug money, however, you don't find a ton of cash in terrorist operations. The 9/11 attacks cost only few hundred thousand dollars, and a crank call that bottles up security can be done from a pay phone for a quarter.

Terrorist groups in the 1960s and 1970s obtained most of their funding from ransoms demanded from hostage taking and kidnapping, bank robberies, and the sponsorship of various sympathetic states. Since then, however, their sources of revenue have multiplied and include myriad methods. There is a range of legal and illegal ways terrorists stay solvent:

- **Ethnic and cultural support organizations.** These entities are legitimate and support the goals of various racial groups or displaced persons. They may, however, siphon funds to related groups involved in terrorist activities; charities aiding orphans and widows from war zones are ideal. An advantage is that, up front, the money can be openly banked and transferred. Once money is in the Third World, the trail often goes cold. Prominent Canadian Liberal politicians like Jean Chrétien and Paul Martin have attended fundraising events hosted by cultural organizations strongly suspected of having terrorist ties; CSIS had even warned them not to go.

- **Legitimate investments.** The Palestinian Liberation Organization (PLO) learned as early as the 1970s to channel funds to clean companies. With money from some Arab nations and Libya, the PLO has invested in airlines and duty-free shops in airports.
- **Legitimate businesses.** If you travel to the Middle East, Pakistan, or Yemen you can shop for honey at a number of retail outlets owned by Osama bin Laden and other al Qaeda members. Profits are then used to support the worldwide Islamic Jihad. Terrorists can also make use of illegal trades like drug smuggling and manufacturing. The United Nations believes certain terrorist activities in Africa have been funded by the sale of a relatively unknown drug, khat. The route seems to lead from Nigeria to Somalia. Ethiopian, Somalian, and Yemeni groups move it through our airports, according to the RCMP.
- **Racketeering.** Protection rackets are not new in organized crime; they have been used for ages by Chinese Triads and the Mafia with great success. Today, though, they can be combined with regular services from dubious private security firms, giving you a real invoice for your troubles. This is a common method in Northern Ireland, used by both the Irish Republican Army (IRA) and its protestant counterpart, the Ulster Defence Regiment.

- **State sponsorship.** Due to serious American pressure on the international community since 9/11, state support for terrorist groups is much less important than it was when Libya's strongman, Muammar Qaddafi, used about $100 million of his country's oil revenues annually to support nearly every terrorist waging war on the West. But Iran may still be in the game, and dysfunctional states lacking strong central governments, like Somalia and Sudan, can provide safe havens worth their weight in gold even if broke.
- **Ransoms from kidnapping.** Hostages can make good currency as well being media sensations, as the Revolutionary Armed Forces of Colombia (FARC) found out. It is estimated the group has collected about US$200 million from releasing abducted citizens of that country and well-off foreign nationals.
- **Extortion and blackmail.** According to the Metropolitan Toronto Police and Sri Lankan diplomats, this is a Canadian favourite of the Tamil Tigers. One cop claimed $1 million a month was raised by the Tigers this way in 1998. In addition to "protecting" relatives in their old homeland, Tamil expatriates can be assured that embarrassing information or material about them will not become public — for a fee. "Tributes" can be demanded on a regular basis. The Canadian government has yet to ban Tiger fundraising like Britain and the U.S. have done, despite many calls to do so. Money for terrorism can also be collected from drug cartels for security as FARC has done in Colombia for a 10 percent cut. In 1986, they made over $3 million each month with this type of tax. In geographic areas under majority terrorist control, war taxes can be a portion of a citizen's income. Extortion can be

tacit as well as overt: within mosques, a *zakat* may be collected for the poor and usually makes up 2.5 percent of one's income, a *sadakat* puts one in Allah's good books, while *fitras* are expected during the Muslim holy season of Ramadan.

- **Fraud.** Fraudulent activity can take many forms; stealing manufacturer's coupons or buying them in bulk and later redeeming them via crooked merchants can net a terrorist a fortune. It's estimated that coupon fraud in Canada is worth over $12 million every year, and some criminals even get schoolchildren to sift through garbage for them. In addition, credit/debit card fraud is popular, not only by the traditional means of stealing the actual cards but also by using sophisticated identity theft plans, which can involve stealing electronic data that has been swiped. It's a good rule to "charge it" only with merchants you can trust.

- **Smuggling.** In the U.S., Hezbollah recently ran cheap cigarettes from North Carolina up to higher-tax Michigan in order to send funds to Lebanon and pay for attacks against Israel. When smuggling across international boundaries, it doesn't help law enforcement if a country's seaports are swimming with outlaw motorcycle gangs either, as is alleged to be the case in Canada. Only 3 percent of ship containers arriving in Canadian ports are inspected. People can be smuggled as well as goods.

- **Theft**. Petty thievery kept the Canadian-based millennium bomber Ahmed Ressam in the black, and the FLQ once committed twenty-five robberies in two years, but car theft rings are a new twist. The RCMP claims that top Hezbollah operatives drive luxury automobiles and SUVs stolen from North America by Middle Eastern criminal gangs. Even Canadian construction equipment has shown up in

Shanghai, although the perpetrators are believed to have no known terrorist connections at this time.

- **Illegal banking.** Various inside ways to make a buck are available to terrorist groups if the bank is *really* their friend. The old Bank of Credit and Commerce International (BCCI) was quite cordial to Osama bin Laden, the Mafia, and South American drug cartels until being shut down in 1991. Abu Nidal had forty-two accounts in a BCCI branch in London alone.

- **Counterfeiting.** According to Statistics Canada's *2004 Annual Crime Report*, this was the only crime sharply on the rise here, which should be a matter of concern. Seen the American greenback lately? All U.S. bills were recently redesigned because Hezbollah apparently circulated hundreds of millions of bogus hundred-dollar bills for black market purchases. Documents such as passports and birth certificates can also be forged for funds, keeping terrorist organizations in good practice when they need their own false papers. As well, you know that a Rolex watch offered by a street vendor for $20 likely gives slightly inferior Swiss time; some say that up to half the world's knock-off market could be terrorist controlled.

- **Private donations.** A wealthy champagne Marxist publisher transformed Italy's Brigada Rosa from amateurs into a real terrorist threat, and wealthy patrons sympathetic to terrorist groups' aims are a big problem now, especially in the Middle East. Bin Laden is only one of a million dedicated warriors with deep pockets.

- **Government corruption.** In some countries, vast amounts of commodities and freedoms are exchanged because of payoffs to greedy politicians, customs and immigration personnel, police officers, judiciary personnel, and military personnel.

These include freedom for criminals, weapons used by armed gangs and terrorists, nuclear-grade plutonium, false passports and travel documents, and exported contraband. Many of these are for grabs in the former Soviet Union, some for as little as a couple of cases of premium vodka. Many former KGB officers are out of work. They know their craft well, and some have obtained employment with Eastern European organized crime groups.

After being introduced to the Iranian's Kurdish contacts in Canada, RCMP officer Gabriel Marion led everyone to Rome, where he posed as a capo operating a smuggling ring for the dreaded Costa Nostra. He also brought along a personal negotiator, bodyguards, chauffeurs, an international banker, and a chemist to test the purity of the heroin he was going to buy. All were RCMP and Carabinieri (Italian national police) undercover officers. The criminals were so impressed with the chemist's credentials they offered Marion US$1 million a week for his assistance with quality control in their heroin labs located in eastern Turkey.

Italian authorities flashed US$2 million for the deal, and when three cars driven by Polish "mules" pulled into a garage under Marion's control in a Rome suburb, the game was over. Secured on top of the vehicles' gas tanks were seventy-five kilos of high-grade heroin, and to this day, Project Overtrick remains Canada's largest undercover heroin bust. The Turkish, Iranian, and Polish conspirators would eventually plead guilty in Rome. What does it take to pull something like this off? Marion explains:

Firstly, you need a lot of patience. You must have a good understanding of a target's ethnic background and how they operate. Always study your environment: the geographical space, methods of operation, surveillance abilities, and mannerisms. You also try to remember faces and people around you when dealing with these characters as they may be putting physical surveillance on you once you leave a meeting. Keep a close eye on your rear-view mirror. When one on one, you almost need to think like a shrink in understanding your opponent without letting them know you are actually reading their mind or laying the groundwork by using reverse psychology. After all, you want him to believe who you are is *what* you are.

When I go to a foreign country, I am in their environment and it could be dangerous. Working in high-level covert operations makes you constantly on your guard, because a slip-up in conversation could cause you to lose your credibility as well as the evidence. You could be killed if they believe you are an informant or possibly ripping them off. Or they may want to rip *you* off or hold you for ransom if they feel confident you are in direct control of large amounts of money. People in Bogota will kill you for $100. Never mind if you have $2 million. Things can go wrong, and that is why you need a professional cover team to offer you security in tight quarters and monitor your movements in case.

Lastly, you must never forget what side of the fence you stand for. In this business you have to act professionally and turn on all your talents and skills while undercover and then "turn yourself off" when you go back to your humble existence. You always need to remember the day when you took your oath of office. Those who do not know how to turn off do so at their peril, for the line gets blurred causing your family, social, and professional lives to suffer if your "other life" starts to become a reality and get out of control. You will be in danger of drifting and following the path of many public icons who have tried to conceal a very troubled existence.

On September 15, 2000, Marion was awarded the Meritorious Service Medal of Canada by Governor General Adrienne Clarkson, and soon after he retired after being with the Mounties for twenty-six years. The citation noted that he took a leading role in the operation and showed dedication, commitment, and perseverance throughout.

"Far too often, police forces with good intentions create jurisdictions that are jealously guarded and controlled. Criminals and terrorists don't respect these and do what they have to. The key to my success was the co-operation and support from various police forces around the world," Marion says. "Overtrick was a police operation. But you can't lose sight that similar cases — involving terrorists moving funds in the underground banking system without leaving an audit trail to detect — are widespread or inter-connected. Afghanistan and Pakistan are but some examples. Opium cultivation and production translates to large volumes of cash, arms, training, power, and terrorism."

As for the Toronto-Iranian money exchanger, he might even be back in business here. Although he pleaded guilty for a minor offence under the Proceeds of Crime Act, the police did not press charges for the drug importations in Rome or money laundering, as the cash Marion had washed was not tainted in the first place. He spent no time "in gaol" and promised to be a good citizen.

CHAPTER 7

WELCOME TO CANADA
by Kostas Rimsa

"I've been told a forged Canadian passport can be bought on
Bangkok's Khao San Road for $1,500."

It is important you know that I am a first-generation Canadian. My parents were immigrants. I believe strongly in immigration to Canada for all that qualify, no matter their race or creed. I dare anyone to accuse me of being racist or anti-immigrant. But I would not be surprised if certain "agents of influence" will attempt to do so. Some of the following facts will be difficult to accept, and exposing them will not be to the interest of terrorists, organized crime, and those who have committed gross blunders in Canadian security policy and its implementation.

Canada's falling birth rate is below that needed to replace our population. At the same time, baby boomers are starting to retire and there are fewer Canadians coming behind them. By 2004, more than 70 percent of all new jobs created in Canada required some post-secondary education, and the country is already facing skills shortages in a range of occupations. To remain competitive and keep up with technological change, it's clear that Canada can never stop renewing through immigration and upgrading the skills of its workforce.

But there are some serious problems with our refugees. Infiltration through immigration is a tactic of al Qaeda and other terrorist organizations. According to the United Nations, out of the current 200 million refugees in the world, about 15 million are assisted in their efforts by human smugglers. And 95 percent of refugees are allowed to stay immediately upon their arrival in Canada. In the three years after 9/11, 15,000 refugees arrived in Canada, 2,500 of which were from terrorist sponsor countries or countries affected by internal terrorism. In addition, there were an estimated 200,000 illegals in Canada as of 2004, often working in the black market. Another 36,000, including criminals and security risks, were ordered deported, but their whereabouts are unknown. To halt such abuses with the security resources now in place is like trying to stop people from drinking during Prohibition.

As early as 1999 the Special Senate Committee on Security and Intelligence stated that Canada is used as "primarily a venue of opportunity to support, plan or mount attacks elsewhere and as a conduit to the United States." In a July 1999 report entitled *The Exploitation of Canada's Immigration System: An Overview of Security Intelligence Concerns*, CSIS identified several specific support activities of international terrorists in Canada, including planning and providing logistical support for terrorist operations in Canada and abroad, using fraudulent travel documents for entry, procuring weapons and materials, recruiting members and supporters, manipulating members of émigré communities, and providing a safe haven. The use of Canada as a staging ground for terrorist acts abroad — in particular in the U.S. — has been a real threat for years.

While Citizenship and Immigration Canada had an intelligence function before 9/11, it has formalized this within its Intelligence Branch to provide a focal point for gathering, analyzing, and sharing intelligence on immigration cases and migration trends with partners inside and outside our borders.

Globalization has created major challenges with immigration. Growing numbers of people are prepared to break Canadian laws, and CIC has noted an increase in the submission of false statements and fraudulent documents. But CIC is appallingly tolerant of these — submitting false information results in the refusal of an application at worst — and nothing prevents the applicant from submitting another the next day. The penalties now stipulated in the act are practically unenforceable in other countries as well.

Visa officers need a good knowledge of the infrastructure and social and political conditions in all countries for which an applicant has submitted a police certificate so they can assess its reliability. They also need knowledge of fraud trends in immigration applications and organized crime to make informed decisions. But officers have little information about conditions in countries other than where they are posted and receive very little training in how to determine admissibility, use security profiles, or identify trends in organized crime. Their procedural manuals for security review are over a decade old and desperately need to be revised.

Determining admissibility in the areas of criminality and security requires a high level of expertise. Departmental figures show a decrease in the rate of applications approved in recent years. This represents not only fewer potential immigrants but also an increased workload for visa officers, because they must support their decisions thoroughly when they refuse an application. In the event of a judicial review, they must also defend their position before a federal court. Since the passage of the Canadian Charter of Rights and Freedoms, the selection of immigrants has moved toward a more legalistic application of the act, and this trend reflects applicants' heightened expectations of the right to fair treatment. Numbers of lawyers and immigration consultants are growing. Immigration issues deal with people, and they frequently attract media attention. Politicians, non-governmental organizations, and others often contact program managers about specific cases. Following up requests and interventions from lawyers, immigration consultants, and MPs represents a significantly increased workload in many offices. According to a 1995 report, about one-third of a visa officer's time was devoted to deciding on applications, but the situation has become worse over the years due to increased numbers of applicants and cuts in staff. From 1990 to 2001, federal Liberal governments slashed staff by 20 percent. Low morale due to overwork can lead to a multitude of security problems: the issue of under-staffing is not only one of budget and manpower, but of security and intelligence as well.

The 2002 Immigration and Refugee Protection Act gives the department four responsibilities: citizenship selection, settlement, integration, and protection for refugees. While many functions were transferred to the new Canada Border Services Agency, immigration staff still work with them at major airports and border crossings.

The Immigration, Passport and Citizenship branch is responsible for investigating violations of the act relating to citizenship, passports, frauds, forgeries, and conspiracies. Services abroad are provided through eighty-one offices located in Canadian embassies, high commissions, and consulates. Approximately 210 Canadian officers and 980 locals work in them. Many are also responsible for several countries. Two of the key missions assigned to this branch are passport control and security screening.

Claimants of any category can be turned down for reasons of health, criminality, or security. Between 20,000 and 30,000 persons request refugee status annually in Canada, and they may make a claim for refugee protection at any CIC Port of Entry office (airport or land border crossing) or inland CIC office across the country. In the case of applicants where no initial security concerns are noted by the CIC officer, the refugee claimant's background information is forwarded to the CSIS Security Screening Branch to conduct its checks as time and priority permits. Approximately 80 percent who arrive claiming refugee status do not have any identification documents, and 95 percent are not detained when they arrive. It often takes only one hour to process a refugee from the moment the person claims refugee status until they leave an airport. They are entitled to medical coverage, social assistance, and work permits rather quickly after making a claim.

Waiting periods can be as long as thirty-two months, and this gives refugees plenty of time to disappear with little chance of being found. Over the course of the last six years, 36,000 refugees have been ordered out of the country — only the Canadian government can't find them. An example are the 599 Fujian Chinese who arrived by boat in 1999 off British Columbia; 131 were initially released from detention and 80 of them disappeared. Canada has varied and large ethnic communities, allowing illegal immigrants or terrorists to hide.

Such statistics worry our neighbour to the south. Some may be terrorists and some are undoubtedly hardened criminals. Is it any wonder that CSIS claims there are fifty terrorist groups active in Canada?

Many foreign intelligence officers overseas have told me that entrepreneur-class applications often involve fraud, organized crime, and illegally obtained money. The problem is that many immigrants are not efficiently security screened, if they are checked at all. Citizenship screening is only conducted on the basis of threats to Canada's security as set out in Section 19 of the Citizenship Act. Over the past few years, only about one-fifth of new immigrants have been screened. If refugees do not disappear initially, Canada has a judicial process that prevents us from deporting people without due process, and that gives time to disappear underground. All applicants and their dependants aged eighteen and older undergo criminality and security checks only before they are granted permanent residence.

Screening checks are conducted on only about half of refugee applicants, if that. All people who board an airliner or ship have documentation to get on. In most cases, they destroy their papers in flight or on arrival. Has it never occurred to the government to simply put them on a plane back whence they came? Even evaluating admissibility relies primarily on the co-operation of third parties. It often depends on the goodwill and honesty of local police forces, and in most cases the validity and reliability of the information they provide cannot be verified. A criminal background check is often limited to verifying whether a police certificate is attached to the application, without questioning the document's authenticity or reliability.

Frequently, information cannot be obtained because of the political or social situation in certain countries. For this reason, CIC does not require a police certificate for applicants from more than forty countries, which comprise almost 23 percent of the total. Some immigrants are thus admitted with no assurance that they have not committed crimes abroad.

There are serious constraints on the use of certain information whose source or nature cannot be disclosed. Data obtained from CSIS often falls into this category. The act allows certain information, obtained in confidence from a foreign government or an international organization, to remain undisclosed during a judicial review, but it does not protect the confidentiality of information obtained from Canadian sources, other information agencies, or other sources. And yet protecting information sources is an essential condition of continued co-operation by CIC's partners. In these circumstances, visa officers tend to avoid making negative decisions for fear of being unable to defend them in federal court, even when there is a reasonable suspicion that an applicant has engaged or may be planning to engage in espionage, subversion, terrorism, or violence.

All of these constraints make it difficult to declare a person inadmissible. On average, fewer than 1 percent of applicants are deemed so on this basis.

An interesting aside here is that Quebec has its own immigration program, selection criteria, and offshore offices. In 2001, immigration to that province accounted for 15 percent of the total flow to Canada. Believe it or not, the federal government cannot even monitor this system, which featured weak security policies for such legal documents as birth certificates as late as 2001. Should we be surprised at the number of arrests in Montreal?

In May 2002, the Passport Office introduced the new digitized Canadian passport with enhanced security features in an effort to counter criminal activities, such as identity theft and forgery. As well, a new fraud-resistant Maple Leaf card for immigrants who become permanent residents is also being issued. It is important to note that the Canadian passport does not contain biometric information, and it does not have an electronic chip in which personal data can be stored. The decision to include biometric features in Canadian travel documents has not yet been made by the government. The global community and even entities like the International Civil Aviation Organization have not chosen a particular technology or preferred biometric security measures for passport control. Currently, the only agreed-upon security measure seems to be digital photography. The Americans, British, and Germans are all concentrating on making the photos tamperproof.

In 2004, the government commenced plans to screen the photos of Canadian passport applicants against images of suspect terrorists on "watch lists." The Passport Office tested a computer program that compares a picture of a face with thousands of other pictures and zeroes in on possible matches. It is now seeking approval from the federal privacy commissioner to use the facial recognition technology in processing applications. The selected software program compares twenty characteristics on a face, and the initiative was supposed to complement federal plans to begin issuing high-tech passports with digitized photographs in 2005. Computer security requires rules on access and use, and stringent monitoring of compliance. There are concerns about the level of security in all the offices abroad as personnel do not have all the expertise needed. According to a 2004 Auditor General report, information about the 25,000 Canadian passports lost or stolen annually is not available to front line officers. It is only since this was revealed that the government has taken measures to correct the problem.

Another problem is that in Canada, judges perhaps feel using or possessing fake passports is a victimless crime. This may explain public statements made by Jocelyn Francoeur, Director of Security, Policy and Entitlement at the Passport Office, who added that the "costs of importing witnesses from every island airport in the world is prohibitive." Often stolen passports of legitimate citizens are sold to be altered by professional criminals or terrorists and used in their nefarious ventures. In such cases, it is common to have two and even three passports lost or stolen before the authorities take any action. Even then, the office simply denies new documents or revokes them for up to five years to those who misuse their passport. It's obvious that stricter penalties for those apprehended using or possessing forged or altered passports must be implemented.

Many Canadians believe that Canadians staff our embassies and consulates. They are very much mistaken; I have had dealings with consulates that were staffed *exclusively* by locals. The government does anything to save a buck, especially when the key issue is security. The process of buying one's way into our country is rampant at Canadian missions around the world. Most of the detected incidents involved locally hired staff in Canadian consulates, and there are few security mechanisms in place to stop such activity. Complicity, favouritism, theft of public funds, solicitation, and theft of visas are common. Large amounts of money are also handled, and the forms on hand bring a tidy sum on the black market: visas are now worth several thousand dollars. The department's Office of Professional Conduct reported that in cases under investigation in 1998, an estimated five hundred visas were missing or stolen, and a 2000 audit identified 304 cases of passport theft *inside* Canada, thirty-two of which required police support.

Better controls over documentation at embassies and consulates are required, and the practice of "partnering" should be instituted: one Canadian at least should be involved when issuing papers. Considerably more Canadian citizens could be filling positions overseas; one recommendation would be to use students or young future diplomats.

CIC also employs Canadian physicians to manage the determination of medical admissibility. These departmental physicians supervise local physicians who have been designated to conduct medical examinations. The local doctors forward the results to the departmental ones, who, in turn, submit their recommendations to visa officers. Determining whether or not applicants and their dependants are admissible is ultimately the visa officer's responsibility. The trouble is that contract physicians, especially in the Third World, can be bought off easily. To counter this abuse, secondary medical checks should be performed in Canada while under detention. Even terrorists are sick sometimes; bin Laden has bad kidneys.

I've been told a forged Canadian passport can be bought on Bangkok's Khao San Road for $1,500. They are so exact that officials believe they are largely powerless to detect those who are trying to fake their way into Canada. With these passports, illegal immigrants often leave through Hong Kong, the busiest Asian embarkation point for Canada. According to the 2003 *Report on the International Terrorism Threat*, CSIS stated that Thalayasingham Sivakumar, a high-ranking member of the Tamil Tigers, travelled to Canada on a false passport in June 1989. The Tigers' chief of procurement is still known to travel internationally using Canadian and other forged passports. Here at home, the good forgeries are made in Montreal, while most of the smugglers for illegals travelling south of the border are based in Toronto. An RCMP raid in Montreal in 1998 upset Russian and Asian mobsters by seizing hundreds of bogus passports from different countries. Also in the cache were Canadian visas, citizenship cards, and immigration forms; passports are not the only problem. Intelligence reports have revealed that other immigrants who try such schemes admit to paying up to $6,000 for a covering letter and counterfeit seamen's books, which allow easy access through our seaports.

New fraud-resistant Permanent Resident Cards have been issued by CIC since June 2002. They are highly resistant to alteration and duplication because they include a laser-engraved photograph and signature and many other advanced features. Now that new immigrants have been taken care of, I feel it is our turn, as citizens, to receive a national identity card. This is a provocative issue, but I do not believe that it is the beginning of the end to personal freedoms: the time has come to protect our identity as well as our privacy. Identity cards exist in one hundred countries around the world; in Europe every nation has one except Ireland and Great Britain, which have launched public consultations on their introduction. Australia and New Zealand are even considering biometric IDs. It may also be possible to put this technology to friendly use that will allow the card to be used as a driver's licence or credit card. This seems to be the way of the future as the Canadian Air Transport Security Authority (CATSA) plans to issue biometric cards for its workers, and under the Smart Border Action Plan we have agreed to develop common standards for biometrics with the Americans.

Another major intelligence problem for CIC is human smuggling and trafficking. One Immigration Control Officer received eight death threats during his three-year posting in Bangkok, six from Chinese gangs. The department created the Immigration Control Officers' network to provide international leadership in responding to this smuggling, but the officers have many more responsibilities on their plates. In 2004, a cargo of ten Chinese migrants was headed to Canada. In China, gangs charge between $22,000 and $75,000 per head and have even killed their own agents for failing to deliver people to the right destination. This shipment never reached Canada because CIC caught it, but many others do.

The money involved is substantial, and work by foreign agents cannot always be depended on for that reason. According to the department's Intelligence Branch, more than eight hundred people with ties to organized crime were deported or denied entry into Canada since 9/11, and about twenty thousand cases involving immigrants and visitors have been forwarded to the department's Organized Crime Division since its creation in 1994. The major concerns in the past few years have been predominately Asian, Eastern European, and Italian organized crime, as well as motorcycle gangs. This division was set up as a result of the increased threat from Eastern European groups and the expected increase of activities by Chinese Triads expected at the time of Hong Kong being returned to China. Immigration officials believe that better training, intelligence sharing, and communications systems would strengthen future efforts.

Illegal workers inside Canada number approximately two hundred thousand. This figure cropped up after an unofficial investigation with the support of different unions across Canada, which was conducted to determine the number of those working versus the estimated available. Though the number is considered the projected average of all estimates, former Minister of Immigration Joe Volpe quoted it at a summit held in 2005. No alarm was expressed in regards to security at the meeting, but rather how industry could make use of this illegal labour pool. The minister was more concerned that industry should provide more mobility for these illegals in order to relieve job openings in different regions and thus aid the need for skilled labour. Where are these illegals that are taking jobs away from Canadians and landed immigrants? Who knows? Remember that there are approximately six hundred thousand honest potential immigrants waiting in line.

This lack of concern can also be found in the statements of then Deputy Prime Minister and Minister of Public Safety and Emergency Preparedness Anne McLellan when she brushed aside opposition concerns regarding thirty thousand outstanding deportation orders. According to her, they are only people that have overstayed their visitor and student visa allotted times, certainly not a security threat. And then there was Judy Sgro, minister of immigration, who in 2004 was called on to resign after the husband of a Romanian stripper admitted he and his wife helped out on her re-election campaign in order to get fast-tracked through the immigration system. Anyone operating in Eastern Europe could have told the minister that many of the companies that bring strippers to Canada from there are fronts for organized crime. More importantly, these groups have connections to intelligence agencies of foreign countries. It is not uncommon to find that there is joint ownership of such companies. In 1999 in the former Soviet Union I personally made inquiries into this after I found out that the company in question had already shipped five girls to Canada. One owner worked the black market, another was from the Communist Central Committee, and the third was "retired" KGB. Sgro could have easily been compromised not only by organized crime but by a foreign intelligence service to boot. Why should we tolerate a minister of immigration who totally ignores security? Why did we have a minister charge of key intelligence and security forces in Canada ignoring thirty thousand deportation orders? This is absurd.

A mention here is required of the Immigration Task Force (ITF), a joint force of federal and provincial police that has captured 2,500 people across the Greater Toronto Area during the past ten years. About 150 arrests each year are deemed high risk. It's clear that the ITF should be increased and other groups like it instituted in every major city in Canada. All ITF units should be given improved intelligence co-operation and capability to eliminate the potential terrorists that are hiding among what now is revealed to be 230,000 illegals in Canada.

The government still doesn't seem to be getting it. In 2005, about five thousand tsunami victims from Sri Lanka were fast-tracked into Canada. Special personnel were sent over there to scour the land for would-be immigrants. Those with relatives here can be sponsored easily: faking a family tie by offering money or by threatening real family members is very easy for terrorist groups like the Tigers. Documentation would have been washed out to sea. How can a person prove he was a victim of the tsunami? The Liberal government was under pressure from a well-organized Tamil community that is a force in about ten ridings they held. Although it is good politics for the Liberals and portrays Canada as providing humanitarian assistance, this program will, without a doubt, be used to bring Tiger terrorists to Canada.

With the Maher Arar case receiving widespread media attention, the public eye has been drawn toward the subject of immigration and intelligence in a critical way, yet there is an aspect of this story that the press is either unable or unwilling, to tell. It concerns citizenship. You possess dual or multiple citizenship when more than one country recognizes you as its citizen. Unlike the law in effect until 1977, the current Citizenship Act allows Canadians to acquire a foreign nationality without automatically losing their citizenship. Consequently, you may have the rights and obligations conferred by any of these countries on their citizens. Whenever you are in a nation that recognizes you as a citizen, its laws take priority over the laws of any other country of which you may be a citizen. Dual citizenship may carry with it certain benefits, but it can also bring unexpected difficulties: legal proceedings, tax and financial responsibilities, military service, denial of emigration, and even imprisonment for failure to comply with obligations in one of the countries.

If you, your parents, your grandparents, and your spouse (if you are married) were all born in Canada and you have not become a citizen of any other country, then you are exclusively Canadian. But if one or more of them were born abroad or acquired another citizenship, this might result in your having dual citizenship, depending on the laws of the countries concerned, even if you never asked to be one. This occurs because citizenship can be obtained in more than one way: through country of birth, naturalization, parents, grandparents, or possibly marriage. According to international law, Arar was a citizen of two countries, Canada and Syria. He therefore could be deported from the United States to either, legally. The Americans chose to deport Arar to Syria. It was their legal choice to make. Canada could do absolutely nothing to alter this decision as the government had no legal ground to stand on — moral ground, perhaps, but not legal. I have always known that this can happen to anyone with dual citizenship. I have two passports as well.

Only by using additional Immigration Control Officers overseas, working in many cases in joint groups with the U.S. to receive additional intelligence and support, will it be possible to alleviate some of the pressure currently on the system. Once again, it will be up to the Americans to bail us out. Between the lack of security and intelligence and the apathy on the part of the federal government, terrorists, criminals, and other illegals know they will not be investigated or harassed by intelligence services. They know they will always have the right of appeal and will be able to bring their families over, have children born in Canada, and evade our justice system, usually indefinitely. This situation must be changed. All of us have a stake in the outcome and all of us have a role to play in defining the solution. We should not be living in our own little bubble — today's risks are far too grave.

CHAPTER 8

THE UNUSUAL SUSPECTS
by Dwight Hamilton
with files from anonymous

"I was lucky. One day, we may not be so lucky."

Here's a story from the papers I think you should take note of. At an altitude of 2,400 feet, Delta Air Lines pilot Parry Winder was on his final approach to Salt Lake City International Airport in December 2004. But what was to be a routine landing quickly turned into a deadly matter as he radioed the control tower that they had just been hit by a laser beam that appeared to originate from the ground and lasted approximately six seconds. An "intensely bright green light" illuminated the cockpit of his aircraft, affected his depth perception, and disrupted his ability to land the plane in a normal manner, he later said. Despite the startling nature of the incident, Winder initially brushed it off and went home after the flight. It was not until he awoke the next day with severe pain in one eye that he became aware of the gravity of the situation. As a result, he saw an eye surgeon and was treated for a swollen retina. It took two weeks for his right eye to heal, and although he was permitted to return to flying after three weeks, he still has abnormal sensitivity to bright lights.

In late January 2005, the U.S. Transportation Department began requiring pilots to report all such incidents immediately to air traffic controllers so the information can be shared with federal security authorities. The safety chief of the Federal Aviation Administration, Nicholas Sabatini, advised the House Aviation Subcommittee that a task force researching the incidents would announce their findings that August. Despite Winder's account and a number of open source reports, Sabatini stated, "No accidents to date have been blamed on lasers disabling crew vision." Further, he stated that the Department of Homeland Security "assures us that they have no information that would suggest that any of these incidents is in any way related to terrorist activity." It is less than comforting that American officials were quick to assure the public that "they have no information that would suggest that any of these incidents is in any way related to terrorist activity," yet they failed to explain what or who is exactly behind them.

Here in Canada, securing the critical elements of the air transportation system is the mission of the Canadian Air Transport Security Authority. The agency reports to Parliament through the minister of transport and is responsible for the pre-board screening of passengers and their belongings. CATSA also handles the acquisition, deployment, operation, and maintenance of explosives detection equipment at airports and collaborates with police in civil aviation security measures, working with the RCMP to provide police on board aircraft. The implementation of a restricted area ID card for people who have access to aircraft and the screening of non-passengers entering restricted areas at airports are also part of its mandate. In addition, CATSA personnel conduct searches of planes, food containers, and aircraft stores at eighty-nine airports on a regular basis. More than 90 percent of all aircraft passengers in Canada are screened according to the agency's procedures.

There is cause for concern. In December 2004, documents obtained through the Access to Information Act by CBC News revealed that over one thousand uniform items belonging to Canadian airport screeners were lost or stolen in a nine-month period. Nearly a quarter of those had a CATSA logo on them. Among the missing items are ninety-one metal shields that act as security badges, which prompted sharp criticism from Senator Colin Kenny, chair of the Standing Senate Committee on National Security and Defence. Kenny stated unequivocally that Canadian travellers were not getting the security they need, and some American news organizations also held these losses and thefts as evidence of continued security problems in Canada. Later, federal Transport Minister Jean Lapierre said the missing uniform items did not constitute a threat. "We have no report of any security breach," he insisted. "At this time, there's not one security incident that has been reported from this."

The Canada Border Services Agency is tasked to ensure that all travellers coming into Canada are admissible, comply with Canadian laws and regulations, and pay applicable duties and taxes. The agency processes all commercial shipments at ports of entry to ensure Canadian laws and regulations are adhered to and that no illegal goods enter the country. On the immigration side, a multi-layered approach means identifying and interdicting high-risk people, whether at the point when a visa is issued, when the individual attempts to board a plane overseas, or when the individual tries to enter the country once arriving at the border. CBSA also has a network of Migration Integrity Officers around the world. As part of their work, the agency checks documents to prevent people from using improper papers to board planes destined for Canada.

In January 2004, the government established the National Risk Assessment Centre (NRAC) within CBSA. The NRAC, which operates twenty-four hours a day, seven days a week, acts as a focal point and an interface between intelligence agencies at the international, national, and local levels to protect Canadians against current and emerging threats. Through the analysis and sharing of information, the centre increases Canada's ability to detect and stop the movement of high-risk people and goods into the country. The NRAC ensures the distribution of information to intelligence and law enforcement and field officers. Terrorists, high-risk people, illegal contraband, drugs, and weapons are all targeted. The NRAC receives much of its information via the entities of the Smart Border Action Plan.

It's clear something needs to get smarter. At five British Columbia border crossings, twenty-six vehicles blew by the ports without stopping during the week of February 7, 2005. In Stanstead, Quebec, the count is consistently well over 250 unidentified vehicles illegally entering Canada each month by using two unguarded routes, namely Leeball and Church roads. CBSA has documented more than 1,600 vehicles entering Canada in 2004 and failing to report to Customs. What happens then?

Ron Moran, national president of CBSA's union, has stated, "Our members have stopped bothering to call police to intervene and catch vehicles illegally entering Canada because police interventions simply don't happen, they don't exist anymore." Police openly admit they don't have the resources to deal with border runners. About 140 posts are staffed by one person and are classified as work-alone sites with little or no hope of getting quick support from police or other border officers when there is an emergency or a surge in traffic. The practice is exceptionally risky for the officials.

"Imagine telling hundreds of customs officers hired to protect our nation's border and ensure the safety and security of Canadians, 'Don't stop the really bad criminals, they may be too dangerous for your own safety, run or hide, let them cross our borders, then call police and hope they find those criminals before somebody gets hurt.' How absolutely ludicrous is that?" asks Moran. "We wouldn't be surprised if legal minds looking at this were to call such decision-making a product of wanton recklessness or pure criminal negligence."

On March 1, 2005, a man drove a car to a border post seeking entry into Canada. The man was listed in the FBI database as a possible terrorist, and the U.S. Department of Homeland Security, upon further checking, confirmed this. "I had to search the male and the car without the ability to defend myself," said the agent, noting that officers at CBSA are not issued firearms, only protective vests, batons, and pepper spray. American authorities identified the male as a suspected suicide bomber living in the U.S. who had a close association with individuals (and family) in Canada. He was returned to the U.S. without incident after being briefly detained. The border agent feels fortunate: "I was lucky. One day, we may not be so lucky."

The federal government has done its best to perpetuate an illusion of minimal security dangers at our borders by, among other things, trying to deny information that would support the need of an armed presence. This is an issue of safety not just for customs officers, but for the public. Our government must abandon its paternalistic instinct and the practice of hiding the truth from Canadians. In an April 2005 meeting with Standing Senate Committee on National Security and Defence witnesses, Moran stated that there have been a number of detentions and apprehensions of terrorists at the various American and Canadian border crossings by both countries' agents, and for every thirty apprehended, one might be publicly reported. It's not surprising that Moran says, "It is clear that CCRA's senior bureaucrats do not possess the law enforcement experience and/or background to adequately run Canada customs border security."

Opening diplomatic mail or mail that seems to be a national security threat is a tradition that spans thousands of years. By the fifteenth century, every government in Europe was doing it. Canada is no different from the rest of the world in this regard, except that it has the required legislation and the checks and balances system of a modern democracy, which many of the countries in the world today still do not have. But with seven thousand post offices and twenty-two major processing plants across Canada, it is not a simple task. With millions of letters and parcels processed each day, with limited resources available, it is impossible to check everyone's mail, even if that was allowed. To monitor the situation there is a system of postal inspectors who conduct internal investigations into employee wrongdoing. They work closely with customs, immigration, and CSIS in a variety of endeavours.

Once a threat has been identified, CSIS can be granted a warrant to monitor an individual's mail. The physical work is conducted by specially vetted private CSIS contractors who work undercover as inspectors. The warrant can be for different levels of intrusion by CSIS. One level would allow only the external information on a letter or package to be copied down. Other levels allow the letter or parcel to be opened and the contents to be photocopied or photographed and then analyzed, for things like codes and secret writing by the CSE. These warrants are often issued in conjunction with others that permit other types of surveillance activities by CSIS and supporting agencies.

Customs has always had the power to open mail or have mail opened in their presence if the mail was from outside the country. Customs officials regularly pass along the information they find to other government departments, such as the RCMP, CSIS, and CIC. In some cases customs will confiscate documents and send them to other departments; in others, documents are merely copied and the copies sent along, while the original mail continues on to the addressee. Officers are not required to obtain any warrant before opening and photocopying the material. The law authorizes customs officers to act as agents for CIC's Intelligence Branch in its business of identifying, intercepting, seizing, and/or copying suspect mail or courier packages without warrant and without just cause. Toronto-based RCMP, CIC, and customs officials recently intercepted twelve packages of Iranian-Canadian documents on their way to Dubai. These included passports and social insurance cards, credit cards, library ID, and fishing licences, which are often passed on by members of a particular community trying to help people from their homeland immigrate to Canada.

CIC has created a centralized database that catalogues the documents and information passed along by customs; the database can be accessed by immigration officials all across the country. A twenty-four-page manual instructs them to record the names, birth dates, family information, destinations, and travel histories, and to describe any other documents seized. If a package contains travel documents, it recommends recording airline tickets, baggage tags, and seat numbers. The manual also says that the database is scheduled to be upgraded with digital scanning capabilities, allowing officials to enter photographs and text images. Both regular and couriered mail can be legally intercepted in accordance with the law. Such operations are also carried out by other democracies. For example, the Dutch authorities picked up a package of ten counterfeit Canadian passports and passport laminates being sent from India to a Sri Lankan in the Hague.

According to a press report in 2004, less than 5 percent of the mail coming into Canada is X-rayed. By law, no inspection can be done on mail that weighs less than thirty grams. Government documents obtained under Access of Information legislation show that guns, tear gas, ammunition, explosives, and drugs are routinely smuggled into Canada via the mail to the five main mail centres in Toronto, Montreal, Vancouver, Calgary, and Winnipeg. The main concern, though, is that terrorist campaigns using the mail are always possible and have been carried out in other countries over the past fifty years, a recent example being the use of anthrax in the U.S. in October 2001. Another is a letter or parcel bombing campaign, which can be easily carried out, as co-author John Thompson found out courtesy of the Animal Liberation Front.

Canada has the largest coastline of any country in the world, and the St. Lawrence Seaway, its inland waters system, is the world's longest and most complicated. Our coasts are very challenging. The Atlantic Ocean has severe summer and winter conditions, including towering waves and gale-force winds. Freezing spray and ice cover compound operation problems in winter, and fog is a factor year round. Things are similar on the Pacific coast, but without the extreme winter cold. Marine conditions in the Arctic are harsh due to the low temperatures of air and water, the presence of ice and snow, and the prolonged hours of darkness.

Still, the oceans generate a substantial part of Canada's gross domestic product from commercial fishing, shipping and shipbuilding, tourism, manufacturing and services, and the oil and gas industries. Within our Atlantic Ocean area alone, an average of 350 merchant vessels and more than 150 fishing vessels use the waters every day. A daily average of more than four hundred boats can be found operating on the Pacific side. This is significant: with air travel being better secured, terrorists attempting to reach the shores of Canada — and later, perhaps, the U.S. — may travel by ship rather than plane.

The Department of Fisheries and Oceans' key current contributions to our national security effort are its conservation and protection program and the Canadian Coast Guard, which monitors our coasts. The coast guard liaises closely with the navy, which assists in some functions. The conservation program supports the security community through an air surveillance program that uses specially equipped aircraft to gather intelligence on the positions and activities of vessels operating off the coasts. All surveillance information is passed on to the defence department. The Canadian Coast Guard Auxiliary was established in 1978 and is made up of volunteers who assist in marine search and rescue operations and prevention. Its units are concentrated within those high-risk areas where the requirements are greatest. Its members' intimate knowledge of their own waters and coastline is often vital to a successful rescue and could be invaluable in intelligence collection in support of national security.

There are many challenges faced by the coast guard in its new assigned role in national security. It must secure a good portion of the perimeter of North America. Our navy is primarily a "blue water" fleet, mandated to fight battles away from Canada's shores. Its ships are generally too big, too slow, and too expensive to efficiently deal with threats in littoral waters. The navy does own a fleet of what are known as maritime coastal defence vessels, but their primary role is in training naval reserves.

Canada's coasts are virtually undefended. In Nova Scotia, for example, the Criminal Operations Branch of the RCMP has only thirteen officers dedicated specifically to the 7,400-kilometre coast of that province, backed up as required by thirty-two other officers, trained for armed boarding, who act as an emergency response. Neither our coast guard vessels nor the personnel on board them are armed. Before the national security role was tacked on, coast guard ships did, upon request, conduct security surveillance and carry officers from customs, CIC, the RCMP, and Fisheries and Transport on interdiction missions, but this was not common.

Today's coast guard cannot protect our perimeter. It does not have the weapons, training, or vessels for this task, yet no institution is more familiar with our waters. The majority of coast guards throughout the world have a policing role; they are most often defined in this respect and have the necessary equipment and trained personnel to do the work. It's only common sense that our coast guard should be given the responsibility and weapons to secure our own waters, but that would mean a sizeable increase in funding for new ships as more than 50 percent of the fleet is past its half-life. It would cost an estimated $350 million just to bring them up to strength to perform the roles that they are mandated to play now. Even though the government is investing $276 million for the acquisition of six new oceangoing vessels and four new ships for the Great Lakes and St. Lawrence Seaway, this is not enough. By comparison, Australia is currently pumping $500 million into a stand-alone coast guard distinct from its navy, and the United States has increased the budget of its coast guard to a point over that which was requested, and it is even being up-gunned.

Ideally, the coast guard should be an independent agency with its own mandate separate from the fisheries department. Already in existence are U.S.–Canadian Joint Rescue Co-ordination Centres, responsible for the planning, coordination, conduct, and control of search and rescue operations. These centres, staffed by search and rescue coordinators from the Canadian military and coast guard, are on full alert twenty-four hours a day, seven days a week. The best way to coordinate the surveillance of our coasts though is through Northern Command (NORTHCOM). A new organization formed by the U.S. for the military defence of North America, NORTHCOM's headquarters is located next to NORAD in Colorado. Though it is already part of NORAD, Canada has not yet decided to join the new alliance.

In December 2002 the U.S. and Canada signed an agreement regarding emergency assistance and the use of their troops on each other's territory. As Canada has limited defence and emergency response capability, this is required in the event of a terrorist strike involving weapons of mass destruction. There are some maritime implications. The September 1999 U.S. National Intelligence Estimate on ballistic missile threats, for example, discusses a variety of alternatives to long-range ballistic missiles that terrorists might employ, including short-range ballistic missiles launched from forward-deployed ships, land-attack cruise missiles launched from (even commercial) aircraft or ships, and non-missile means. Covert delivery could be by ship, plane, or land.

Canada does very little monitoring of its coasts, due predominately to a very restrictive budget and the aging equipment currently used. Increased satellite surveillance would improve the maritime security of the Canadian coastline, as would joining NORTHCOM and arming our ships. The use of the coast guard in intelligence collection could be instituted with a minimum of additional training.

The Public Health Agency of Canada's Centre for Emergency Preparedness and Response (CEPR) is both a collector of information and an end user of intelligence. The centre is Canada's central coordinating point for public health security issues and uses intelligence to develop and maintain national emergency response plans. The CEPR assesses public health risks during emergencies and uses the intelligence it collects to keep health and emergency policies in line with other federal and international health and security agencies. Intelligence is also used when the CEPR fulfils its responsibility for determining federal public health rules governing laboratory safety and security, quarantine, and similar issues.

The CEPR is the government's health authority on bio-terrorism, emergency health services and response, and nuclear emergencies. As the lead department, it is responsible for coordinating the nuclear emergency response of at least fourteen federal departments and six agencies. In the event of a terrorist act involving radiological or nuclear devices, the agency's Technical Advisory Group would support the Solicitor General's National Counter-Terrorism Plan by providing technical and operational advice on potential radiological impacts and protective actions. Part of the collection and analysis of information is conducted via the Centre for Surveillance Coordination and its Geographic Information System, which ties together many health professionals, laboratories, and institutions, in addition to federal agencies and emergency preparedness centres.

The Canadian Nuclear Safety Commission (CNSC) receives intelligence about potential threats that have been constantly monitored in close collaboration with many agencies, especially the U.S. Nuclear Regulatory Commission. The CNSC then passes on intelligence on a need-to-know basis to the appropriate agency using a three-tiered system of nuclear sites for which it is responsible. Those in the first tier are considered major licensees and include some research facilities at universities and isotope processing labs. The second tier includes uranium refineries, mills, and fuel fabricators. The third tier comprises another 4,500 licensees of lesser stature. Intelligence is used to design realistic exercises, enhance training of on-site security personnel, and inform agencies of potential problems.

Information is keenly guarded. For example, CNSC regulations prohibit disclosure of the location, routing, and timing of nuclear material shipments, such as spent fuel. The shipment of radioactive material is also governed by Transport Canada's Transportation of Dangerous Goods Regulations, which require shippers to have emergency response plans in place.

Although on the surface it may seem that Environment Canada would have no reason to have an intelligence unit, it does. The problem is that it is viewed as only a support service for inspections and investigations, despite the fact that its officers must participate in the National Support Plan from the

Office of Critical Infrastructure Protection and Emergency Preparedness. This complements and supports all other emergency planning frameworks in Canada, including the National Counter-Terrorism Plan, the Federal Nuclear Emergency Plan, and the Marine Spills Contingency Plan, which defines the way the coast guard will operate during events involving marine pollution. There is also a Canada–U.S. Joint Inland Pollution Contingency Plan, which provides a framework for the countries to prepare for, and respond to, accidental and unauthorized spills and the release of pollutants that may cause damage to the environment. It covers the shared inland boundaries of both nations.

There is a real possibility of a terrorist act that could have a devastating impact on the environment, especially if it involves the use of improvised nuclear, biological, or chemical weapons. In addition, smuggling networks that would be monitored by Environment Canada investigators could be used for bringing terrorists and/or their equipment here.

Transport Canada is not only responsible for securing road, rail, and air transport of people and goods, it must also cover the security weaknesses of Canada's port system. This is significant. Former CIA director George Tenet has directed attention to ship containers as being the "potential Trojan horses of the twenty-first century." Marine security is currently the country's weakest link. Transport Canada is the lead agency in countering a marine threat and is supported by National Defence and Public Safety and Emergency Preparedness Canada, which includes the CBSA, CSIS, the RCMP, and the coast guard.

To protect our coasts effectively we must ensure that security extends from our ports beyond the two-hundred-nautical-mile economic zone. This will not be accomplished without substantial financial support for security and intelligence programs already established in response to U.N. regulations and the threats posed since 9/11. Collaboration with the Americans, no matter how they are represented by their government, is key to success in this area.

In compliance with the new international security requirements of the U.N., the government-required ports and their facilities to have approved security plans in place and operational by July 1, 2004. Under the federal program, ports and marine facilities were able to apply for funds to assist with new security equipment. Transport Canada also implemented a plan for a new security clearances program in 2004. All Canadian vessels and ports now have to register their International Ship and Port Facility Security (ISPS) code with the International Maritime Organization. Also, commercial vessels over one hundred tons now require security plans.

Of the 370 port facilities that need to comply with the ISPS code, fifty-seven are owned and operated by Transport Canada. Private or local interests operate more than 150 facilities, and 81 are located in our three main ports of Montreal, Halifax, and Vancouver. The department also assists with security assessments and plans for locks on the St. Lawrence Seaway and between the Great Lakes. Restricted regions known as Customs Controlled Areas were implemented by the CBSA.

Transport Canada's Intelligence Branch has the dual role of managing security-screening programs for the department's employees and transportation-sector workers as well as acquiring, analyzing, and disseminating political and economic intelligence in support of departmental strategic policy. It also liaises with other national and international agencies on security intelligence and counter-terrorism matters. Clearances are issued to departmental employees who require access to sensitive information and to those who need access to a restricted area of a Canadian aerodrome. Assessments of tactical and strategic intelligence involving threats to the transportation system are given to other departmental decision-makers and stakeholders.

Canadian and American authorities have been working together to enhance marine security and share intelligence on ships entering the Seaway and Great Lakes. The security screening procedures include pre-screening of foreign ships before they arrive in the system and onboard inspections of them prior to proceeding to port. Boarding protocols have also been refined to improve response to any threats before ships arrive at port.

Intelligence is distributed by the branch to such end users as CATSA and the Security Operations Branch, which manages the National Transportation Security Awareness Program. This is directed at all areas of the transportation industry, staff at transportation facilities, and the travelling public. This branch designs and delivers training for the professional development of Security and Emergency Preparedness inspectors and for the use of the transportation industry, also in all modes. It is the departmental liaison with the RCMP and other police on security and criminal matters and performs air carrier inspections at offshore destinations.

The operations branch assists in the development of multi-modal policies, standards, legislation, and training courses to ensure a high level of security for the national transportation system. It acts as the functional authority to help industry achieve compliance with security legislation, monitors the consistency of inspection and enforcement of the system across the country, conducts reviews of regional security offices, and performs external audits.

Intelligence is also key in the Canadian Transport Emergency Centre, which assists response personnel in handling dangerous-goods accidents. Situation Centres (SITCENs) are the departmental focal points for response, providing information on emergencies to senior management, other government departments and agencies, other countries, and NATO. They include full-time informatics support as well as a desk officer who, among other things, regularly trains emergency responders in the use of the centre's resources. In addition to the SITCENs, a National Situation Centre is located in Ottawa with regional offices in Moncton, Montreal, Toronto, Winnipeg, and Vancouver. It is responsible for the National Emergency Preparedness Program, which consists of planning, training, preparing responses, creating awareness, and assuring quality.

Intelligence liaison extends from domestic to international agencies. One example is the agreement signed between Transport Canada and the RCMP to share sensitive information on organized crime and criminal association to assist in screening airport workers.

Maritime security is multidimensional. Terrorist threats can come from sea, air, land, and even underwater. Canadian ports are still relatively open to infantry-style raids, suicide missions, and combat swimmers or divers. Today, re-breather scuba tanks (also known as closed-circuit or Drager systems) can be used that produce no telltale trails of bubbles on the water's surface. High-speed boats, canoes, kayaks, inflatables, and craft disguised as police or coast guard vessels could be utilized in any attack. Marjacking (marine hijacking) and using a mother ship to dispense terrorists in smaller boats who would commit acts of sabotage along a coastline were common tactics used in Palestinian attacks on Israel. The PLO has trained with mini submarines and the Tamil Tigers with electric-powered human torpedoes. Infiltration can also come from the air by parachute, hang-glider, helicopter, or ultra-lights. In addition, infiltration by using custom-built containers can be used to gain access to either the port or a ship for the purpose of marjacking. Such containers have been used in the past to smuggle terrorists around the world.

On October 28, 2001, Amir Farid Rizk, an Egyptian-born Canadian citizen, was arrested in Italy after arriving inside a cargo container from Egypt. It had been specially modified to include a chemical toilet and sleeping area. Also found inside were maps, airline tickets, a laptop computer, and a satellite phone. Back here at home, a 2002 survey of dockworkers for the Standing Senate Committee on National Security and Defence stated that 187 of five hundred longshoremen at the port of Halifax had criminal records.

CHAPTER 9

DIPLOMATS
by John Thompson

"Dead ones, however accidental, cause much awkwardness."

As a rule, being outspoken is a good way to meet lots of foreign diplomats, consular staff, and military attachés. It's a bad way to meet your own. In twenty years of providing research and commentary on security issues to both Canadian and international audiences, I've only twice been invited into the sacred halls of our Department/Ministry of External/Foreign Affairs, DFAIT, or whatever it's being called this year. The name does keep changing — and we'll all see how long the new moniker of Foreign Affairs Canada (FAC) stays.

The first time was while I was serving as the escort for a pair of visiting Chinese generals, and this got us a superb meal with elegant service on the upper floor at 125 Sussex Drive with some of the senior people on Asian and Pacific desks in the department for a quiet exchange of views on regional security issues. Any progress this trip might have made was derailed the next year by the Tiananmen Square massacre.

The second time was shortly after 9/11, when I was trooped in along with a squad of Canadian academics (almost all of whom were the usual suspects) for a groupthink session on responses to terrorism. My blunt views and disdain for giving much importance to "root causes" were shared by the lone representatives of the RCMP and CSIS at the table, and I suspect none of us *realpolitik* types have been invited back.

I've also seen the panic that can affect senior members of the department when they find their minister has slipped his leash and is getting some independent views, having helped facilitate this once in a small way with a member of the opposition party from an African nation. It turned into a very educational afternoon. I have met with ambassadors, consuls, and embassy staff from some twenty different countries on a professional basis. One or two had taken umbrage at things I had said about their nations; most wanted to swap opinions and information on the subjects that comprise my professional interests. There was also the one rather liquid lunch with a consulate staff in Toronto who believed they had been reconnoitred for a possible terrorist attack and wanted a second opinion as to how likely this was and who the prime suspects might be. There was also the poor old military attaché from a then Warsaw Pact member, scurrying around the defence and security studies community in Toronto once a month trying to fill his assigned "norm" of material lest he be summoned home in disgrace.

Canada's diplomats tend to be, like most of their counterparts from other nations, extremely civil, very well spoken (in public circumstances anyway), and precise in their communications. These are the professional characteristics we should expect from career diplomats, and FAC recruits and selects accordingly.

The roles, rights, and responsibilities of ambassadors and diplomatic staff are entrenched in customs and practices that go back to the Greeks and Romans, if not even further. They are supposed to be protected persons and were even regarded as sacred in some cultures. Whatever else could be said about Genghis Khan, he was particularly circumspect about honouring the safety of ambassadors and went into Central Asia in a genocidal fury after his own were murdered there. The principles about protecting diplomats were well understood in Europe even before the rise of the modern nation state, and aside from those killed by the French Revolutionaries and Napoleon, diplomats generally remained inviolate until the start of modern terrorism in the 1960s.

Diplomats are supposed to be clear and lucid communicators who pay close attention to nuances, protocol, and their manners. This is because they must avoid deliberately giving offence, yet must make sure there is no misunderstanding about the messages they are asked to deliver or the answers they must carry back. The apparent failure of an American diplomat to clearly communicate to Saddam Hussein that he was to keep his mitts off Kuwait in 1990 is a case in point, though one should bear in mind the ability of totalitarians to hear only what they want to.

Ambassadors and their staff also have a vital secondary function: diplomats are expected to acquire information so that they can provide an accurate picture about other nations and events to their own governments. This is a form of intelligence gathering.

Regardless, diplomats will be the first to strenuously tell anyone who listens that they are not intelligence agents, and they certainly seldom regard themselves as "spooks" or spies. Nor are they. Diplomats and their staff can gather information openly and cleanly; this is expected of them. But looking for secure or protected information in other countries is considered espionage, and this is usually grounds to withdraw recognition of a diplomat's credentials from the host government.

The histories of intelligence gathering organizations and diplomatic services around the world are often closely intertwined, and this was particularly true after the start of the Cold War. In most European societies before the twentieth century, diplomacy and foreign intelligence gathering were strongly connected — but this was not so for Britain and America. The roots of most of the older intelligence agencies in Great Britain and the U.S. lie with the military, with code-breaking functions that started during the First World War, and with domestic police agencies. Canada, having developed in the Anglo-Saxon tradition, could really only number the RCMP's Security Service as an intelligence agency before the Second World War, and our biggest post-war development resulted from signals intelligence (SIGINT) activities directed against the Soviets in concert with our allies.

But there were Canadian civil servants with a penchant for intelligence matters in the then Department of External Affairs, like Norman Robertson, who was the acting undersecretary of state for the department when he facilitated Canadian involvement in wartime Allied code-breaking operations. Robertson later handled much of the work generated by the defection of Igor Gouzenko, keeping the files out of External Affairs' system and using a private one instead. Robertson also played a key role in developing the Security Panel in the Privy Council

Office, whose successors still receive almost all of the intelligence collected for Canada that gets placed before the prime minister and Cabinet.

The relationship between FAC and the intelligence functions in the PCO continues, but this certainly does not mean that Canada's diplomats see themselves as a direct part of the world of intelligence gathering. They do tend to be fairly aware of this world, however, and know that the foreign affairs officers of other countries may be more likely to be aggressive intelligence officers than any Canadian would be. As often as not, personnel from FAC are involved with the PCO's Coordinator of Security and Intelligence and the Security and Intelligence Secretariat.

The history of other nations' intelligence gathering through their diplomatic corps is much more aggressive. The Soviet Union, right from its inception, strove to limit the mobility and access of foreign diplomats on its territory while actively using its own embassies for every conceivable intelligence function. Igor Gouzenko's revelations were by no means unusual, and the treasure trove of material from the old First Directorate of the KGB that was published in *The Mitrokhin Archive* reveals the vast extent of Soviet spying through their embassies. There was usually a "legal," a known representative of the KGB, on the staff of every embassy, just as the Americans have a CIA officer attached to many of their legations. The Soviets also made extensive use of "illegals," intelligence officers operating from behind diplomatic cover. Often the man actually in charge of an embassy staff was not the ambassador but one of his seeming subordinates who was there to oversee the collection of intelligence.

The RCMP Security Service detachment in Ottawa was kept gainfully employed for decades, following Soviet embassy staff around to catch them, often quite successfully, engaged in espionage. *The Mitrokhin Archive* also mentions episodes of agent recruitment, influence operations, passing clandestine funding to Canadian and U.S. communist parties, and systemic commercial/industrial espionage being run out of the old Soviet embassies. Their Warsaw Pact allies and the Cubans were similarly busy, particularly through their various consulates in Montreal and Toronto.

By many accounts, the People's Republic of China uses its diplomatic posts just as aggressively nowadays, particularly with respect to acquiring technology and conducting influence operations. They have also been noted using their embassies and consulates to monitor the Chinese community here, seeking to limit the influence of dissidents and Fayun Gong sect members. The same has been observed of the Iranians, the Iraqis during Saddam Hussein's regime, and allegedly the Saudi embassy with its support to the activities of sundry Wahhabist missions here.

A last personal observation: my father was an Air Force officer and a defence scientist for many years, specializing in electronic warfare and remote sensing. Once I received my commission as an officer in the Canadian Army he opened up about a few things that technically were not part of his business but that always irritated him, and he took me to view the rooftops of various embassies in Ottawa. The forest of antennas — particularly on the Soviet embassy rooftop — included a great many that had no business being there except to eavesdrop on Canadian government and commercial communications: clear proof that that the protected grounds of these nations' embassies were being used to illicitly gather intelligence. I've never seen a similar setup on the roof of any Canadian embassy, nor have I ever heard of Canadian diplomats behaving like so many others have.

The role of Foreign Affairs Canada is fairly basic: it supports Canadians working and visiting abroad, works in co-operation with other branches of the Canadian government to enhance our national security and interests (and the department maintains a very broad view of what this entails), and acts as PR agent by "promoting our culture and values internationally." The promotion of international trade was tacked on to FAC back when it was DFAIT, but now it is a somewhat separate function again.

Currently, FAC maintains some 270 offices in some 190 countries. This includes embassies, high commissions, consulates, and delegations to the Organization for Security and Cooperation in Europe, the North Atlantic Treaty Organization, the Organization for Economic Cooperation and Development, the Organization of American States, the European Union, and several United Nations offices. There are eighty-one possible postings for a Canadian diplomat in Europe and much of the former Soviet Union, sixty-three in sub-Saharan Africa, sixty-two in Asia or the Pacific, sixty-two in Latin America and the Caribbean, twenty-four in the Middle East and North Africa, and twenty-four in the U.S. and Mexico.

There are worse places to serve than, say, with the consulate in San Francisco or our embassies in Copenhagen or Vienna. But somebody has to stay in places where the inhabitants have no great respect for a Canadian ambassador or his or her car or wristwatch, and security is tight around our embassies in Tirana, Albania; Port-au-Prince, Haiti; and Abidjan, Liberia. We have embassies in Afghanistan and Colombia, and we are reopening the embassy in Iraq — places where the risk of an attack on our diplomats is very high.

Unfortunately, most of the security for our ambassadors and their staff tends to be passive: stout locks and bright lights. A very few embassies have a military police officer along as an escort for the ambassador, and fewer still have the full security team that often (very discreetly) accompanies ambassadors and consuls from more threatened nations. Until the terrorist threat to our embassy staff translates from hypothetical to historical, this state of affairs is likely to continue. Of course, most Canadian diplomatic postings are in no need of armed security.

To staff our offices, FAC recruits about fifty personnel a year for placement as trade commissioners, Citizenship and Immigration Canada officers, Management and Consular Affairs officers, and political/economic officers. This last group tends to be the pick of the applicants that make it through the selection process; historically, they either stay in the diplomatic service the longest or gravitate to other senior positions in the civil service. Many of the senior policy mandarins in other government departments entered the civil service through External Affairs. About 3,500 Canadian citizens also staff our overseas offices in supporting roles, as do about 5,000 local employees.

An embassy might also include a military attaché (or a whole section of them), a liaison team from the RCMP and or CSIS, and other people serving in security or intelligence roles. Again, their functions are quite open and they work to facilitate legitimate information gathering or liaison work with their counterparts in the host countries. A military attaché in Moscow during the Cold War would have been expected to watch the great annual parades where the Soviets openly displayed some of their newest weapons systems; today he might be engaged with dozens of other routine duties with the Russian military. The RCMP officer might be acting as a liaison with the national police to facilitate the sharing of intelligence or co-operation on international investigations.

The annual take of foreign service recruits are carefully screened; academic and linguistic qualifications are not enough. They also need to demonstrate that they understand exactly what is expected of a diplomat and can behave accordingly.

In a hypothetical situation during the screening program, a prospective political officer might be expected to imagine that he is to meet a dissident in some unsavoury nation as a part of his duties. Such a meeting would not be quite clandestine but would certainly be discreet — the subtle differences are important. Would the candidate think of turning up in disguise (a very bad idea) or would he merely pay attention as to whether or not he were being tailed on his way to the meeting? If he were being tailed, would he immediately speed away in his car (another bad answer) or take a leisurely drive back to his residence?

If, during the course of the meeting with the dissident, armed police burst into the room, would the candidate immediately declare that he is a Canadian diplomat and that the dissident is under his protection (a truly bad idea), throw himself out the window to escape arrest (likewise exceptionally wrong), or calmly sit down, quietly identify himself when asked, and seek to report the whole incident to Ottawa once back at the embassy?

Another hypothetical situation involves discovering a party of thieves in the midst of making off with the embassy's silver tea service — any other answer besides immediately fading into the background and calling the police when it is safe to do so is a failing grade.

Adventures of this kind for Canadian diplomats are almost unknown — almost, but not entirely. Between arranging for scholarship exchanges, reviewing travel plans for non-governmental organizations, reading the local newspapers, and passing the canapés when networking with peers, a political officer, especially a junior one, might receive any number of interesting assignments. During the abortive putsch that signalled the end of the Soviet Union, a Canadian political officer was in the crowd; apparently there was one at Tiananmen Square when the Chinese military rolled in; and one was scrambling off the grandstand at the assassination of Anwar Sadat. One need not be James Bond to keep an eye on history as it unfolds.

It usually is not policy to drop someone into harm's way ahead of time, but rather to get a first-hand impression of ongoing events; if gunfire looks to start up, the diplomat is expected to get well out of the way. Training them is expensive, and dead ones, however accidental, cause much awkwardness. But Canadian diplomats have met with the leaders of terrorist groups and guerrilla movements, kept in contact with endangered dissidents in dozens of countries, and otherwise developed political intelligence through open means. They are not intelligence officers and never see themselves as such.

Intelligence gathering involves the collection, collation, interpretation, and dissemination of information. Most of the intelligence that an agency develops is through open sources: newspapers and wire service reports, television footage, and the Internet. Even the CIA or MI-6 will sometimes admit that 90 percent of information comes from open public sources. Much of the remainder comes from open discussions with people. Police detectives, CSIS officers, and Canadian ambassadors are alike in this: they give you their business cards before they start to talk to you. The ambassador is far more likely to see that you are at your ease in settings that are as conducive as possible to the exchange of opinions and information, however. The ambassador will never resort to wiretapping or "good cop/bad cop" interview techniques, and if they do lie to you, it will be a very polite misdirection rather than some bald-faced fabrication.

The cop, the CSIS agent, and the diplomat also must all file regular reports on who they have met and what they have learned. In the service of some countries, diplomats must do this for every meeting that they participate in; Canadians might not be that different. As the minutiae of every particular floods the department, consulates, missions, and embassies tend to file routine reports and summaries on political and other professional developments and then fire them back to Ottawa. While the sources that FAC's officers amass are usually open ones, the contents of the reports themselves betray Canada's interests and intentions and so are often classified.

Canadian diplomatic staff cannot spend all of their careers outside of the country and must usually be rotated back to positions inside their headquarters. Usually, one tour outside Canada is followed by another two to three years back home. FAC's internal organization includes the usual spectrum of divisions, bureaus, and desks, which reflect its functions and interests. There are seven regional offices — North Asia and Pacific; South and Southeast Asia; Middle East and North Africa; Africa; European Union and North and West Europe; Central, East and South Europe; and Latin America and the Caribbean — that are subdivided again with specific desks for different countries.

There are also branches located under International Security and Global Issues. The first includes International Security, Security and Intelligence, International Crime and Terrorism, Global Partnership Programs, the Ambassador for Mine Action, Peacekeeping and Human Security, and Area Management. Global Issues includes the Science Advisor, Economic Policy, Environmental and Sustainable Development Affairs, International Organizations, Global Issues, the Ambassador for Circumpolar Affairs, and another Area Management Section.

Many of the personnel in International Security or Global Issues are not political officers, and many were seconded from other government departments. This is also the area where a lot of the routine work of international relations is done. An officer in the international security desk might be staffing requests for port visits to Canada from foreign navies, sitting in on arms control conferences, or overseeing the facilitation of travel to Canada for dependents of foreign military personnel located here. Most of the work for staff in the Security and Intelligence Section is of a similar nature.

A recently returned junior political officer might find herself back from Angola to sit for a spell in the African section, but perhaps reviewing material from South Africa rather than Angola. At the same time, she might also be tasked with sitting in on committees formed under Global Issues that work to restrict small arms trafficking, and sometimes may be farmed out to liaise with the non-governmental organization involved in this area of interest. Besides reviewing material, she must write briefs, position papers, and outlines for policy development, distilling her own experience and incoming data for the mandarins and, perhaps, even the minister's staff.

Next time out, she might be the Second Political Officer in Portugal or Brazil, unless she took language training suitable for another part of the world. Upon her return, her fundament might be planted in the Latin American desk with time spent on the OAS and sitting in on International Crime and Terrorism meetings, and so it goes on up the career ladder.

FAC's ability to generate information is profound, and well beyond its own ability to process all of it. When Canadians comment on the need to generate an overseas intelligence agency, they should remember that they've got 90 percent of one already and it usually does a fine job. But the most common problem in the history of generating intelligence stems from a single source: the ability of the receiver of that intelligence to reconcile it with his or her own misconceptions. Historical examples of this are plentiful, and many are cited in the century of British military blunders chronicled by Norman F. Dixon in *The Psychology of Military Incompetence*. Dixon wasn't necessarily picking on the military, but he was pointing out that failure in a military environment is absolute: lost battles, ruined armies, and many more dead soldiers and civilians than there ought to be.

Failure in a civil service environment or a political party that has governed much too often is less difficult to recognize, but both environments have the same problem that a blundering military does. Dixon points out that an environment that rewards conformity will attract anal-retentive conformists and that they will crowd up the promotion ladder a little faster than the truly gifted will. Diplomatic corps (even Canada's) have seen their fair share of talented mavericks, and there are many splendid examples of exceptionally bright and independent-minded ambassadors in our country's service. It is not impossible for such to rise to the top, but it can sometimes be difficult.

What goes for Canada's civil service can also apply to the political party that has governed it for some 70 percent of the last century. We have had good ministers of external affairs and we have had some appalling ones, and some have held the portfolio for longer than they should have. Karl von Clausewitz once observed that officers are either energetic or lazy and either stupid or clever. Much can be done with an energetic and clever one, or even a lazy and clever one; a lazy and stupid one won't do that much harm, but an energetic and stupid one is an absolute disaster. We have had ministers like that too.

The temptation to tailor information for ministers is often strong, although one can get the impression that nobody in FAC expects to do that for their colleagues in the PCO or other federal departments. The ability of members of various Canadian governments, including ministers from both major parties, to disbelieve the intelligence they get or to fail to act on it has been clear. The ability of an energetic but not-so-clever minister to shape the department cannot be understated either, particularly if he or she holds the portfolio for a number of years. This helps explain why FAC still has its devotees of "soft power" traditional peacekeeping or small arms control, or why Global Affairs tends to be cluttered with celebrity-cause issues.

Yet, under its various names and through its history, FAC has generated an extraordinary number of able civil servants that have served Canada well, despite everything their own government can throw at them. They may not see themselves as an intelligence organization, but they have a better claim to that role than many others.

CHAPTER 10

EAVESDROPPERS
by Kostas Rimsa

"Seeing no visible connection between the two computers, I asked,
'How the hell did you do that?'"

I believe that today, a computer is as deadly as a gun. In the light of possible cyber-terrorism operations mounted by hostile intelligence services, hactivists, hackers, or crackers, and with increasingly poor security practices by its own employees, computer security is a growing concern in the Canadian federal government. The Communications Security Establishment is a critical agency in this battle, not only as a collector of information but also as a protector of Canadian cyberspace.

The availability and quality of technology commercially available has also severely reduced the advantage that the CSE once had. Terrorists use encryption for radio, phone, and computer communications; computers are used to collect intelligence and store encrypted analysis, and orders or operations are communicated by passing information encrypted on floppy or compact discs. They also use steganography (the art of writing hidden messages in such a way that no one apart from the intended recipient knows of the existence of the message) in digital pictures to communicate. Money laundering and fraud are conducted via computer. Computers can also be used to delete critical information and to commit acts of sabotage, either in support of an operation (for example, by interfering with 911 responders) or as a stand-alone action. This type of cyber-sabotage could have disastrous effects on the Canadian economy and could even kill thousands. The trend will continue.

Terrorist groups can develop hackers/crackers with relatively little expense, and sponsor-state intelligence organizations can provide training if required. They can use hacking and cracking in support of operations, intelligence gathering, group financing, and propaganda (perception management). All sponsor states have special units geared toward these ends.

Established in 1946, the CSE has been an agency in the portfolio of the Minister of National Defence since 1975. Its headquarters in Ottawa has an old nickname, "The Farm," indicating a past connection with Camp X (see Chapter 11). Current strength is approximately one thousand employees, but since 2002 there has been a rumoured recruiting campaign that will expand this figure by about one-third. This is due to a new tasking involving the protection of Canada's infrastructure that only got into swing last year. The CSE has a mandate to:

1. Acquire information by using signals intelligence from the global information infrastructure and use it to provide foreign intelligence in accordance with government intelligence priorities. The collection of SIGINT is conducted by the Canadian Forces Supplementary Radio System, which operates under the direction of CSE. It remains responsible for the operation and maintenance of facilities dedicated to SIGINT collection.
2. Provide advice, guidance, and services to help ensure the protection of electronic information and information infrastructures that are important to the government.
3. Provide technical and operational assistance to federal law enforcement and security agencies.

In 1947, an agreement was signed between the U.K. and the U.S. bringing the SIGINT organizations of Australia, Britain, Canada, New Zealand, and the U.S. under one umbrella. The countries divided responsibilities into spheres of influence and intercept coverage. The participants adopted terminology, code words, intercept procedures, and security. NATO members and others such as Japan and South Korea later signed on, but with restrictions on the data shared. Based on this agreement, they developed a worldwide SIGINT collection network and associated software under the code name of ECHELON. Many of ECHELON's collection stations are now fully automated. DICTIONARY consists of hardware, software, and supercomputers that conduct searches for keywords — such as *bomb*, *sabotage*, or *hijacking* — or the name of a place or a specific person. When such a keyword is located in phone, fax, or radio communications, the communication is captured for future analysis by HUMINT sources.

Voice recognition technology is also being constantly tested and integrated into ECHELON. If the voice of a targeted individual is detected, the conversation is recorded and analyzed at a later time. ECHELON is estimated to intercept up to 3 billion communications every day. Because of the wide net it casts, many people who have placed international calls have probably been monitored. Since many Canadians are immigrants, overseas calls are to be expected on a large scale. But it is key to understand that no human source will eavesdrop on your communications if a keyword has not been detected. In addition, speech recognition hardware and software will identify only known criminals, foreign intelligence agents, and terrorists. Even if a keyword is detected, the human analyst determines if there is a threat, and if there is no threat, the conversation is deleted and no further investigation is conducted. There is not enough time or resources to do otherwise.

Can CSE spy on Canadians? The last amendment to the National Defence Act established ministerial authorization as an instrument by which CSE may be allowed to collect, under certain circumstances, private communications, which the Criminal Code defines as those that originate or terminate in Canada. The overriding condition is that the interception be directed at foreign entities outside of Canada. The amended act lays out criteria that protect the privacy of Canadians, which must be met before the authorization is issued. It also ensures that the commissioner's mandate is extended to include the review of CSE activities that are conducted under ministerial authorization.

When people first learn of the capabilities of the CSE to monitor phone, fax, computer, and radio communications, some have feared potential abuse and have openly campaigned for greater oversight of the CSE. Some of these people have what I call "capability fear," others do it for political purposes, and yet others (like foreign intelligence services) may do it to erode CSE capabilities, thereby weakening Canada. There are also ex-employees with personal axes to grind who take advantage of capability fear.

Based on the CSE's relatively small staff size and the numerous tasks that must be performed, it is highly unlikely that CSE employees have the time or energy to expend on superfluous monitoring of Canadians. People are made to be afraid of all intelligence agencies. There is a mystique around them, which can work both to their benefit and detriment. There is very little need for Canadians to fear wrongdoing — the CSE is very tightly controlled. The minister of national defence is accountable to Cabinet (controlled by the prime minister) and to Parliament for all CSE activities and provides direction to the CSE concerning the performance of its functions. In turn, the defence minister is supported by two individuals of deputy minister rank. The deputy clerk of the Privy Council and the counsel and security and intelligence coordinator are accountable for CSE policy and operations; the deputy minister of national defence is accountable for its administrative matters.

To provide additional oversight of the CSE, a commissioner was appointed in June 1996. The commissioner's mandate is to review CSE activities to ensure their compliance with Canadian law. The commissioner has access to all CSE information, except Cabinet documents. He submits an annual report to the minister of national defence, which is tabled in Parliament. He also submits classified reports to the minister when his reports on completed reviews contain sensitive information that requires classified handling.

The days of the Cold War may be long gone, but the threat of foreign agents operating on Canadian soil, engaging in scientific and technical espionage is still increasing. Even though the following examples of CSE operations are from the Cold War era, they illustrate how the CSE cooperates with the RCMP and CSIS on joint operations against spies. In one incident, a Soviet scientist by the name of Khvostantsev, while working at the National Research Council, was reported as trying to buy sensitive documents. CSE was brought in and verified "burst" transmissions from the target's residence. When a raid was finally conducted, a hidden antenna was discovered in addition to the transmission set. The scientist was declared *persona non grata* and deported. In a second incident, Lieutenant Colonel Smirnov tried to buy secrets from Bell Northern. After he was verified as a spy by CSE, he and his Soviet military intelligence cohort were also deported. Spies must communicate with their handlers, and this is one of the weaknesses of espionage. At one time, there were more than thirty agents from the former Soviet Union alone being tracked by our counter-intelligence service. Remember that intelligence is war in the shadows. Canadians are never informed and rarely discover what occurs.

In March 1995, JTF-2 operators boarded the Spanish fishing trawler *Estas* based on intelligence provided by CSE. The information that sparked this operation came from CFS Leitrim, a SIGINT collection station. Intercepted Spanish fishing fleet transmissions indicated that quotas had been surpassed, and this was passed on to the fisheries department, who in turn asked for the support of both the coast guard and JTF-2. The CSE had been a catalyst for the first JTF-2 "blue" operation. In 1993 and 1994 the agency monitored the Mohawk Warriors Society. The target of this operation was the automatic weapons shipments from Akwasasne to other reservations.

Because the CSE is part of the U.K.–U.S. agreement, information from the U.S. National Security Agency (NSA) and Britain's Government Communications Headquarters (GCHQ) was used in support of JTF-2 while they were hunting Osama bin Laden in Afghanistan.

On April 4, 2004, it was reported in the media that from their base in Maryland the NSA via ECHELON had intercepted messages that led to Operation Crevice in Great Britain. On March 29, 2004, eight men were arrested at the same time in and around London. A ninth man was arrested two days later. Seven hundred police raided twenty-four suburban homes and commercial properties. Computers were seized along with six hundred kilograms of the bomb ingredient ammonium nitrate at a warehouse linked to the suspects.

The SIGINT also led to the arrest by the RCMP on March 29, 2004, of a Canadian in Ottawa, Momin Khawaja. He was a software developer at the department of foreign affairs. He is now named as a co-conspirator in a British court. Eight others in Britain were arrested at the same time. Khawaja was charged under Canada's anti-terrorism law with participating in or contributing to the activities of a terrorist group and with facilitating terrorist activity. His father, who was working in Saudi Arabia as an administrator in Yanbu College and who is known for being outspoken against Saudi and U.S. policies, was picked up by Saudi Arabian security forces for questioning. Other members of the Khawaja family living in Orleans, a suburb of Ottawa, have stated to the media that they have since been followed and photographed, that their mail is being opened, and that someone is eavesdropping on them.

It is unclear at this time if Khawaja will be extradited to face charges in Great Britain. The suspects there were charged with the commission, preparation, or instigation of an act of terrorism and face ten years in jail if convicted. The plot involved mixing explosives with osmium tetroxide, which would create a toxic cloud upon detonation. This could have had lethal effects if the bomb had gone off in a fairly confined space, but it is not a traditional chemical warfare agent and would dissipate quickly. Khawaja is the first Canadian to be charged under the new laws. By analyzing communications it was determined that this cell was linked to one of al Qaeda's top men, Abu Musab al-Zarqawi.

Fateh Kamel is a Canadian citizen from Montreal and the owner of a craft store. Described as very religious, according to the previous storeowners he was well-known in Montreal's Islamic community. He currently stands accused of being the head of the Canadian cell that included millennium bomber Ahmed Ressam. It is known that he and others communicated by cell phone overseas as well as by encrypted e-mail.

On June 23, 1985, the bombing by Sikh terrorists of an Air India Boeing 747 flying from Toronto to London killed 329 people, most of them Canadians. On the same day, an Air India flight from Vancouver to Tokyo was also targeted, but the bomb, which was in the luggage, exploded while being off-loaded from the aircraft. Two Japanese baggage handlers were killed thirty minutes after the flight arrived in Tokyo with

390 people on board. Although this attack was not detected in time, the CSE was already in the process of targeting Sikh terrorists by monitoring their communications from the Canadian embassy in New Delhi, having set up operations in March 1983. The success in New Delhi assisted in gaining CSE carte blanche from the Canadian government for embassy collection operations.

In 1988, I was sitting in court listening to the testimony of a witness regarding a Sikh terrorist. I had been invited to Hamilton, Ontario, to see if I could be of service to the prosecution as an expert witness. At the time, in addition to being a military intelligence officer, I was an instructor at Toronto's Humber College, where I had developed a program in the study of terrorism for security, police, and intelligence personnel.

In 1987, six Sikhs living in Hamilton had been arrested planning a terrorist act. The case was eventually thrown out because the RCMP wiretap evidence supposedly violated the Charter of Rights and Freedoms. Little did I know at the time that the CSE was supposedly behind the eavesdropping and as a source could not be mentioned by investigators and police to ensure that future operations would not be compromised.

The Internet is creating new and unexpected vulnerabilities. All aspects of Canadian society are becoming increasingly dependent on telecommunications — electronic banking and finance, transportation, electrical power, oil and gas, water, emergency services, and government operations. As this dependence increases, so too does our vulnerability to any disruption of our national information infrastructure. Imagine that the power outages that affected Eastern Ontario and Quebec in January 1998 were brought about by a major cyber-attack rather than by an ice storm. It illustrates the devastating impact a serious disruption could have on Canadian lives and on their security.

The CSE is a key player in protecting Canada's critical infrastructure, even more so since 9/11. But it is the Public Safety and Emergency Preparedness Canada portfolio that has the leading role in implementing the integration framework set out in the National Security Policy. The Canadian Cyber Incident Response Centre, created only in 2005, is the focal point for activities in this area. It is important to realize that PSEPC is only setting policy and coordinating the effort in the different fields of security, much of which was recommended by the McDonald Commission more than twenty-five years ago but was never acted upon by subsequent governments. In the case of cyber-terrorism it will be up to the CSE to solve most problems on the ground.

The U.S. is advanced in its work securing its critical infrastructure, while Canada is just beginning. The Americans began to take measures to address this vulnerability beginning with Presidential Directive 39 in 1995. The Canadian government began thinking about this only after 9/11. Canada, as usual in matters of security, has been extremely slow off the mark. The results of Canadian vulnerability tests performed in certain departments to replicate a cyber-attack have not been comforting. The lack of infrastructure protection in Canada is of great concern to the U.S., as we are linked in so many ways that the impact of any significant event in either country is almost certain to be felt in the other.

At the time of writing, a task force that is part of the National Security Policy commitments to develop a national cyber security strategy had not yet been created in Canada. It will lay the groundwork for the strategy by taking stock of the critical components of the national computer infrastructure and describing the nature and scope of the threats to it. The task force will consult with the private sector, examine Canada's state of readiness to respond to and recover from a cyber-terrorism incident, and recommend action plans to strengthen our critical information infrastructure.

CSE is mandated to advise the federal government on the security aspects of its automated information systems; it is also developing a threat and vulnerability database, evaluating the threat posed by hacker tools and technologies, seeking partnerships with industry, and developing and evaluating new security devices to thwart a cyber-attack.

When laypeople envision this threat, they think of a broad virus distribution attack that targets all computers, both government and corporate. These types of attacks have been seen in the past from crackers, a nickname for those who cause damage to information or systems they hack into. Another option considered is specific targeting of 911 service communications that would affect fire department, ambulance, or police dispatch. Others think of computers as a support means used by terrorists to collect information for conventional terrorist attack.

At this time, the intelligence assessment is that cyber-terrorism will eventually be used in support of a conventional action to compound problems for responders and compound physical damage. The use of cyber-terrorism in such an attack would not only be a force multiplier but would be spectacular in the media. Others in the field of communications security (COMSEC) — or INFOSEC, as some call it — believe that a widespread attack could be prepared for over a period of years. One of the difficulties of both hacking and cracking is that the search for appropriate targets may take a long time, and once found, access must be gained, a process that also takes time. Part of this process would include the preparation of new viruses and other forms of attacks; for this, mercenaries could be hired. The information would then be stored, and when the time was right an attack could be launched on a mass scale by having implanted the "malware" (viruses, etc.) to be activated on command or by a time-release system. Conventional attacks could also be launched. Fortunately, these types of attacks are still to come.

The first "cyber war" broke out in September 2000 between Israel and the supporters of the Second Intifada (Palestinian uprising) operating from inside Israel and the occupied territories and also from Lebanon, Iran, and Saudi Arabia. The crackers attacked Israeli government websites and systems, calling it an "electronic Jihad." The theory was that the more money Israel spent having to fix and protect its computer systems, the less money would be available to buy bullets, guns, and missiles to be used against Palestinians. Such an attack can also enlist the aid of those who may not be able or prepared to offer armed resistance to Israeli occupation, thereby widening the war effort against Israel. It could also have involved mercenary crackers. Relatively little preparation by the Palestinians had been undertaken, but the effect would have been much greater if several years of recruiting, planning, and preparation had taken place. This was actually minor in comparison to what is possible.

Based on intelligence obtained in 2003, al Qaeda is preparing to target digital devices controlled by computers. The capture of certain computers in Afghanistan revealed a concentrated effort to seek out information on programming physical switching devices that either send information back to a computer via the Internet to automatically regulate a physical function or initiate a specific action like opening a dam to release water. They are remote controlled and are divided into two categories. The simplest are known as distributed control systems (DCS). These collect measurements, throw railway switches, close circuit breakers, and adjust valves in pipelines for water, oil, and gas, in addition to other uses. The more complex are known as supervisory control and data acquisition systems (SCADA). These control an area of DCS, sifting through incoming data and directing certain physical switching actions.

Many are currently connected through the Internet with only low-grade security measures, if any, in place. Both types of devices can be found in oil and gas utilities, many manufacturing plants, electrical power facilities, dams, water storage and distribution facilities, nuclear power plants, emergency telephone systems, etc. Access to such systems would allow terrorists to misroute passenger trains, change pressure on gas pipelines, cause oil refinery explosions and fires, disrupt air traffic control, turn off electrical power, and open dam floodgates — causing economic havoc and costing lives.

Once into a system and with knowledge of how these devices are programmed, terrorists could affect specific targets like an electrical substation, cutting power only to a specific area, such as a downtown core, in support of a more conventional attack. There are 3 million SCADA systems in use in the U.S. today, and more than 1 million in Canada. They are programmed for instantaneous response, cannot tolerate authentication delays, and most lack memory for integrity checks to be installed. Unless the computer system can be fully protected or is self-contained on a LAN, these devices are vulnerable to attack and in time should be replaced with new technology that could receive encrypted communications. To replace millions of them would be extremely costly. It is also important to remember that 85 percent are in the hands of the private sector, which would resist such a modernization attempt due to the expense.

In 1998, a twelve-year-old broke into Arizona's Roosevelt Dam computer system and accessed the SCADA system, which gave him control over 1.5 million acre-feet of water, or 489 trillion gallons. That is enough to cover the city of Phoenix, not far downstream, in five feet of water, which would have affected 1 million people. Fatalities would have been expected.

On April 23, 2000, Vitek Bodin was arrested in Queensland, Australia. In his car at the time of the arrest were a stolen computer and a radio transmitter. He had attacked the Maroochy Shire Waste Water System forty-six times in two months, causing the leakage of hundreds of thousands of gallons of sewage into parks and rivers. These were the first premeditated attacks against SCADA and DCS. The reason behind the attacks? He was angling for a consultant's job at the company. He had quit his job at Hunter Watertech, a supplier of remote control and telemetry, which provided SCADA and DCS equipment to the targeted corporation. There were three hundred SCADA nodes in the system. Bodin learned how to use the controls as an insider, and he obtained the required software openly. Nothing special required — he found the manuals on the Internet.

It is important to note that even if a system is a LAN using radio-controlled communications instead of the Internet, it can be interfered with. Additionally, if the SCADA and DCS are on a LAN, a well-placed infiltrator can cause extreme havoc. Background checks must be conducted in utilities at the appropriate level of scrutiny.

Such attacks are possible, and the risk will increase with time, as al Qaeda becomes more proficient. Al Qaeda's goal of mass destruction has not changed. It is a question of when, not if. The view that problems in cyberspace remain in cyberspace is false. Computers on an increasing scale control and run physical assets. Digital devices are used by millions in infrastructure essential to the minimum operation of the economy and government. Luckily, terrorists have not yet struck, but they are heading in that direction and there is not much time left to correct the numerous security problems currently faced in Canada.

In 1989 I was in Tyson Corners, Virginia, home of CIA technological research, attending a trade show and conference on surveillance techniques and technology. An old friend suddenly grabbed me and said, "You have to see this!" We rushed over to a booth where a gentlemen who knew my old friend was sitting behind a PC, with another PC about ten feet away. "Look at this screen and then look at the other screen," he said. As he typed on one computer, everything appeared on the other PC's monitor. Seeing no visible connection between the two, I asked, "How the hell did you do that?"

In April 1985, Dutch scientist Wim Van Eck published a paper and named the effect Van Eck Radiation. Computers, monitors, printers, keyboards, and fax machines all give off electromagnetic signals, or data leakage. A monitor produces the strongest signal. This means that with the assistance of the appropriate equipment and another PC, all information on one screen, including passwords and user ID, could be captured on another. This process, known as electromagnetic emission monitoring or remote screen capture, can be done from a building across the street or a van parked close by. At the time of the demonstration I received, the emission receiver could be built for US$5,000 and had a practical range of five hundred metres, but under certain conditions the range was up to double that. As in the case of most technology, it could be improved upon. The plans of building the intercept system were being sold for US$75 and were readily available if you knew where to look.

To curb data leakage, and for other reasons, the military developed a NATO program called TEMPEST (Transient Electromagnetic Pulse Emanations Standard). In Canada, this measure falls under the control of the CSE. Along with curbing data leakage, it also assists in saving equipment from the electromagnetic impulses created by a nuclear blast and protecting against radiation interference if a dirty bomb is used. The CSE develops and certifies computers, printers, and cryptographic equipment. To be approved, equipment must be designed to suppress unwanted radiation by arranging electrical shielding either within the equipment itself or around a "secure" room it is contained in. A weak point is the cabling that connects different hardware, although optical fibre helps. Other techniques are also used to protect against this threat. Corporate espionage agents of hostile intelligence services are aware of them, but are Canadian corporations?

The CSE needs to be on top of ever-new security problems that emerge with new technology. One example is the wireless fidelity (Wi-Fi) systems that allow wireless computer interaction. With this, individuals have Wi-Fi network cards in their laptops that allow access to the Internet.

Another problem of the near future will be virus attacks on cell phones that are connected to Internet. At this point cell-phone viruses are rare, but they are already out there. The first was detected in Japan on phones running the Symbian operating system in June 2004. The Cabir virus spread by using the Bluetooth protocol and caused infected phones to have interruptions while in service. Also in June, a virus hidden in an e-mail targeted NTT DoCoMo Internet-enabled phones. It caused the infected cell phones to call the fire department, police, and ambulance services, tying up Japan's emergency lines. The biggest challenge in designing anti-virus software for cell phones has been writing efficient code that is compact enough to fit in the phone's limited memory. McAfee VirusScan has written an anti-virus package that has been available in Japan since November 2004. It automatically scans incoming e-mails and data and can be updated remotely by sending a signal from the phone tower to the user. This type of technology is about to enter Canadian and American markets. Although security with many new technologies is partially the responsibility of the corporate sector, the CSE must stay on top of developments and forecast how they will affect Canada's critical infrastructure.

The British government was the first to recognize that organized crime groups have hired hackers to assist them with information warfare, both offensive and defensive, in addition to having their own internal resources for such activity. The Latin American drug cartels based in Colombia, Peru, Mexico, and elsewhere began to operate at a high level of communications technology as far back as the early 1990s. To counter this threat, the British have formed a new specific joint tasked unit, the Serious and Organized Crime Agency (SOCA), which has five thousand personnel and became operational in 2006. Britain's Government Communications Headquarters will be an integral part, and laws regarding phone taps and e-mail evidence have already been strengthened in support of this operation. Lawyers, bankers, and accountants will be forced to give information or face jail time. SOCA will draw from members of all intelligence agencies, and GCHQ supercomputers at Benhall and Oakley eavesdropping centres in Cheltenham will be used.

The CSE gives support to the RCMP in many criminal matters, but the integration of resources here does not equal that of the British, who were the first in the world to fuse the abilities of the GCHQ and law enforcement. In Canada, we should do the same. The new organization would integrate already existing Joint Task Forces and organizations like FINTRAC into a much more powerful integrated force. This recommendation is for future consideration; the CSE currently has enough on its plate securing our critical infrastructure.

So little has been written or is truly known about the CSE. If an agency is veiled in secrecy, certain concerns, like the lack of security planning and preparation regarding critical infrastructure, can easily be overlooked, and key intelligence organizations may be left ill-prepared to handle emergencies that may arise. In intelligence, it is imperative to be able to plan years in advance and foresee problem areas. In this case, the problem was foreseen by the CSE, but without being discussed in public, increased government funding is hard to get.

Much information and intelligence provided by the CSE cannot be acted upon because of the sensitivity of the methods of collection involved in intelligence, security, and criminal matters. You can get a glimpse of this problem from the case involving the Sikh terrorist trial in Hamilton. Canada needs an elite agency able to act on the information gleaned from CSE sources and its allies. Release of information to other Canadian agencies is often limited, as it must be used cautiously. The enemy, for example, cannot find out that their codes are compromised. This new intelligence group, under control of the CSE, could also engage in other operations like targeting foreign diplomatic intelligence gathering by gaining access to codes and signals equipment, conducting deception operations, and providing *agents provocateur*, tactics currently not implemented by the CSE. Such internal groups exist in support of both the NSA and GCHQ. Why not Canada?

I personally ponder the quality of leadership chosen for matters of Canadian security. Take this quote from Margaret Bloodworth, deputy minister for public safety, to the CSE Cyber Protection Forum on January 19, 2005:

> Let me assure you that if Canadians are depending on me to protect their cyberspace, they are in deep trouble. I'm very much on the, I wouldn't say completely

illiterate, but the lesser-literate side of the cyber world. It needs those of you who understand and know what it is about to actually tell those of us who have an interest in pursuing it what it is we need to do in a practical, pragmatic way because we know we can't change the world tomorrow.

No offence to the deputy minister, what Canada needs is leadership with technical or practical expertise in these matters. Things in national defence are similarly handled. "My knowledge of the [CSE] was very superficial indeed when I was minister of defence," Jean-Jacques Blais once said.

In addition, fewer than a quarter of the CSE staff was engaged in COMSEC in 2002, at a time when our critical infrastructure has to be secured. Promotion based on political correctness and not ability complicates matters: you can speak eight languages, as many in CSE do, but if you don't speak French, you don't get promoted. Most government quotas for this intelligence organization are easily met because of its nature and requirements, but the lack of justified or perceived promotion leads to "moles," a dilemma that has not been considered by government.

DND also needs new intercept equipment on the tactical level, like unmanned aerial vehicles (UAVs) to be equipped for SIGINT. A more in-depth study of tactical electronic warfare capability will reveal a need for new technologies for the units reporting to the CSE. As well, terrorists' tactical use of communications must be countered when Canadian units are deployed overseas. This includes, but is not restricted to, electronic interception of cellular and satellite phone communications. Again I would recommend UAV technology, which is currently being used by some of our allies in Afghanistan and Iraq. We do not always have access to this intelligence, however, and so desperately need our own equipment. The problem with funding to modernize is affecting all intelligence organizations in the Canadian Forces at all levels.

On a final note, we need to conduct more intrusive background checks on employees within Canada's critical infrastructure. CSE can assist agencies like CSIS and the RCMP in identifying those individuals that would require such attention, and there are many. Finally, corporations must do their part; it's clear they can't wait for the government to protect them before it's too late. The threat to our infrastructure is immediate.

CHAPTER 11

IN THE ARMY
by Dwight Hamilton

"Just the type of man we need in intelligence, actually."

It was a typical damp, cold, and grey Remembrance Day when I first found myself at an extraordinary piece of Canadian geography — Camp X. Also known as Project J or Military Research Centre No. 2, it was here that Ian Fleming, creator of the world's most famous secret agent, James Bond, cut his teeth in the world of operational intelligence. It was here that he donned scuba gear in the dead of night and placed a limpet mine on the hull of an old tanker moored just offshore in Lake Ontario. It was here that he was tasked to place a fake bomb in Toronto's main power station, which he did by conning his way into the facility using his Old Etonian upper-crust British accent. And it was here that he found that he could not kill in cold blood, unlike his fictional character, who has often done so in books and movies.

Each year on the eleventh hour of the eleventh day of the eleventh month, two minutes of silence are observed here by members of the Canadian Forces Intelligence Branch. So rare a breed are they that it was the first time I had seen personnel wearing my old uniform in many years. The compass rose insignia bears a striking resemblance to that of the U.S. Central Intelligence Agency.

Originally set up by the Canadian government and British Security Coordination (BSC), Camp X trained agents for Britain's Special Operations Executive (SOE), a division of MI-6, and for the American

Office of Strategic Services (OSS), the precursor to today's CIA. It was located near the town of Whitby, just east of Toronto. There, both men and women learned Morse code, demolition techniques, map reading, and how to size up partisans when operating behind enemy lines. The legendary Lieutenant Colonel William Fairbairn also taught the art of silent killing, bringing Far Eastern martial arts secrets that he had honed when chief instructor of the Shanghai Municipal Police Force. Canadians, Americans, Yugoslavians, Italians, Romanians, Chinese, and Japanese, among others, endured courses before some were sent to finishing schools in Great Britain and India. Live ammunition only was used by instructors and students.

In addition to its school, the camp also was the location of one of the world's most advanced communications centres at the time — HYDRA. For security, the building's windows were seven feet above-ground, but it's hard to imagine that unauthorized personnel could even get within a mile of its doors. After all, the camp guards didn't use blanks either. HYDRA was essentially a group of radio transmitters and receivers wired in series for extreme power. They were bought from various Canadian ham operators and even a radio station in Philadelphia. Three sets of diamond-shaped rhombic antennae fed into a single triple-diversity receiver. The antennae covered the greatest number of frequencies in the least amount of space and provided very high gain and slow fadeout effects; the public was told they were towers for the Canadian Broadcasting Corporation.

Outgoing Morse code was encrypted in a fascinating way due to the work of a Canadian electrical engineer, Benjamin Bayly. He took commercially available Western Union teleprinters (which utilized punch tape) and replaced their ten-minute repetitive spindles with two-hour unique ones. There were two identical tapes for sender and receiver and they were never reused, so the codes were unbreakable. This innovation, which he called the Rockex, also allowed the camp to use commercial landlines and transatlantic cables. In addition, it reduced the time of getting a Top Secret message to Europe to one minute. Going the diplomatic pouch route took six hours.

Camp X was run by BSC, which was headed by an enigmatic Canadian millionaire, Sir William Stephenson, now widely known as the "Man Called Intrepid." Ian Fleming once said that James Bond is "a highly romanticized version of a true spy. The real thing, the man who became one of the great agents of the [Second World War] is William Stephenson." In the foreword to the first book on his exploits, *The Quiet Canadian*, Fleming wrote that Intrepid "worked himself almost to death during the war, carrying out undercover operations and dangerous assignments (they culminated with the Gouzenko case that put Fuchs in the bag) that can only be hinted at."

For its part, BSC was a remarkable outfit. Located on American soil, employing about one thousand mainly Canadian personnel, it served British intelligence needs in North America from 1940 to 1945. Housed in the Rockefeller Center's International Building in New York City, BSC provided a confidential route for communications between Churchill and Roosevelt, engaged in political warfare by countering American isolationism before Pearl Harbor, and protected British transatlantic shipping from Nazi sabotage in U.S. ports. In addition, Stephenson, as a "passport control officer," placed agents in various embassies throughout the Western hemisphere, helped William Donovan set up the OSS, and provided liaison between American, British, and Canadian embassies and between the military and the RCMP. Mail censorship centres were established in Bermuda and Trinidad where BSC scoured letters for hidden messages and the newly invented microdot. While the political relationship with J. Edgar Hoover and his Federal Bureau of Investigation was precarious, BSC handed over 75,000 letters to the FBI during 1941 alone, which led to the arrest of several German agents.

Filing clerks, journalists, code and cipher specialists, civil servants, linguists, a New York private eye, future advertising mogul David Ogilvy, and even actor Noel Coward all found a strange wartime home at BSC. The last time I was in Manhattan, I was surprised to see that a Berlitz language school is still just down the street from headquarters, as it was in Stephenson's day.

After the war, Stephenson commissioned an official history of BSC's activities, known in intelligence circles as "the Bible." Now publicly available, it makes for fascinating further reading. Noted espionage author Nigel West has called it "one of the most astonishing documents in history," and it is likely still classified Top Secret in Britain. Its creation was equally astonishing. Extensive files from which the book was gleaned were moved under military guard from New York to Camp X in 1945, and only twenty copies of the book were printed. The books were then placed in separate locked boxes, and up to ten were distributed to Churchill, Britain's Secret Intelligence Service and SOE, and perhaps to the White House. Intrepid kept two, one went to Norman Robertson of External Affairs, and the rest were stored in a Montreal bank vault, only to be destroyed the following year.

Shortly before I enlisted, Stephenson was appointed the first colonel commandant of the new branch that had split from the old Canadian Forces Security Service, which had also included the military police. Here is the message he sent for our inauguration mess dinner on October 29, 1982:

> Since I am unable to be present because of serious and urgent preoccupation elsewhere, I have asked my friend Vic Ashdown to speak for me at this timely and most important gathering of members of the new Intelligence Branch.
>
> Let me say firstly that today, intelligence in the context you are aware of, is not only the first line of defence but might very well be the only defence. We must know before the event when the enemy intends to strike and thereby strike him first.
>
> Those who favour our unilateral reduction of atomic and high intensity radiation missilery are advocating, not Russian roulette, but absolutely certain suicide.
>
> The issue is quite clear, death, slavery or freedom. Due to the extensive penetration at all levels by the enemy you must be completely objective in your analysis of information.
>
> I shall say no more as you all have urgent business to attend to which directly affects the future of our beloved Canada, and indeed, the whole planet.
>
> Good luck and God bless you with your endeavours.

The debate concerning Stephenson's role and importance in world affairs has been bitter and often petty. Some say he was instrumental in saving the free world; others, including a former Liberal member of Parliament, have dismissed him as a liar. It's now common knowledge that the most famous book written about him, *A Man Called Intrepid*, contains some fiction. As a result, it spawned a feeding frenzy among certain civilian intelligence "specialists." But the reasons for the work's falsehoods are unclear even today. Disinformation furnished by the protagonist? Carelessness or deliberate embellishment on the part of the author? These are not small details; the book was reclassified from the non-fiction category after several scathing reviews. Nevertheless, it became an international bestseller, made its author a fortune, and is still in print today. When I met him in 1988, he was ensconced in Toronto's Rosedale neighbourhood, and when his wife, a producer for TV's *60 Minutes*, answered the door I mistook her for his daughter.

In September 1983 Stephenson was awarded the William J. Donovan Medal, given to those "who have rendered distinguished service in the interests of democratic process and the cause of freedom." For the presentation, U.S. President Ronald Reagan wrote, "All those who love freedom owe you a debt of gratitude." Yet about a week later, a Canadian academic referred to Stephenson as a "minor intelligence official" when talking to retired CIA staff officer Thomas Troy at a conference in Annapolis, Maryland. Such confusion.

As some intelligence officials like to say, "Intelligence is the second oldest of professions, is only slightly more respectable than the oldest one, and, like it, suffers from the activities of enthusiastic amateurs." Academics, journalists, and self-styled investigative historians delving into the world of espionage would be wise not to jump to conclusions based on their glimpses of publicly available material. Just because you don't find something in the files does not mean an event did not occur. It is well-known that Stephenson was loath to leave paper trails, and this is often a standard operating procedure.

No Canadian likely knows the complex world of international security better than John Starnes. Not only was he the first civilian director of the RCMP Security Service, he was also an assistant deputy minister in External Affairs and an ambassador to Germany, Egypt, and Sudan. He began his career with the intelligence section at Military District No. 2 Headquarters in Toronto. In his memoir he writes, "Some decisions, particularly in security and intelligence, never were committed to paper. Modern researchers who assume that they have the whole story sometimes can be quite mistaken in their assumptions."

For the record, Stephenson was the first foreigner to receive the U.S. Medal of Merit, the highest civilian decoration possible from that country. The citation stated that he provided invaluable assistance to America in the fields of intelligence and special operations. As well, he received a knighthood and the Order of Canada. If he was merely a minor player, he certainly did a pretty good job of fooling a few major governments. Just the type of man we need in intelligence, actually.

The Intelligence Branch that chose Intrepid as its first honorary colonel has an equally heroic past, albeit somewhat less mysterious. It began its official life as the Corps of Guides in 1903 and included twelve intelligence officers for each military district across Canada. They were mounted, as was the RCMP in those days. Its director general was tasked to "gather information on foreign armies, militia, military engineering and to prepare reports for any army in the field." In 1913, with the Great War looming, the country had just three thousand militia. When war broke out, the Canadians came under British command, which had no parallel formation, so the guides were absorbed into other units and worked at a variety of tasks; there were then 499 men all ranks. Many went into cyclist battalions but were not used for reconnaissance and liaison purposes until the final Allied offensive in 1918, when they suffered severe casualties. There was also a counter-espionage section known as I(b) that apprehended hundreds of enemy agents engaged in clandestine work.

The years between the world wars were lean ones for Canadian intelligence, and the Guides were disbanded in 1928, but not before a bizarre footnote in the nation's history. Lieutenant Colonel J. Stewart "Buster" Brown was the director of military operations and intelligence for the Canadian Army from 1920 to 1927 and was convinced that the United States was planning to invade the Great White North. So he hatched Defence Scheme No. 1, which was a pre-emptive strike aimed south of the border. Brown actually scouted the northern U.S. with fellow senior staff officers for strategic positions to be captured — in disguise no less! Those must have been very strange days.

When war was declared against Hitler in September 1939, Canada again decided to copy the British organizational pattern, and intelligence officers were assigned to various units at several levels. But the immense pressures of the global conflict acted as a catalyst to bring the trade together, and the Canadian Intelligence Corps (the corps) was born in October 1942.

Canada will likely never field an entire army again, so the time leading up to D-Day is unique in our armed forces' history. Headquarters in London was a beehive of planning activity. In addition to a massive background study on Germany, its military, and its people, the corps sifted, examined, and analyzed intelligence from myriad sources. Resistance group members, refugees from Axis-occupied states, wireless transmissions from covert agents, aerial photographs, every form of media, results from raiding parties along the French coast, and intercepted mail all flowed into the mix.

Troop strength, what defences they had, any armaments and dispositions, the state of German morale, reinforcement capabilities, fighting ability, and personality characteristics of enemy senior officers were all factors that would be needed by the assaulting Allied commanders. It was a Herculean task, but at least the corps was now several hundred strong.

Once ashore, corps personnel began practising operational principles they had learned. As the forward edge of the battle area closed toward Berlin, Nazi saboteurs and sympathizers were exposed and rounded up. Their caches of explosives from underground storage were discovered and destroyed. Instances of sabotage were isolated and sparse, so successful were the corps' efforts.

In the Pacific theatre, a wide variety of undercover operations were undertaken by corps staff seconded to British and American organizations. Interrogations and document research also continued after the fall of Japan.

Back home in Canada, the corps trained its soldiers for overseas duty and screened applicants for SOE, who would later be sent to Camp X.

Many volunteers failed due to the intense physical and psychological requirements, but some became the best Canadian agents provided to the British. The job was extremely dangerous and often fatal; Captains Frank Pickersgill and John Macalister were two who paid the ultimate price. Less than a week after insertion in France, they were captured by the German Gestapo and tortured hideously for more than a year, eventually being strangled at a concentration camp in 1944. But neither broke, which gives you an idea of the level of courage each possessed. Sixty years after the fact, Toronto's 2 Intelligence Training Company laid a wreath at the foot of the University of Toronto's Soldiers' Tower in their honour. The Canadian Army is not for the weak; half of the men in my infantry platoon dropped out of basic training, and we were not even at war.

After the Second World War, the Gouzenko affair placed an emphasis on national security duties, and the corps began focusing mainly on counter-espionage. But it wasn't long before the Cold War turned very hot on the Korean peninsula and Canada was called to arms once again, this time under the euphemism of a "United Nations police action."

Putting out that international fire required more than a few cops, however, and the men who comprised 1 Field Security Section faced a formidable foe oblivious at times to the Geneva Conventions. It comes as no surprise then that an Anglo-American-Canadian study team later debriefed Allied prisoners who had been captured by the Chinese in order to formulate training guidelines to resist interrogation.

The corps was busy with more than on-the-job training. In 1947, the corps founded a school at Camp Petawawa for both regular and reserve intelligence staff, and the militia was authorized six training companies in Montreal, Toronto, Halifax, Vancouver, Edmonton, and Winnipeg. These provided a pool of expert manpower to augment the regular forces, which was strengthened by the diverse skills that reserve personnel brought to the service from their civilian lives. In 1952, the school moved to Camp Borden and today is located in Kingston.

The amalgamation of the three separate services of the Canadian Armed Forces in 1968 saw the formation of the Security Branch, which included the corps, the army and air force police, and the intelligence personnel of the Royal Canadian Air Force. The Royal Canadian Navy had no separate trade but instead employed operational staff on intelligence duties. At the time, the theory was that personnel were to be cross-trained between intelligence and security so they could eventually perform either role. This rarely occurred in practice, however, and this era is not regarded fondly by most. Three formal studies were conducted from 1968 to 1981 to examine the wisdom of the merger, and it was finally decided to split the two branches. Re-badging occurred in late 1982, which was just about the time I walked through the door.

In a nutshell, military intelligence is the knowledge required by command staff who formulate policy, plan, and make decisions. It is the brain behind the sword. Strategic intelligence is required for national policy and planning on a worldwide basis. Tactical intelligence directly relates to operations in the field. Counter-intelligence denies the enemy any information by protecting against espionage, sabotage, and subversion. This field security is usually conducted in conjunction with the military police.

At its most rudimentary level, intelligence is general reference material regarding the capabilities and resources of the enemy in addition to the potential theatres of operations. Capabilities include the enemy's intentions, organization, tactics, equipment, and general modus operandi. The weather is also important. The wind, precipitation, atmospheric pressure, temperature, and hours of daylight all can have an effect on the enemy's equipment and supplies, movements, observational powers, and ability to mount air operations. Terrain is also vital. Key observation posts, avenues of approach, and areas of cover, concealment, and fire all play a role.

On land, the factors of terrain and enemy methodology will affect a commander's mission and are obtained by combat surveillance, carried out by army reconnaissance units. If a particular forward enemy unit is spotted (or a prisoner captured) intelligence staff can paint a picture of what likely lies behind them. This information is combined with the known orders of battle. Armies are made up of divisions, which are made up of corps, then brigades, then regiments, then battalions, and finally platoons, which are split into sections of a dozen men each. And that's it down to the last rifle. Combining all the previous information with personality profiles of enemy commanders and mission templates, intelligence staff try to predict for the commander what will happen next.

For intelligence staff in a command post, the job is a tough one. What are the enemy's traffic capabilities? What are the critical targets within its structure? What are the likely routes, artillery positions, and kill zones? Have you considered the assembly areas and landing zones? Operators must also be well versed in the complex jargon of military radio voice procedure, including call signs and pro words. Air reconnaissance is referred to as "spyglass," armour as "ironside," infantry as "foxhound," and artillery locators as "crackers," to name just a few. Sometimes all this must be done in the midst of flying shrapnel. "Roger so far?"

The intelligence cycle is a sequence of systemic activities leading to the production of intelligence, which is information from the battlefield (or proposed area of operations) that has been analyzed and processed. This includes four major steps: direction, collection, processing, and dissemination.

The process of ascertaining training requirements, planning, tasking changes, and reviewing training productivity occurs at the direction stage. Intelligence staff must determine the information required by command, develop a plan, task sources and agencies, issue orders and requests, and continually check on productivity.

In the collection phase, sources must be exploited and the information obtained must be delivered. The plan must allow time for briefing, collecting, reporting, and collating. When organizing a collation system, relationships become apparent and relevant facts become available for intelligence reports or summaries. One must be careful that information is not obscured by trivia and that any gaps in knowledge are emphasized, allowing for a minimum of rephrasing when disseminated.

An intelligence operator must show command staff specific information in priority order and list all sources and agencies that have been tasked. Timings, places, the form of reports required, and the collection burden spread must be communicated as well. The processing stage is the evolution of information into intelligence. It is here that data is evaluated, analyzed, integrated, and interpreted by intelligence staff.

The final step in the cycle is dissemination. Intelligence must be conveyed in an appropriate form to those who need it. It must be clear and concise. After all, the Intelligence Branch's motto is *E Tenebris Lux*

("From darkness, light"). Standardization and urgency must be adhered to in regular distribution, all the while utilizing the need-to-know principle regarding security classification, whether Restricted, Confidential, Secret, or the close to thirty levels of Top Secret that are assigned. Some documents contain information that has been derived from sensitive sources and methods, and these details are released only on a strict need-to-know basis and then to "CAN/UK/US EYES" or "CAN/US EYES" only, as indicated. Needless to say, violating the Security of Information Act is a very serious offence (see Appendix II).

Another item that intelligence personnel take seriously is the watch list of countries they should not enter. None of these hostile states would treat you kindly upon discovery of your entry, and you are told that quite bluntly.

It should be mentioned that the military police also play an intelligence role with the Canadian Forces National Investigation Service, which includes a counter-intelligence unit with four regional offices and two sub-detachments across Canada. Personnel may be in civilian attire or posing as soldiers from other units. The service's mandate is to investigate and counter espionage, sabotage, subversion, terrorism, and other criminal activity in relation to the military and its members, as well as to screen foreign nationals who attend military programs here. Its activities seldom reach the press. One odd exception was an investigation of the purchase of a building in 1998 by a group of University of New Brunswick Muslim students who intended to convert the dwelling into a mosque.

It is not just in times of international conflict that the Intelligence Branch has been instrumental to Canada's security. Life within our borders may be docile today, but the climate in Quebec in the late 1960s verged on anarchy. "Have you ever seen a bus full of English blow up? Have you ever seen a Protestant church burning? Be sure you soon will." Such was the message of a pamphlet distributed to Canadian students in those days by the FLQ.

FLQ bombings had begun in March 1963. Thereafter, the terrorist group repeatedly hit the army, the RCMP, the Canadian National Railroad, the Montreal Stock Exchange, and the CBC, among many perceived "Anglo" targets. The group's manifesto and propaganda had strong Marxist-Leninist overtones, which was a sign of the times. Cell leaders, including a Belgian and a Hungarian, had been schooled in terrorism in Algeria and Cuba, and others had received training from the PLO. Police also uncovered plots to kidnap the American and Israeli consulate generals.

As well as having stolen a considerable amount of dynamite from commercial sources, break-ins at armouries as early as 1964 had put scores of .308 cal. FN rifles, 9mm Sterling sub-machine guns, and Browning thirteen-round automatic pistols, as well as crates of standard-issue NATO ammunition, into FLQ hands. Complicating matters further, a former Canadian major general has subsequently indicated that French soldiers had been permitted by Paris to finish their army stint in Canada, working as language teachers and "members of the insurgent organization."

By September 28, 1970, the Canadian military had been placed on red alert. A week later British trade commissioner James Cross was abducted from his Montreal home, and five days after that Quebec Deputy Premier Pierre Laporte was taken. H-Hour had arrived: at 1:07 P.M. on October 15, infantry, light armour, and air support were ordered to secure key positions in both Montreal and Ottawa. As they say in hockey, the government had dropped the gloves. Code name: Operation Essay. At 4:00 the next morning, the War Measures Act was proclaimed, suspending citizen's rights for the only time in Canada's peacetime history. Arrests without warrant and indefinite detention — deal with it. On the steps of Parliament, a reporter asked Prime Minister Pierre Trudeau how far he was prepared to go. "Just watch me," he calmly replied.

On October 17 an FLQ communiqué was found at Montreal's Place des Arts: "Pierre Laporte, minister of unemployment and assimilation, was executed at 6:18 tonight by the Dieppe (Royal 22nd) cell. You will find the body in the trunk of the green Chevrolet (9J-2420) at the St. Hubert base. We shall overcome."

James Cross was eventually freed and the kidnappers were flown aboard a Yukon military aircraft to Havana, where they were permitted political asylum, and Operation Essay ended on January 5, 1971. The public knows the time as the October Crisis. But it's not very public that

Canadian military intelligence had been operating undercover for this eventuality long before the call to arms.

According to one of the leading members of the FLQ, the origins go back as far as 1960, when the planning section of the military's Quebec command drew up contingency plans for an insurrection. As a test it sent one thousand troops to St. Vincent de Paul Penitentiary to quell a prison riot the next year. In 1963, the military set up liaison with the provincial police there. But the key point in this story was B Category Plan 210, devised in about 1965. The plan entailed the infiltration of Quebec's labour movement, universities, and political parties. Personnel were to monitor agitation and become involved in demonstrations and labour disputes. Plan 210 made projections, built scenarios, and prepared counter-offences.

At about the same time, U.S. military intelligence, the RCMP, the provincial police, and the Montreal city police began to forge relationships, likely due to American experience dealing with the urban riots that were sweeping the country in the late 1960s. There may even have been CIA involvement. An internal memo dated October 20, 1970, read, "Subject: Quebec. Sources advise that urgent action be taken to temporarily break contact with FLQ militants since the Canadian government's measures may have undesirable consequences."

It has been well documented that the intelligence of the RCMP and provincial and municipal police was woefully lacking before and during the crisis; Trudeau's take on their shortcomings was extremely sharp. Given this void, many have stated to me that military intelligence was the key player. Although political problems remain to this day, the FLQ kidnappers were caught and the violence extinguished quickly. Without a doubt in my mind, it was the expertise of our branch that provided the crucial margin in the federal government's victory to re-establish a semblance, at least, of national unity.

What is the current state of the Intelligence Branch and what lies in its future? Just three months before 9/11 an alarming planning document from the Department of National Defence surfaced in the press. In part, it stated, "Successive budget reductions have caused an erosion in the intelligence-staffing capability to the point where the associated risk is barely acceptable." Branch personnel have always been in short supply and high demand, so the story is not a new one. But it would appear we are now at a crisis point. And we are now at war. While DND's needs are also being addressed by soldiers seconded to intelligence roles and some civilian analysts, the branch itself could only muster a little under six hundred regular and reserve force personnel at the time of the attacks on the World Trade Center and the Pentagon. Amazingly, half are reservists and on active operations. And about 250 are attached to National Defence Headquarters. Obviously, regular non-HQ staff needs more backbone.

Yet they represent an invaluable asset. Canadian intelligence can interlope with American forces better than any other NATO country, and whether people like it or not, Uncle Sam is the point man in the New World Order and will continue to be so for the foreseeable future. The community also benefits enormously from our historical ties to Britain and the U.S. with respect to intelligence sharing agreements, often taking more away from the tables than we deliver. And our country's level of development in information technology is second to no other nation at the present time.

The small numbers limit those with diverse language skills, however, and it's difficult to predict where the next firefight will be. The nature of low-intensity operations, which may dominate the future of warfare, place a premium on human intelligence, so this is of particular concern. Our equipment is aging, and only the army's Coyote reconnaissance vehicles and the navy's new frigates can be considered state of the art. Tragically, in Canada, funding, not needs, dictates capabilities.

At the same time that the shortage of personnel is the branch's greatest weakness, their quality is its greatest strength. Our allies regard us as well trained and professional. What sort of person makes a good intelligence operator? American General George Patton's intelligence officer typified them as "possessed [with] imagination, initiative and mental flexibility. Each was a willing worker, a methodical detail man and organizer. Everyone got along well and could supervise others, and was able to think on his feet and express himself well." Most importantly, each had "matter-of-fact feet-on-the-ground common sense."

Some lament that our services don't recruit from universities. Testimony to the Standing Senate Committee on National Security and Defence claimed, "Part of the government's problem is that it does not recruit potential recruits from Canada's universities ... government decision-makers lack confidence in their intelligence advisors. Canada's intelligence personnel are too often perceived by decision-makers to be guessing, rather than knowing." It went on to point out, "This should not come as a surprise. Recent Canadian governments have not treated intelligence with the priority it deserves, have not done thorough searches for talented people outside government to upgrade the quality of analysis, and have not dedicated sufficient resources to keep personnel fresh and well-informed."

This is a disturbing but perhaps self-serving view, as it came from a history professor with no operational experience in intelligence. While it is true that Canadian governments have likely ignored the services' advice on many occasions, it is doubtful it is because staff are undereducated and their reports of poor quality. A private who was in my unit has his doctorate from Yale. A corporal had attended Harvard. We were all trained with weapons of various sorts. And it is difficult to understand how the professor can comment from a quality standpoint since only those with appropriate security clearances are privy to intelligence reports.

It is bizarre to believe this situation could be rectified by additional recruitment from the ivory towers. Would it be prudent to pit Mr. I-wrote-a-great-grad-paper against men who have been trained to kill, steal secrets, and manipulate governments? If you're looking for a good school to pick from, try Camp X.

CHAPTER 12

VERY SPECIAL FORCES
by Kostas Rimsa

"Our politicians don't care about security. It is no surprise they have not publicly honoured JTF-2 as have foreign leaders."

I could not believe where I was or what I was doing in September 1991: standing on a firing range in the middle of Lithuania, one of the Baltic republics, and still behind the Iron Curtain as far as the Russians were concerned. The presence of the Soviet Army everywhere was proof of that. The KGB was present in force, also operating in high gear.

Standing in front of me was a group of very fit men dressed in casual civilian clothes. Every one of them was a good six inches or more taller than me, and I am five feet eleven inches. All were athletes, some even Olympic contenders. All had university degrees or were close to completing them, but none of the men that stood before me had any security or military training of any kind. Few had ever fired a weapon — let alone in anger.

These men were all volunteers for the new secret service (then known as ATAS, which later evolved into the current VAD) of an independent Lithuania. Their perceptions of what a bodyguard should do were based on a few books and movies from the Soviet Union. This was going to be their first course. The service was to protect the new political leaders, who had already declared independence from the Soviets. The country was the first Soviet republic to do so but Moscow had not accepted it. At that time, neither had any country from the West except Iceland. Canada, the United States, and Great Britain would all take months to recognize this tiny state that dared face off with the Russian Bear.

The men in front of me were exceptionally brave. At any time, the KGB Osnaz, Soviet Army Spetsnaz, and MVD OMON (local police SWAT), in addition to the numerous conventional troops in the country, could have swept down and killed everyone. Thirteen people had already died during a demonstration in Vilnius when the army and OMON moved against them. If this happened, I would probably die beside them. The Russians would make sure that I did. How I got there would be of no concern to anyone.

My partner and I were in Lithuania to teach these giants how to defend themselves, their leaders, and their country. My function was to train the bodyguards of the unofficial president and the prime minister, teach surveillance techniques and intelligence analysis, and advise in the formation of the organization. I was given only three months to accomplish these tasks. There was no time, if Lithuania was to make its way into the arms of the West. Western intelligence organizations were to follow our lead in providing assistance to the new government, but only in time. We were all this group had to cling to for knowledge and survival.

Some thoughts went through my head: Were the Soviets going to use force? If so, when? Should I remain and fight? I probably would not have a choice anyway — I was expendable. Are the candidates suitable? Who picked them? Are there any infiltrators? If infiltrators are present, will they kill me in a shooting accident? Or slip me a round that will explode in the chamber of my 9mm Makarov pistol or AKSU? Or will I die on the firing range because of an accident by inexperienced students? Is anyone in the group an agent for the purpose of collecting information on tactics? If I teach everything I can within the time allotted, would that be wise if some of the men were later corrupted by organized crime and became dangerous? I would be responsible. What if they eventually made an error in judgment and a VIP were killed? Would I be blamed for not training them well enough?

Within one week, we had already received our first death threat from the KGB: "We know who you are and what you are doing ..." This was the first of ten death threats that I received working in the former Soviet Union in a decade.

JTF-2 did not exist when these events took place. But JTF-2 operators will recognize that my confession above is the truth, as one of their taskings is to guard VIPs. Convincing, organizing, training, leading, and advising are also often elements of their operations. JTF-2 troopers working in foreign internal defence operations know this type of experience, which is sometimes linked with covert ops.

One of the first things taught to a special operations forces (SOF) operator is that there are different truths in the world. There is the truth that is superficial and then there is the truth that is real. This is called a "ground truth." JTF-2 operators quickly learn how to tell the difference. If they do not, they will soon be dead. To learn the ground truth you must listen, observe, question, and think for yourself. Initially, you are trained to do this consciously. In time, it becomes second nature. The search for ground truth is meant to keep the operator aware of his or her surroundings. It allows them to see things for what they actually are, not what they are portrayed to be.

This must come as a surprise to those Canadians, including some of our politicians, who believe soldiers are nothing but mindless individuals who follow orders and cannot manage to think for themselves. That attitude is bizarre to the SOF operator because it is obvious that such individuals probably do not search for ground truths themselves. Truth is often difficult to accept because it can be ugly: The world is full of people who do not have our values or even our logic. I know this because I have worked or travelled in more than fifty countries around the world.

To understand units like JTF-2 you must know what is known in the SOF community as the four SOF truths: humans are more important than hardware; quality is better than quantity; SOF troops cannot be mass-produced; and competent troops cannot be created after emergencies occur.

Governments can pick and choose what is released to the media and the public, and JTF-2 represents an elite body going to a combat zone, so there is always a positive media response. Negative responses are generally reserved for when conventional troops are sent to war. Low casualties because of superior training, tactics, and experience are the hallmark of JTF-2 operators. Therefore, there is a low risk of political fallout. The unit is also flexible and versatile. They are deniable, trained for counter-terrorism or unconventional warfare — in short, today's war. JTF-2 can do jobs no other units in the Canadian Forces can and so are valued by our allies. The last director of the U.S. Central Intelligence Agency, George Tenet, presented an "attack matrix" in December 2001, in effect a plan to combat terrorism through covert action in eighty countries around the world. JTF-2 and other allied SOF units will have increasing and more dangerous roles if the War on Terror is to be won.

JTF-2 is a strategic military asset that conducts direct action operations as well as intelligence collection and support operations. It supports strategic and operational levels to complement national- and theatre-level operations and collection efforts. Operations are conducted in order to achieve military, political, economic, or psychological objectives by unconventional means in hostile, denied, or politically sensitive areas in both war and peacetime. The unit should never be deployed for missions that can be accomplished by conventional forces; to do so would squander a strategic resource that is difficult to replace.

As of September 11, 2001, there were 297 personnel in JTF-2. The unit was split into three squadrons of seventy-person troops (or platoons), then further divided into "bricks" of four troopers. Headquarters staff make up the remainder. Its organization borrows from the British Special Air Service, American Delta Force, and SEAL Team 6.

The general objectives of all SOF missions are to disrupt, degrade, detect, deter, delay, and destroy the enemy. Most missions, whether of long or short duration, are clandestine; few are even aware that activities are being carried out. They can be divided into two general categories: black ops (counter-terrorism and hostage rescue missions) and green ops (training foreign commandos and gathering intelligence).

These are further broken down into unconventional warfare, direct action, strategic reconnaissance, counter-terrorism, foreign internal defence, non-combatant evacuation, psychological warfare support, collateral special ops, combat search and rescue, and aid to the civil power. JTF-2 is supposed to be self-sufficient and able to deploy with minimum dependency on others — it must be ready to quickly deploy anywhere in the world.

JTF-2 operations are usually ordered or approved by senior officers in Ottawa in the case of a request when working jointly with allied troops overseas. The commander on the ground has the final say only after a mission has commenced. All operations are conducted on the need-to-know principle. JTF-2 is small and its operators often work in pairs. It should, in theory, be able to employ different methods of insertion and attack than do conventional forces.

SOF units utilize the concept of force multipliers, which allow them to take on a considerably larger or well-prepared enemy. Since these units are in most cases fighting against superior numbers, force multipliers are key. They are a mix of actions by the operators, which are permitted by superior training standards, weapons, and equipment available. One multiplier, surprise (gained by stealth, deception, and means of transport and insertion/extraction), allows for greater mobility than the enemy, which in turn allows for rapid concentration of force in a given location on the battlefield. This allows SOF teams to overwhelm the targeted enemy force. The means of transport and insertion/extraction should be integral to the unit, but are unfortunately lacking in JTF-2. Speed is another multiplier, and is often dependent on transport available that lets JTF-2 move around in the enemy's rear areas. A lack of transport is therefore of great concern. Yet another multiplier is violence of action to produce shock in the enemy. This is gained by training SOF operators to be aggressive and to employ good offensive tactics, and by providing every operator and subunit with firepower that is above and beyond that of the conventional infantryman. It takes a superior selection of personnel, training, tactics, and weapons. In addition to the firepower a SOF unit carries into battle, firepower availability means having on call its own operationally dedicated close air support or land-based or naval artillery. JTF-2 is lacking in all forms of on-call fire support and depends exclusively on our allies to bail them out or to assist in accomplishing a mission. It is also questionable whether the JTF-2 operators and subunits are actually supplied with the best weapons available on the market.

For direct-action ops, JTF-2 needs timely and accurate intelligence, which is yet another multiplier. The better the intelligence, the better the chance for success. The unit does have its own intelligence support staff, as do all SOF units, but JTF-2 also requires additional intelligence that can only be supplied by external sources and agencies. Intelligence is also key to proper planning and preparation. Comparable American, British, and German units all have excellent intelligence resources available, both technical and HUMINT. Not so for JTF-2: when operating in foreign theatres, we often depend on intelligence from our allies. The Canadian Forces has limited resources and capabilities in overseas environments and should be given a budget to increase such. The budget of 2005 did not even consider this as an important factor; yet the government and the media presented it as a great boost for the troops.

Good planning is the final multiplier. "Perfect planning prevents poor performance" is an adopted saying from the SAS. Planning consists of design, preparation, rehearsal, infiltration, execution, exfiltration, and debriefing. This, JTF-2 does very well; it is an internal function of the unit dependent exclusively on the skills and experience of the personnel assigned to the task. But is merely the ability to plan well sufficient to be a force multiplier? It is not a ground truth for JTF-2: if you do not have transport to even get into the area of operations, or you have to spend time planning *ad hoc* measures, you are not concentrating on the mission itself. You then have to have a considerably larger operations staff at headquarters (which is unlikely in the Canadian Forces because of budget restrictions) or planning officers will be overworked, as often is the case in JTF-2. In SOF missions time is often limited, and mistakes can happen under these conditions.

Another problem is that thin resources limit the options available to JTF-2 planners to increase the chance for success and to limit casualties. Equipment, transport, and weapons available are often weak links. These three factors also limit how JTF-2 can be employed in joint operations overseas with our allies. It is the use of force multipliers that allowed American SOF to accomplish the job of an estimated sixty thousand conventional troops in northern Iraq. A force of over one hundred thousand equipped with tanks and armoured personnel carriers were defeated by gaining the support of irregular Kurdish forces.

In Afghanistan, SOF with JTF-2 personnel among them did the same. It was not until cleaning up with Operation Anaconda that conventional troops were used. JTF-2 contributed to this quick victory over Osama bin Laden and the Taliban, and bin Laden certainly knows this, which is why Canada is a potential target for terrorist attacks. Our government does not understand that when you send people to hunt down and kill or capture a terrorist leader, they will somewhere down the road seek payback. This is a ground truth. The bombings in Madrid and London are prime examples.

What follows is an assessment of current requirements that should be met immediately to support JTF-2 and the missions assigned to it. Having a specialized quick-response unit like JTF-2 is of little use if it does not have the transport required to travel the required distances. Renting strategic lift aircraft from Russia and Ukraine resulted in JTF-2's late deployment into Afghanistan. Believe it or not, we stood in line behind commercial clients. Survivability of the unit and its operators is another concern. JTF-2 deserves the best equipment on the market today. Their operatives' lives depend on it. The following recommendations are only examples of the possible solutions to the problems encountered by JTF-2. Due to space constraints certain recommendations were not included.

Currently, JTF-2 receives SOF helicopter transport from either the British or Americans when deployed overseas, if it is available. The right transport helicopters would enhance the force multipliers of speed, surprise, shock, and even intelligence. The MH-53J/M Pave Low would be a wise purchase. It is a low-level, long-range helicopter capable of undetected penetration into denied areas, day or night (even in adverse weather) and can be used for infiltration, exfiltration, and resupply. Well-armed, it has in-flight refuelling capability, allowing it to be ferried anywhere in the world. Another candidate is the MH-60L "enhanced" Black Hawk. Also well-armed, it is now used to transport U.S. Army Rangers and could actually be used by all Canadian Forces deployed in combat theatres. JTF-2 now receives close air support from the Americans if they can spare it. Dedicated close air support would enhance surprise, speed, and violence of action. The Canadian Forces currently has the CF-18 Hornet in its inventory. While definitely not the best close air support aircraft, it is better than nothing until an appropriate purchase can be made. Our air force could deploy these as it has in the past, such as in the first Iraq war. But the chief problem for its overseas deployment is a lack of strategic lift transport, maintenance personnel, and munitions. A lack of political will to deploy them is also a key problem. A better choice is the AC-130U Spectre gunship. It has the advantage of quick deployment because of in-flight refuelling, and the fact that the Canadian Forces already has qualified pilots and mechanics for the C-130 Hercules would make this weapon platform attractive to JTF-2 as well as regular Canadian troops. Another idea is to obtain the AH/ MH-6 "Little Bird" helicopter. These are equipped with FLIR, can be armed with 2.75-inch air-to-ground free flight rockets, Hellfire and Stinger missile combinations, or a 7.62 six barrel mini gun. Because of its small size it can be used for infiltration into urban areas using the "fast rope" technique and has greater possibilities in finding a landing zone in urban terrain. With a range of up to four hundred miles, it can carry a brick of troopers and is used primarily for reconnaissance, command post liaison, small unit logistics, and close air support. A Hercules transport can carry three of them, and it takes only fifteen minutes to reassemble one and fly it away. Little Birds can actually kill three birds with one stone: providing helicopter transport, close air support, and enhanced intelligence gathering capability.

Currently, JTF-2 receives tactical air transport from American forces when deployed overseas. Picking up some planes like the MC-130 E/H Combat Talon or Combat Talon II would stop this bit of freeloading. The aircraft are well-suited to the air insertion and resupply operations of SOF units. Based on the C-130 Hercules design, the plane can also drop bombs of various types. In addition, the MC-130 P Combat Shadow can refuel helicopters in flight as well as insert and extract personnel. All foreign-deployed Canadian Forces could utilize these aircraft.

At the present time, JTF-2 receives strategic airlift transport from allied forces when deployed abroad, if available. If the U.S. cannot help we rent them from Russian or Ukrainian civilian companies. To enhance the force multipliers of surprise and speed some C-141s should be purchased, which could also be used by all the Canadian Forces deployed overseas.

JTF-2 usually receives its covert intelligence support from the Americans, the British, and sometimes the French and Germans during overseas ops. This is inadequate — we are clearly not bringing enough to the table. We should form a military intelligence collection and support unit that would directly serve Canadian troops and be under our command. The new unit would also give a career path for those who have served in JTF-2, the Intelligence Branch, and other security and intelligence agencies. It could be relatively small and well worth the money spent.

Another recommendation is the purchase of long-range patrol vehicles (LRPVs). The first LRPV that I saw was the Chenowth back in 1989 at a restricted counter-terrorism exposition called COPEX held in Baltimore. Manufactured by different firms throughout the world, LRPVs are six- or eight-wheeled light attack vehicles that look similar to dune buggies and are used by U.S. Navy SEAL teams. As well, additional Hummers will be required after the government's planned expansion of JTF-2. In Afghanistan, JTF-2 was deployed in commercial SUVs because we had no strategic air lift capability. We then had to borrow Hummers before an embarrassed Canadian Forces was able to convince our federal leadership that such vehicles were required, and funds were eventually allotted for an emergency purchase. It must be noted here that American SOF Hummers and LRPVs usually mount the MK 19, a 40mm automatic grenade launcher that has a 1,600-metre range and can fire a grenade every second with a kill radius of approximately ten metres. The MK 19 has been in service for more than thirty years in all branches of the U.S. military. We have nothing like it, despite the fact that it is relatively inexpensive.

On December 8, 2004, JTF-2 was awarded the U.S. Presidential Unit Citation for heroism in battle. It is only the second Canadian military unit to ever receive the honour. American president George W. Bush made the presentation in California. JTF-2 had been part of the multinational force in Afghanistan from October 2001 to April 2002, and the unit was praised by American commanders in Afghanistan and by politicians and journalists at home more than once. But it was never honoured by our own Canadian government. Why?

On August 9, 1995, in the Montreal suburb of Anjou, the unit was discovered in training. Concerned citizens called the police. Quebec

Premier Jacques Parizeau complained publicly. Then Prime Minister Jean Chrétien claimed he was not even aware of the existence of JTF-2 at the time. This is how much the threat of terrorism meant to the prime minister in 1995, two years after the first World Trade Center bombing and the year the U.S. federal building in Oklahoma was destroyed. Our politicians really do not care about security. It is no surprise that our politicians have never publicly honoured JTF-2 as have foreign leaders. It's about time to break the conspiracy of government silence on matters of security, defence, and intelligence.

The following will no doubt be disapproved of by Foreign Affairs, the department that sets foreign and domestic policy in Canada with respect to Canada's image. JTF-2 operators will also likely object to my recommendations. I agree that JTF-2 had to be secret while it was getting off the ground, and that's why Canadian political policy made an exceptional attempt to keep the unit hush-hush. But today JTF-2 should be more like the SEALs in the U.S. and conduct public demonstrations, which could be then covered by the media. The RCMP's Special Emergency Response Team had an active campaign in media relations and assisted in its funding and even survival at certain times of budgetary restraint.

The SAS allows its retired members to publish books to ensure funding continues to flow and to instill pride in its accomplishments. It also allows for pride to develop in the ordinary British citizen — that his or her country has people like this. It gives a sense of security. The same is seen in American books on the Green Berets, SEALs, Delta Force, Underwater Demolition Teams, and other specialists such as snipers. With military censorship applied, ex-JTF-2 members should be permitted to write books, even fiction books, on their experiences. The Canadian Forces currently has a video on JTF-2 and it should be released for everyone to see. A movie could be made funded partially by the Canadian government, or a *Survivor*-style reality TV program with past members of JTF-2 could be shown.

The Australian Special Air Service allowed some select soldiers to become known to the public. Some of its medal recipients were honoured as members but were referred to only as "Trooper X." This allowed for secrecy and good public relations. The British have a similar system. Why not Canada? It's clear that an attitude change is required by the Canadian public. With public support would come funding for all force multipliers.

Still more crucial than public support is the public service. It runs the Canadian Forces — literally. The staffs of the deputy defence minister and the chief of defence staff are one and the same. They make and enforce policies, many of which are common for federal government departments without exception. All are to be run like businesses. Civil servants enforce gender quotas, First Nation quotas (yet some of my best instructors were Natives or of mixed blood), visible minority quotas, and disabled persons quotas. In time, as it is government policy in other departments and they must be uniformly maintained, there will be an attempt to impose these quotas on JTF-2.

Political correctness rules in our government. It does not matter what ability you have but rather whether you fulfill a quota. Do you read and write French like a native of Quebec? One cannot even become a lieutenant colonel without French; many of history's greatest generals would never have made it past major in the Canadian Forces. This also goes for anyone of equivalent rank for civilians in the defence department. Yes, civil servants have equivalent military ranks, and vice versa. This ideology also explains the rise of incompetence and corruption in both. The best are not promoted, as ability is trumped by quotas and language policy.

The solution is to separate the staff of the deputy defence minister and the chief of the defence staff. The Canadian Forces is not a corporation and *cannot* be run like one; it's time to rethink political correctness with respect to our military. There is definitely no place for this in JTF-2. Politicians do not have to die because of political correctness — our troops do. Remember the SOF truths? Humans are more important than hardware, quality is better than quantity, operators cannot be mass-produced, and competent troops cannot be created after emergencies.

Government interference also affects military procurement. Take the case of a remote piloted vehicle from France that crashed consistently during its tactical deployment to Afghanistan. On March 20, 2004, a $2-million Sperwer UAV cracked its wing and nose cone in a farmer's field just fifteen minutes after taking off from Camp Julien. It was the fourth to meet this fate, and another two have developed cracks in their wings. They were not even battle tested. By the way, the Canadian Forces will have to pay for these UAVs as they do not own them. Who knows where the money will come from, as nothing was allotted in the 2005 budget? The Iltis light utility vehicle (manufactured by Bombardier) and the H-101 Cormorant helicopter have also had serious problems. Many observers feel that all these purchases had ulterior motives, such as providing jobs to Quebec and other political considerations. It's clear that future purchases should be solely in the hands of the branches of service, including JTF-2. You get what you pay for.

Budget limitations also limit the knowledge and experience of JTF-2 operators. After my training for the Lithuanian secret service, its operators received training from the U.S. State Department, sometimes travelling to America for courses.

In 1994, I started training the Lithuanian national police SWAT team. It was the only unit in all of the former Soviet Union with a nationwide, one-hour hostage negotiation response ability employing Western tactics. To my knowledge, it still is. The operators were later trained by the FBI and the French national police group RAID in hostage negotiations.

In 1997, I began a three-year quarterly contract with a SWAT team in Riga, Latvia, that had already received training from members of the SAS and the Israeli MOSSAD. In the fall of 2000, an observer from an allied intelligence agency and I were monitoring an exercise of the YPT (the Lithuanian equivalent of JTF-2) that included a moving vehicle take-down, terrorist investigations, interviews, interrogations, and finally negotiations and building assault. Some of them had already received training from the French military's GIGN and others had been my students in ATAS. The point is you should never stop learning if you are a JTF-2 operator. You must be cross-attached from foreign teams and vice versa, as each instructor will teach nuances others will not. And the JTF-2 thirst for knowledge is expensive.

But when you are prepared there is no better training than to gain experience in live operations: a fighting edge must be maintained. Funds must be allotted to allow JTF-2 to participate in live operations. Much of this information is filtered down to parent units of the operators, so that all benefit from this approach.

In December 2001 the federal government stated that it would increase JTF-2 to six hundred personnel, doubling it by December 2006. But with a dwindling recruiting pool, Canada is breaking one of the four truths. In 1993 our military was 80,000 strong, seven years later it was reduced by a quarter, and today we can muster about 52,000. The SAS, with about six hundred all ranks, can choose from a military force double our size; current levels are difficult to maintain, let alone expand. In JTF-2, entry standards have had to be lowered from corporals with four years service to privates with only two years served. And it takes three to four years to get a JTF-2 "flash," or shoulder patch. Recruiting and training will not be able to sustain the rate of expansion without lowering standards even further.

So by evaluating the needs of JTF-2, anyone can see that the current budget and the timing of money made available are completely inadequate. Politicians are playing with the lives of all Canadian soldiers. Issuing them with the Iltis in Afghanistan because armour was not available borders on manslaughter. If a civilian corporation behaved in such a fashion by not providing required safety measures or equipment to its employees and they were injured or killed, the company would be sued because it would be liable. The government demands safety in the workplace for everyone except the Canadian Forces.

On February 1, 2006, the Canadian Special Operations Command was formed. The new leader of this organization is Colonel David Barr, an old hand at SOF operations. He will be responsible for coordinating current special operations and planning for JTF-2's expansion. In addition, a new 750-troop regiment is to be formed that would undertake roles similar to those of the U.S. Green Berets and/or Rangers. One of the best means to defeat terrorism is to use unconventional-warfare troops. This is a ground truth.

Previous page: A father with his children at New York's Ground Zero in April 2005. Plaques on the fence are inscribed with the names of 9/11 casualties. Top: A long shot of the World Trade Center site. "Is this real world or exercise?" a military official asked after al Qaeda rammed jumbo jets into the twin towers. Above: Urban downtown cores with skyscrapers, like this one in Toronto's financial district, are ideal targets for terrorists due to the extreme congestion of potential victims. Opposite: A security consultant overlooking the Tarmac at Pearson International Airport. It could happen here.

Note: Unless otherwise credited, the illustrations contained herein are a selection of my work as a photojournalist from the years 1982 to 2005. Some are my subjective interpretations of the many events described in this book.
— Dwight Hamilton

Photo courtesy Gabriel Marion.

Photo courtesy anon.

Top: RCMP officers with the take from Operation Overtrick, the largest under-cover heroin bust in Canadian history. Above: Warsaw Pact weapons used in train-ing. Opposite: A co-author fires an extremely rare M16 re-bored for old AK-47 rounds (7.62 mm). It looks identical to our rifles, but the ballistic evidence it leaves behind is different. Use your imagination.

Photo courtesy anon.

Top: Some of the Intelligence Branch's innovative training methods of the Cold War era included selecting women from non-combat arms units to pose as enemy special forces during exercises. These Soviet Spetsnaz troops are armed with AKMS-47s and RPG-7 rocket launchers. Above and opposite: Our man in Havana? How much Foreign Affairs Canada contributes to the national security equation is difficult to gauge, as it is not officially in the business of espionage. But some of its embassies have military attachés even behind enemy lines; a supervisor of mine was once posted to pre-Perestroika Prague. And while our embassy in Havana didn't have a military attaché at the time, a senior Canadian official attached to Washington has admitted that the U.S. made "far greater use" of our intelligence during the Cuban Missile Crisis than has been revealed. What else doesn't the public know about the department's clandestine activities?

Top and above: The front entrance to the International Building at Rockefeller Center in New York City, which once housed the headquarters of Intrepid's British Security Coordination. This was the hub of one of the most significant covert intelligence organizations of all time. Opposite: The British-born author of *A Man Called Intrepid*, William Stevenson, in 1988. A globetrotting foreign correspondent for many years, he published the international bestseller in 1976 and immediately drew fire. Who knows if the full picture will ever emerge about the biographer's subject?

CBT INT CRSE 8801

Top and above: The Intelligence Branch often teaches courses to other personnel like this class at CFB Borden. Note the flag of the U.S.S.R. to the extreme left. The instructor with the Canada Decoration bar on his uniform is a co-author. Today, the Canadian Forces School of Intelligence and Security is located in Kingston, Ontario. Opposite: Two of our men stand in silence at Camp X on Remembrance Day. All that remains today of the top secret operatives' school is a cenotaph. The Intelligence Branch flag — along with those of Canada, Great Britain, and the United States — flies at half-mast. The solidarity among the countries predates their governments.

Top: Deep inside the featureless, sprawling infrastructure of the Downsview air base were my unit lines; today, it is an industrial wasteland. Above: In Rome, the mark of the Brigada Rosa was everywhere during the heavily guarded trials of the early 1980s. Opposite: My unit's Officer-in-Command. Overleaf: High-risk missions undertaken by units like Joint Task Force 2 sometimes include airborne infiltration. Here, a paratrooper exits a C-47 Chinook helicopter.

CHAPTER 13

OUTSIDE CANADIAN INTELLIGENCE
by Robert Matas

"The gross inaccuracy of the SIRC review report will be immediately evident to anyone who reads it."

The Air India trial brought out piles of dirty laundry from the back closets of CSIS and the RCMP. At the top of the heap was a memo written in 1996 by the officer who was at that time in charge of the Mounties CIS crime section at E Division Headquarters, Inspector Gary Bass. I had been reporting on developments in the horrific Air India case for the *Globe and Mail* for sixteen years when the memo surfaced.

As a national correspondent in the newspaper's British Columbia bureau, I had written since 1987 about the activities of the main suspects, the CSIS and RCMP investigations, and the families' futile efforts to push the federal government to appoint a commission of inquiry into the disaster. I was extremely familiar with every twist in the mammoth case. I had heard all the rumours, partial truths, and denials. I did not know what really happened.

The court had issued thirty-five rulings over two years of pretrial hearings. As the trial was finally to begin, I requested access to the material filed in court from the pretrial motions and applications. Lawyers from CSIS, the RCMP, and the prosecution team tried strenuously to block every avenue available to access the documents. With the full support of my editors, I worked with the newspaper's lawyers to push for the documents' release. Other media outlets joined my paper in pressing for release of the material.

CSIS, the RCMP, and the prosecution repeatedly forced us to go through the expensive process of going to court to obtain an order requiring release of information and returning to court to have them comply with the order. Even when they were complying, they moved so slowly I had the impression they were ignoring their legal obligations to provide public access. My paper spent thousands of dollars to press for access.

The public release of the memo at the trial provided a rare opportunity to peek into the shadows and see how the system of independent review of the country's most prominent intelligence agency performed. The revelations were unsettling. The review committee had rubber teeth. The watchdog had the appearance of biting hard and leaving its mark. But when the veil of secrecy was lifted, it was obvious the Security Intelligence Review Committee was more lapdog than watchdog.

The attack on the national airline of India by a group of Vancouver-based radical Sikh separatists on June 23, 1985, led to the death of 331 people in two bomb explosions at opposite sides of the world. It was the deadliest mid-air attack in aviation history. To an outsider, it was clear after reading the Bass memo that SIRC had fumbled the ball on the Air India file. Its failure pointed to a fundamental problem that could affect the network of review bodies created over the years to keep an eye on the operation of government agencies and departments in Canada's intelligence community. We don't know how serious the crack in the system is because outsiders don't often have the chance to check up on the independent review process. But what Bass exposed cannot be ignored.

Bass had been working during the previous few months with the Air India task force that was still hoping more than a decade after the disaster to make arrests, helping with preparation of court applications to intercept phone calls of several suspects. The inspector was clearly frustrated by what he discovered. After reviewing how CSIS handled the case in 1985, he realized that prosecutors would face significant legal hurdles in preparing evidence for court. He expected CSIS would be under intense criticism for its handling of the case. He feared a mistrial.

If the Mounties could not round up the suspects, Bass assumed a public inquiry was inevitable, and he was concerned about what it would reveal. "I am confident that the result of such an inquiry will be to direct severe criticism to the CSIS, and to a lesser extent the RCMP … handling of the investigation. The fact that some part of the criticism will be with the benefit of hindsight will not soften the blow to any great extent," he wrote.

His harshest words were saved for SIRC. The committee had conducted a special audit of the CSIS investigation into the Air India disaster in 1991 and 1992. The common perception in the early 1990s was that the security agency performed poorly in the case. CSIS agents listened to suspects testing a homemade bomb three weeks before the disaster without realizing what they were listening to. CSIS also intercepted phone conversations of the prime suspect at the time of the disaster and then erased the recordings.

The committee confronted the accusations of incompetence from Opposition members of Parliament and from observers in Sikh and other communities across Canada. In the end, it tried to deflate the allegations. The watchdog put its seal of approval on CSIS's activities. In a summary of its final report, SIRC assured the public that a thorough investigation had been conducted. They reviewed many thousands of documents in CSIS files. They interviewed numerous CSIS personnel involved in the investigation of Sikh extremism before and after the disaster. They met with representatives of the victims' families and officials of the most vocal Sikh lobbying group, the World Sikh Organization.

SIRC made a point of stating that they had the co-operation of the commissioner of the RCMP. The commissioner responded "in a full and frank way" to their request for a briefing on issues related to the inquiry. RCMP staff responded to requests for information. The Department of Justice provided "a useful briefing." If they were to be believed, SIRC had fulfilled its mandate and its conclusions could be trusted.

But Bass disagreed. He believed the committee did not report the full story. Offering his assessment of their work, he did not mince words. "The gross inaccuracy of the SIRC review report will be immediately evident to anyone who reads it," he said, setting out in his memo in detail how the SIRC report was misleading and, in some respects, outright wrong. The report did not accurately reflect the facts on the central issues, he said. He warned them to be ready for the controversy when "a great deal of what some will classify as embarrassing correspondence will be disclosed."

Some agencies, such as the Department of National Defence, are not subject to any independent review. But Parliament has provided reviewers for the RCMP, the CSE, and CSIS. A public complaints commissioner looks into complaints about the conduct of RCMP officers and provides a forum for citizens to appeal the conclusions of internal police investigations of complaints. The commissioner does not have broad powers to access information in RCMP files, and the courts are occasionally asked to rule on the commissioner's reach into the Mounties cupboard of secrets. The commissioner does not initiate reviews of RCMP operations to check if they are operating within their mandate, breaking the law, or violating the rights of Canadians.

Another commissioner reviews the CSE to check whether its activities comply with the law. Reporting to the defence minister, this commissioner also investigates complaints. An inspector general conducts independent reviews of CSIS, the main task being to assess the director's annual classified report for the minister of public safety. They have authority to access almost all information held by CSIS. The exceptions are advice to the Cabinet and correspondence between its ministers. In the annual report, the inspector general must assure the minister that CSIS has not broken its own rules, has followed directions issued by the minister, and has not made any unreasonable or unnecessary use of its extensive powers. The inspector general does not deal with public complaints.

SIRC is the outsider's window into CSIS. But SIRC is different from review bodies set up in the U.S. government. The U.S creates oversight committees to evaluate investigations as they are going on. Canada created a review committee to assess performance after an intelligence agency has completed its activities. Foremost among its mandates, SIRC was expected to balance the extraordinary powers of the security intelligence service with aggressive protection of Canadians' rights. SIRC was to ensure the security intelligence service complied with the law and did not violate the Canadian Charter of Rights and Freedoms. The intelligence community was allowed to intrude into the private lives of Canadians, but the spooks were not allowed to trample over the civil liberties of Canadians in their pursuit of terrorists and criminals. SIRC is required to submit an annual report to Parliament to reassure Canadians that their rights and freedoms are being protected.

Many observers over the years have concluded that SIRC succeeded in making CSIS more accountable. Its track record includes some impressive accomplishments right from its earliest days. In the 1980s, SIRC drew attention to questionable files in the CSIS counter-subversion branch on thirty thousand individuals and files on six hundred thousand individuals throughout all branches of government service. The review committee questioned whether Canada really had so many suspected subversives and whether CSIS really needed to keep files on so many Canadians.

When creating the review committee, Parliament also gave SIRC the authority to report on any matter relating to CSIS performance, but SIRC rarely conducts a Section 54 review. Only seven were held in the ten years preceding March 31, 2004. On October 4, 1991, SIRC announced a review of CSIS involvement in the Air India case under Section 54 of the Canadian Security Intelligence Service Act.

The Air India case was a story of religious fanatics and violence beyond the imagination of anyone in Canada's law enforcement and security agencies. The prime suspects were British Columbia–based Sikh radicals who were out for revenge against the Indian government. Within hours of the disaster, police seized on the theory that the terrorists took the bombs to Vancouver airport and put them on flights connecting to other Air India flights. One bomb blew up on June 23, 1985, on a flight over the Atlantic Ocean, near Ireland, killing all 307 passengers and twenty-two crewmembers. The second bomb exploded fifty-four minutes earlier at Tokyo's Narita airport, killing two baggage handlers and injuring four others.

Auto mechanic Inderjit Singh Reyat was convicted on May 10, 1991, of manslaughter in the death of the two baggage handlers in Japan. The case was based on forensic evidence. Japanese investigators found fragments of the homemade bomb that Canadian investigators linked to Reyat. Twelve years later, he pleaded guilty to collecting the material for the second bomb, which blew up on the Air India flight.

The investigators failed to find any other physical evidence that could be tied to a suspect. Mr. Justice Ian Bruce Josephson, of the British Columbia Supreme Court, acquitted Vancouver businessman Ripudaman Singh Malik and Kamloops mill worker Ajaib Singh Bagri in March 2005 after finding that witnesses testifying against the accused were not credible. CSIS had fingered Vancouver Sikh priest Talwinder Singh Parmar as the mastermind behind the attacks moments after the bombs went off. The agency had been keeping an eye on Parmar since the early 1980s. They had begun to intercept his phone conversations on March 27, 1985, three months before the explosions. CSIS agents also had Parmar under physical surveillance, following him as he went about his daily activities for months before the disaster.

Their activities placed CSIS at the centre of any court case against Air India suspects. Two CSIS agents followed Parmar and Reyat as the Sikh activists went into the woods and tested an explosive device three weeks before the disaster. Interviews conducted by a CSIS agent in 1987 — two years after the disaster — brought out evidence that appeared to incriminate a suspect and became key evidence at the Air India trial.

Parmar was never charged, or even arrested, in the case. He left Canada in 1988, after Reyat was arrested. His friends said Parmar wanted to see whether Reyat was convicted before deciding if he would return to Canada. He was killed by police in India in October 1992, possibly after being tortured. Before his death, Parmar had on several occasions denied he was involved in the disaster, leaving it up to the public to decide whether the police or Parmar should be believed. CSIS's handling of the case was under a cloud when SIRC announced its review in 1991, a year before Parmar was killed. CSIS had already acknowledged that they had erased some tape recordings of intercepted phone calls of Parmar. In its defence, CSIS claimed the information on the tapes was not that important to the Air India case and that the erasures occurred as a result of a routine administrative practice to wipe out intercepted phone calls that did not include information related to national security.

The federal government, the RCMP, and CSIS were under pressure at the time for arresting only Inderjit Singh Reyat. Many blamed an inept security service and a police force unfamiliar with fighting terrorism for bungling the case. Opposition politicians were pressing the government of Brian Mulroney to appoint an inquiry into the disaster and the subsequent investigation. Meanwhile, Toronto journalists Zuhair Kashmeri and Brian McAndrew have suggested that the Indian government might have played a role in the disaster. On November 20, 1992, SIRC released a summary of its report on the agency's handling of the investigation. The objectives for the review were set out in its summary. It is worthwhile to quote the objectives in full, in order to realize how far off the mark SIRC was:

> Our objective was to learn what information CSIS possessed about any threats of terrorist action against Air India or other Indian interests in or relating to Canada prior to June 23, 1985, and whether it fulfilled its mandate to investigate such threats and to advise the appropriate government and law-enforcement agencies in a timely and comprehensive way.
>
> We also wished to learn whether CSIS assisted government and law enforcement agencies by providing, to the extent possible under its mandate as an intelligence gathering organization, all information and intelligence in its possession relevant to the criminal investigation of the disaster. As an adjunct to our primary objectives, we wanted to determine whether CSIS complied with all policies relating to the collection and retention or erasure of audiotapes. Also we reviewed whether CSIS policies or prevailing practices governing the collection and processing of those audiotapes ensured that all information relevant to the disaster was evaluated for its intelligence value or its significance for any criminal activity and that no valuable information was lost. As a final objective, we sought to determine if CSIS had any information

or intelligence pointing to the involvement of any agency or representative of a foreign government being implicated in the destruction of the aircraft.

SIRC maintained a thorough review had been conducted. For more than a decade, their conclusions remained unchallenged. But many observers felt uneasy about the report. They did not accept the summary as the final word. In the end, the report did little to dispel the sense that CSIS had something to hide. The Air India trial provided a rare opportunity for the public to find out about events at the time of the disaster. It was not an intended purpose of the trial, but the court proceedings cleared the way for outsiders to go back to the 1992 report and assess the work of the review committee.

Disclosure rules in court required the prosecution to share with the defendant information gathered during the investigation. The court required CSIS to release thousands of pages of documents, classified Top Secret and Confidential, that otherwise would never have become public. The defence team saw internal CSIS and RCMP material, the prosecution submitted the documents to court as part of the case, and the media gained access to the records. Bass's memo was among a stack of internal CSIS and RCMP documents that revealed holes in the SIRC report.

The review committee had concluded that CSIS was working in a way consistent with the threat as perceived before the disaster. CSIS provided information to the appropriate government and law enforcement agencies in a timely and comprehensive manner. The review committee also decided that the lack of co-operation between RCMP and CSIS and the disputes over the conduct of the investigation tended to be isolated and on a personal level. Regarding the erasure of wiretap tapes, the review committee concluded it was unlikely CSIS destroyed important information relevant to the disaster and subsequent investigation. The review committee also concluded that the information collected by CSIS did not support the theory that a foreign government was complicit in the bombing of the aircraft. The SIRC report was not completely one-sided. The report included some mild criticism of CSIS management for failing to provide direction.

A different story emerged in court. Correspondence between senior RCMP and CSIS officials released at the trial confirmed the agency began erasing wiretap tapes before the disaster, under administrative policies that permitted retention of the tapes only if necessary for national security reasons. CSIS failed to anticipate that Parmar would mastermind the terrorist bomb explosions and did not identify any national security reasons for retaining the tapes. But CSIS continued erasing tapes for several months after the bomb explosions, documents revealed. It may be understandable why CSIS wiped out Parmar's tapes before the disaster. But CSIS has never explained why they did not preserve the tapes after they identified Parmar as the prime suspect in the colossal crime. And SIRC apparently did not ask the question.

Even more outrageous, the correspondence also revealed that CSIS was erasing wiretap tapes while negotiating with the RCMP on conditions to allow the Mounties to have access to the recordings. Needless to say, CSIS did not tell the RCMP they were acting less than honourably by continuing to erase the tapes. The correspondence shows CSIS thwarted efforts by the RCMP to push the investigation forward. Erasing the tapes stopped only after a ministerial order was issued in February 1986. That's more than seven months after the attack.

SIRC members said they believed the tape erasures had no serious detrimental effect on the CSIS or RCMP investigations: "It is unlikely that the prevailing practices resulted in the loss of important information relevant to the disaster and the subsequent investigation." How did SIRC conclude CSIS was providing the RCMP with all the information in their possession that was relevant to their investigation in a timely and comprehensive way? How did SIRC decide that difficulties over cooperation between the RCMP and CSIS "had no serious detrimental effect on the [CSIS and RCMP] investigations?"

It is of course impossible to know what would have been achieved if the two agencies had worked together. Would they have collected enough information to bring charges against the suspects in 1985? Would others have been arrested? Likewise, the significance of the missing information remains a mystery. CSIS decided that Parmar was speaking in code in the intercepted phone conversations. But the spy agency realized what was going on only after the bombs had exploded and several dozen tapes had been erased. How can SIRC reach conclusions about the missing information — which may have been in code — without transcripts of the conversations? At the 2002 trial, Judge Josephson ruled that CSIS demonstrated "unacceptable negligence" in erasing the intercepted tapes. He concluded that CSIS violated the defendants' Charter rights to a fair trial. SIRC was supposed to be particularly sensitive to violation of Charter rights. How did it miss that?

Bass had access to the entire SIRC report, not just the summary released to the public. In his memo he dealt with the details. According to the report, Bass said, there was no evidence of the RCMP asking CSIS to retain the wiretap tapes. SIRC also stated that the RCMP told them that the erasure of the tapes did not wipe out any evidence. The truth, Bass stated, was that RCMP spoke to CSIS four days after the bombing. At that time, CSIS agreed to keep any intercepted wiretaps that could be evidence. Nevertheless, none of the tapes was retained until a ministerial order was issued in February 1986.

"The explanations surrounding how and when tapes were erased are replete with contradictions," Bass said. "There are several statements in the SIRC report relating to the timing of CSIS advising RCMP of specific intercepts, which do not match RCMP records on the same transactions. The efforts by the RCMP to access CSIS wiretap information surrounding the bombings went on until 1990." Bass was explicit in his condemnation. "Valuable wiretap evidence in the possession of CSIS was destroyed when tapes were erased." He did not cut CSIS any slack. Difficulties in co-operation — which stretched over five years — had serious consequences. "Lack of disclosure by CSIS in the early days allowed the RCMP to seek a wiretap authorization on the wrong targets," he stated.

He did not elaborate on whose Charter rights had been violated or what the consequences were when the wrong person was subjected to a wiretap or had phone conversations intercepted. Once again, it seems SIRC failed to alert the public to a violation of a Canadian's rights by the spy agency. Bass also directly contradicted SIRC on the significance of the lack of co-operation to the ongoing investigation. "There is a strong likelihood that, had CSIS retained the tapes between March and August 1985, a successful prosecution against at least some of the principals in both bombings could have been undertaken," he wrote. SIRC also fell down on the assessment of rumours that a foreign government (i.e. India) played a role in the bombings.

"We reviewed the CSIS information," stated the publicly released summary. "Based on the material we examined, the information collected by CSIS does not support the theory of complicity by a foreign government in the crash of Air India flight 182." Bass had more to say about foreign government involvement. "The SIRC review had serious concerns over CSIS' handling of this issue. CSIS' reply to this possibility was that it had passed it to the RCMP to investigate. SIRC reports that the RCMP looked into this aspect and determined the allegation to be without foundation," he said. "The truth of the matter is that the RCMP never thoroughly investigated the issue, which means that apparently no one did."

Here's one final example to illustrate the dubious value of the information provided to the public in the SIRC review. "Based on our review of the information that CSIS possessed prior to the crash, the Service was not in a position to predict that the Air India flight was to be the target of a terrorist bomb," the review claimed. But a different perspective was set out in a memo from the director general of counter-terrorism in CSIS in 1986, which also became available during the trial. CSIS "might have deterred the subsequent presumed bombing of the flight over the Atlantic Ocean if CSIS agents had immediately interviewed Parmar and Reyat after following them into the woods and heard them ignite an explosive device," the CSIS boss concluded.

CSIS may not have possessed specific information spelling out exactly when the bombs were to be put on airplanes and when they would explode. But a senior official with CSIS believed the agency could have taken action that would have derailed the conspiracy. How did SIRC overlook that, especially when you consider that SIRC has what it describes as "absolute authority" to examine all CSIS files and activities, no matter how highly classified? The memos that became available at the Air India trial raise a question about a crucial aspect of the review body. Why should we trust it? This case study of the Air India disaster indicates something was amiss. SIRC claimed an extensive investigation had been undertaken. The public inadvertently learned that senior RCMP and CSIS officials had information and opinions that contradicted key findings. The opinions of the top officials were not reflected in the report. The experience with the Air India case suggests the public needs access to a procedure to scrutinize SIRC findings in order to ensure the committee has done its job.

On its website in May 2005 the committee set out a comment in response to a hypothetical question from those who query the credibility of the work done by SIRC: "The structure is designed to ensure that knowledgeable and respected individuals independent of CSIS and government, but familiar with the security intelligence environment, render honest and fair-minded assessments. Canadians can have confidence that SIRC will remain vigilant to ensure CSIS acts within the law."

The quality of SIRC's work has rarely been challenged, possibly because the basis for the committee's conclusions is not normally open to public scrutiny. The shortcomings of the SIRC report on the CSIS investigation in the Air India case never made it onto the public agenda. SIRC has received the trust of Canadians. But has that trust been misplaced? The review committee is composed of eminent citizens, members of an elite circle of business leaders and former politicians who are given almost unrestricted access to some of the most important secrets in the country. The committee has five members who are also members of the Privy Council, a non-partisan office of government that works closely with the Prime Minister's Office on priorities and matters of national and international importance. SIRC submits a report to Parliament every year, and committee members appear before a parliamentary committee to discuss their operations and annual budget of just over $2 million.

John Bassett, SIRC chairman when the Air India review was started in 1991, was a larger-than-life tycoon for decades. He was publisher of the *Toronto Telegram* for nearly twenty years and a one-time owner of the Toronto Argonauts and the legendary Maple Leaf Gardens. He ran twice unsuccessfully for Parliament, once in Quebec and once in Ontario. Prime Minister Brian Mulroney appointed him to a three-year term in 1988 as head of SIRC. He died in 1998.

When the Air India review began, he tried to dampen expectations. "I caution you that expectations must not be unrealistic or too high," he told reporters. The review was to look into the activities of CSIS and was not to be a substitute for a full public inquiry into the disaster. In the SIRC annual report for 1991, he wrote that the role of SIRC had changed in recent years, reflecting changes that had been made in CSIS. The review body was no longer an aggressive critic of the spy agency, he said. The annual report included much more supportive accounts of CSIS activities, mainly because the secret service was no longer breaking the law. "This progressive but clear-cut change in the tone and substance of our annual reports simply reflects the fact that CSIS is now virtually a new organization, hardly recognizable any more as a direct descendant of the security service of the RCMP," Bassett said. However SIRC has responsibilities that go beyond the issue of whether CSIS complies with the law. It took 9/11 to ring alarm bells in Canada. Potential threats against the U.S. are pushing our government to look more closely at its intelligence agencies. As part of the review of national security, the issue of scrutinizing intelligence agency watchdogs surfaced once again.

The federal government has begun moving toward the creation of a new national security committee of parliamentarians to scrutinize all agencies, departments, and review bodies in the intelligence community. The idea has been bandied about for more than twenty years, but the government had previously rejected the proposal for a parliamentary committee on security and intelligence. Advocates say closer scrutiny is primarily intended to ensure more accountability from the intelligence community and a proper balance between respect for Canadians' rights under the Charter of Rights and Freedoms and the protection of national security.

Another consideration is politics. A parliamentary committee would inject a serious dose of politics into the review of the activities of the intelligence community. It could be a mixed blessing. Politicians sensitive to the moods of the electorate could come armed with the demands of popular opinion. The advisory committee cautioned that the proposed committee was not intended to duplicate the work of SIRC, the CSE commissioner, or the RCMP public complaints commissioner. But the parliamentarians would be expected to have similar authorizations to request and receive unexpurgated reports, the advisory committee on national security stated in its report released in April 2005. The parliamentarians would have powers to subpoena witnesses and compel testimony, to be the forum for consideration of unexpurgated reports from all review bodies. The review bodies were to keep the parliamentarians fully informed of their activities, with detailed listings of operational plans, documents, and reports.

More than twenty years after the Air India disaster, and more than ten years after the SIRC report on how CSIS handled the matter, the public still does not know what happened in the worst crime in Canadian history. Even the passage of time could not convince SIRC to show Canadians what it had done. In response to access-to-information requests from the media, SIRC released a version of its final report. Huge portions remain censored.

CHAPTER 14

LAST SHOT
by Dwight Hamilton

"All the guns are on one side — the American one."

As they say in the CIA, let's "walk back the cat." When Alitalia flight 651 landed at Rome's Leonardo da Vinci international airport at 8:20 a.m. on June 26, 1982, with me aboard, I was still virtually a virgin with respect to terrorism. I was, after all, just a young Canuck with a camera. And I sure dropped my lens quick when two trigger-happy paramilitary types levelled their submachine guns right at my centre of mass and barked, "No pictures." Fair enough in hindsight. I was used to Kodak Moments; they were used to the Red Brigades.

Since that Year of the Gun, I've served with a veteran of the British Special Air Service who would find such occasions mundane and rubbed shoulders with someone who had a hand hacked off by one of the Green Devils and with a counter-terrorism specialist who has left six cadavers in his wake. I've come a long way, baby ... but has Canada?

The series of London bombings on July 7, 2005, proved al Qaeda could still throw a fair punch. Although the causalities were remarkably low, they managed to best the IRA, which has been at the British for decades. The four 7/7 blasts were the deadliest terrorist attack in history on that city so far.

"Until we feel security, you will be our targets," said bomber Mohammad Sidique Khan. "Until you will stop the bombing, gassing, imprisonment, and torture of my people, we will not stop this fight." Al

Qaeda's second-in-command, Ayman al-Zawahri, kept using the term "blessed." More catastrophes are planned, apparently, which should keep our crusader cousins busy for some time.

Should we even care? I think so. We seem paralyzed with a deadly combination of political complacency and public confusion. As a result, national security has been marginalized in Canada — governments have believed that they can delay its discussion without paying a steep political price.

But somebody ends up paying. The federal governments of the last quarter-century have left our military decimated to the point where it may not be able to perform its duties. Anyone who is not aware of and duly alarmed by this trend must not be thinking clearly. Canadian administrations have got to find spending cuts in other areas. "Not enough money to issue recruits with a spare pair of boots" — that's the best one yet.

One of the military's jobs is making sure that the Canadian public doesn't get killed or wounded by people who would enjoy doing so. Next time they split the federal purse, it's worth bearing in mind that some of these people get shot at on the job. And modern combat is not like a video game. It's still sickening enough to induce shell shock in some. The security services have also suffered huge cuts, especially over the last decade. This has to stop.

Here comes the part where the chief says, "Now listen very carefully." Based on proven counter-terrorism tactics, the following steps are required to prevail in the current environment. Although no one likes to admit it to a concerned public, the War on Terror cannot be "won" in the traditional sense of high-intensity conflicts. In this sense, it is identical to criminal activity. The Western democracies can, however, reduce the likelihood and severity of potentially destabilizing attacks against them with due diligence. What follows is a conceptual framework:

- Fight an ideas war. One of the best ways to deter misguided youths from emulating al Qaeda's campaign of hatred toward the West is to enlist the help of moderate Muslim leaders. If they can curb the angry young appetite for destruction, a long-term counter-terrorist objective is met. Think of it as cutting off resupply in a strategic sense.

- Neutralize funding for terrorist groups. Cut the support from sponsor states and trace and freeze or confiscate all monies associated with terrorist organizations. Expose to the press the front groups that receive donations passed on to terrorists, and freeze the front's assets. This is very difficult and problematic: Front groups are often charities that can prove at least some of their money goes to humanitarian causes. If they investigate, intelligence agencies or the press could face a public relations nightmare that includes victims of Western Imperialism or, worse, George W. Bush. Canadian libel law takes care of their other flank until you catch a guy with an AK-47 and his hand in the till. I know at least three Canadian journalists writing in this area who have been effectively muzzled by the possibility of civil litigation while I have been working on this book. One bowed out of writing for me because of it. A charity even made CSIS back down in another case. This battle is currently being lost, which is the reason the names of these organizations are not included here. Utilizing a political system so that its inherent strengths and weaknesses can be turned against it reminds me of Lenin, who is thought to have said, "The Capitalists will sell us the rope with which we will hang them."

- Restrict the movement of terrorists to make conducting operations more difficult. For helpful hints on reforming the Canadian refugee system, reread Chapter 7. Please keep in mind if you start questioning inane positions passing as discourse on public policy, an immigration minister might label you "anti-everybody," as has been done before.

Before this year's election, the former minister, Joe Volpe, was spearheading a major overhaul of the immigration process that will see an increase in admissions 35 percent above levels in effect now. Apparently we don't have enough truck drivers. You go, Joe. Just make sure the next millennium bomber's truck doesn't make it past the gate. With respect to airport safety, read the Standing Senate Committee on National Security and Defence report on our air travel regime, available on the Internet. After perusing the document, flood your MP's office with constructive criticism by mail; you don't need a stamp. Politicians love to be engaged by their constituency. Former prime minister Pierre Trudeau was a big fan of "participatory democracy."

- Destroy or deter terrorist sponsor states. "We are not the public service of Canada," said one of our generals. "We are the Canadian Forces and our job is to be able to kill people." Direct military intervention may be required in certain circumstances, as is being done presently in Afghanistan. Prepare for a long stay; it is impossible to predict the length of time necessary to secure an environment that will be unable to train and export large numbers of terrorists. Moreover, the situation in weakened nation states — or dictatorships, once they unravel due to intervention — is often chaotic. You would be surprised at how many different groups of people around the world want to kill each other. "Along with the Taliban and al Qaeda, one of the three main groups involved is called Hizb-I Islami Gulbuddin. They're not called enemies because they sometimes fight each other when they are not getting along. We call them 'Opposing Military Forces,'" says an intelligence officer about the situation in Afghanistan. "The G2

Section wrote of them as being more like crooks, criminals, and bandits with occasional political and religious rhetoric attached to the two things they really wanted: money and power. People switch sides in Afghanistan more often than they change clothing." In some situations you don't need boots on the ground though. Wonder why Libya has been so polite in recent years? Evidence in Berlin's La Belle discotheque bombing in 1986 pointed toward Libyan involvement, and the Americans sent some carrier-based fighter-bombers on a sort of familiarization flight over Benghazi and Tripoli. Sometimes gunboat diplomacy is all you need, providing the state has some sort of centralized authority, unlike Somalia and Haiti. Do countries such as Iran, Syria, and Yemen see American intervention in Iraq as instructive? They should. Al Qaeda is not the only one with a list.

- Infiltrate terrorist organizations and terrorist support cells by covert means. These adventures are in the major leagues, I admit, but a key activity at this time. Technically, in Canada, being a member of a terrorist group is a crime. The closer an infiltrator gets to the real thing, the closer they come to violating the criminal code. Committing a crime is often a rite of passage to a group, not unlike the mob. Would the government (and public opinion) permit CSIS or the RCMP to engage in such activities? Is either agency sophisticated enough for the task? Recently revealed in the media was an Israeli deception to recruit sympathetic individuals to al Qaeda.

- Use technical surveillance to monitor terrorist communications. By the 2007–08 fiscal year, the budget of the Communications Security Establishment will have been increased by more than half of its pre-9/11 size. But with an increase in data collection ability, personnel numbers must also increase. The agency faces a bit of a specialized skills shortage.

- Develop stronger alliances with coalition governments and others to ensure better intelligence and coordinated action. This entails getting into bed at times with people who are not particularly polite to their fellow man. It's not cricket. But in order to preserve our personal safety as citizens, a bit of situational ethics is called for here. Our values are not the world's values. While I certainly do not condone torture, or even feel that an Abu Ghraib–style photo shoot is particularly productive, not accepting intelligence from foreign states simply because they employ torture as an interrogation procedure makes sense only if you live on Sesame Street. How many police forces in the world would ignore information that could lead to an arrest because it came from a criminal? And of course information could be false due to coercive methodology or the use of sodium pentothal; they know that in the intelligence business. Information is always context dependent and corroborated if possible.

- Monitor hazardous materials, equipment, and weapons sales around the world. Although this is not truly possible in today's asymmetric environment, it is vital to at least attempt it. Today, efforts are weak. There is a need for worldwide government support with this issue. Inventories of nuclear, biological, and chemical agents must be tracked, along with material that could be used in improvised explosive devices like dirty bombs. In the meantime, try to keep an eye out for suspicious purchases of large quantities of ammonium nitrate fertilizer or stocks of peroxide and acetone by those fitting the Islamic

Jihadist profile. What can you do with states that shut out United Nations nuclear inspectors? "The truth is, as [U.S. Secretary of State] Condoleezza Rice has made clear, military action in respect of the Iranian dossier is not on anybody's agenda. I believe it is inconceivable," British Foreign Minister Jack Straw told the BBC in September 2005.

- Harden all targets. There's supposed to be a Senate report on this shortly, so stay tuned. One hopes they look into the situation at Quebec hydroelectric facilities Manic-5 and LG-2, the largest dam in North America. In February 2005, a team of Radio-Canada reporters had no trouble penetrating the perimeters of these installations and walking into control rooms. There were no security guards or cameras in sight.

I close with some thoughts regarding a frequently asked question: What would happen in Canada in the event of a major terrorist strike?

Well, we know that two years after 9/11, during the largest electrical blackout in North American history, the offices of the prime minister and the Privy Council were without adequate backup generating power.

We also know that three years after 9/11, one man with a pistol bottled up 26,000 commuters arriving on trains into Toronto's Union Station during the morning rush hour. To restrict the hostage-taker, police and security had to close the usual exits, and thousands were sardined inside, some taking as long as twenty minutes to get out of the building. Some citizens called for emergency procedures to be reviewed. This transportation hub has been a confirmed al Qaeda target for a while, based upon evidence uncovered in Afghanistan. What would it be like to be pressed next to a man or woman with a suitcase full of radioactive cobalt-60 combined with RDX or C-4 plastic during a situation like that? I reckon you'd remember the ring of their cell phone for the rest of your life.

And we know that you can still drive a truckload of ammonium nitrate and diesel fuel across the Ambassador Bridge without being inspected. All the guns are on one side — the American one. Former Public Safety Minister Anne McLellan is on record as stating that the 9/11 Commission report had little to teach Canada. I wish they would do a report on bridges.

Would our own troops be able to fire their weapons at women and children fleeing the scene of a biological attack, if that is what it would take to contain contamination? This is the type of sickening hypothetical scenario the experts are dealing with now.

And for now, that's about all you need to know. True stories about petrochemical installations in Sarnia being staked out by folks I certainly don't trust and the estimated kill count due to a toxic cloud working its atmospheric way along the Golden Horseshoe can wait for another day. Let's just say that as the United States continues to harden its targets, we become more attractive to terrorists.

Meanwhile, a debate actually exists over the possible introduction of the Muslim legal code of Sharia within our own borders. And in an alarming poll taken in February 2006, more than 60 percent of Canadians said they don't want our troops in Afghanistan, let alone Iraq. Of those who do, one-third would change their minds if significant casualities were suffered. At the same time, some of our own citizens are videotaping things like subway platforms and the CN Tower and getting caught up in a world of international terrorism and Cairo jail cells. For his troubles in this area, a Mr. Mohamed is now suing the federal government for $1 million in compensation. "I'm not a terrorist," he later told the press. "I just don't like Canada."

Message received and understood?

CANADIAN EYES ONLY
by Dwight Hamilton
with files from Kostas Rimsa

*"If this becomes as cool as being a rock star, we've got a real problem
on our hands."*

Some say there's nothing good on television today, but perhaps they just can't find a program they can relate to. Viewers who watched auditions for the show *Canadian Idol* in June 2008 could be forgiven for being a little confused, as a twenty-six-year-old man sang and danced to an Avril Lavigne number wearing traditional tribal Pashtun garb, including their headdress.

Further confusion is understandable when this same man, along with three other Canadian citizens, was arrested just two years later and charged with conspiracy to facilitate terrorism and other offences. Three more Canadians were sought abroad at the time of this writing, possibly hiding out in Iran, Pakistan, Afghanistan, or Dubai. In an Ottawa raid, police found fifty circuit boards to detonate improvised explosive devices and bombs along with instruction manuals and other unpleasant materials, including schematics.

The thing regular folks can't seem to relate to is the revelation that this man wasn't born in an impoverished area of the third world with a reason to fear and loathe enthusiastic flyovers by American Black Hawks. The man was born and raised in the most politically correct, pluralistic, peaceable kingdom on planet earth: our home and native land.

He is a husband. He is a father of three little girls. In the footsteps of the renowned Sir William Osler and Wilder Penfield, he went to McGill

University in Montreal to become a medical doctor. His specialty is pathology, which can come in handy in anyone's bio-weapons program.

What is happening in this country? Just days after the first edition of this book was published, an RCMP joint task force made one of the largest arrests of terrorists in North America. Eighteen persons (including four youths) were charged in June 2006 for plotting suicide truck bomb attacks on the Toronto Stock Exchange, CSIS headquarters, a military base, and the CBC building, in addition to another plot to storm Parliament Hill and behead several politicians, including the prime minister. Many had trained in a makeshift Jihadist camp north of Toronto where they got familiar with white camo coats and guns in the middle of winter. Had they been successful, the installation strikes would have utilized three metric tonnes of ammonium nitrate with the potential for a catastrophic loss of civilian life. Commenting shortly after the arrests on the youthful ages of the accused, I speculated in a television interview: "If this becomes as cool as being a rock star, we've got a real problem on our hands."

As the cases of the Toronto 18 wound their way through court, seven of the group had their charges stayed, but the other eleven pleaded guilty or were found guilty by a jury. Some of the convicted terrorists got out of jail immediately once they pleaded, due to double-credit for time served. At least one had taken an anger management course, and both cell leaders could be walking the streets as free men in under four years. Both will be barely thirty years of age. "Overall, it seems as if the justice system treats an engagement with terrorism as a youthful mistake that will disappear with time," the *Globe and Mail* stated in an editorial that was extremely critical of the penalties. It would appear that in addition to many politicians, the judiciary and the Crown simply do not understand what they are dealing with. As a result of this ignorance, the message the system is sending to the public is that our lives are pretty cheap.

What message do prospective Islamic Jihadists get from this? Now they really know that life in Canada is different from the rest of the world because — believe it or not — one of the cell leaders got a life sentence. One of his convicted friends received an above-the-fold profile on the front page of a major newspaper. And then there was the taxpayer-subsidized play *Homegrown*, whose writer said about her protagonist: "I think he's a guy who showed bad judgment; I don't think he's a terrorist at all."

Since the last chapter was written, this country has come a long way, baby. And with stories like these making headlines around the world, many wonder if we are on the road to ruin.

The Red Chamber

Admittedly, there is no easy road out of the current dilemma, but in the interest of articulating at least one of the problems faced, the following exchange during my appearance last year at the Senate's Special Subcommittee on Anti-terrorism might give you an idea of what the country is up against.

> *Mr. Hamilton:* With the Criminal Code system, intelligence services have a problem. I know this is not classified but I do not know whether the public is aware that the Toronto 18 strike was at least the third cell in Toronto. The first cell was Algerian and the second cell al Qaeda. The problem that the Mounties and CSIS had was that they could not produce Criminal Code evidence, which is needed to hold up in a criminal court.
>
> *Senator Wallin:* That is what I was saying.
>
> *Mr. Hamilton:* The problem in this world of terrorism is that often when you reach that point, it is too late because the terrorist momentum has gone past the chance to catch these people.
>
> CSIS and the Mounties followed a standard operating procedure: they performed a disrupt action. Some of the guys in the cell left the country and some of them did not leave. Basically, CSIS and the RCMP make the cell aware that they are being monitored and they try to put pressure on them. I know that the Mounties and CSIS did the absolute best they could do but, quite frankly, we have to fix the system because it is not good enough.

I believe that I speak for many Canadians when I say that we do not care if they are disrupted terrorists; we simply do not want them running around. We have to find some way that law enforcement agencies and intelligence agencies can deal with some of these people without having to produce that much.

Historically, terrorism wound up in the Criminal Code system. Since more recent events, what has changed is mostly a loss-of-life issue so that they resemble acts of war.

The Chair: Senator Wallin, did you want to add to that?

Senator Wallin: I think we are getting at it. I do not know whether Mr. Crelinsten has anything else to say, but I think we are getting to the heart of it right there with Mr. Hamilton's remarks.

With the specific example above, as more cells are discovered, the obvious problem with simply keeping disrupted terrorists (whom we are unable to deport) under constant surveillance would be an expanded, but prohibitively expensive, watcher service. And with the weapons technology available today, a terrorist strike will be like an act of large-scale war.

I am not the only one who realizes we have a problem on our hands. In a report for the Fraser Institute, Martin Collacott, who was once the Canadian ambassador to Syria, Lebanon, and Cambodia, as well as the high commissioner to Sri Lanka, wrote that "the exigencies of pursuing suspected terrorists require greater flexibility for investigators and prosecutors than is available under normal criminal law." Collacott was also Foreign Affairs Canada's director general of security services at one time and helped coordinate its counterterrorism policy. Even Supreme Court Justice Ian Binnie has stated that it is "absolutely necessary" for the judiciary to defer to the government's security agencies with respect to international security, as that is where the genuine expertise lies. While Binnie admitted that such deference must have limits and that finding where to draw the line is a tough task, he stressed it is imperative to find that mark, as terrorism is the greatest threat to the rule of law known.

And what do citizens who are not sitting on the big bench think? According to one poll taken when the *Anti-Terrorism Act* was being tabled a few years ago, a majority of Canadians favour the indefinite detention of terrorist suspects by the authorities — even without a specific charge.

Secret Asian Men

CSIS Director Richard Fadden certainly stirred the pot when he stated on television in June 2010 that at least five countries' intelligence organizations are unduly influencing at least two provincial cabinet ministers and a number of lesser elected officials in Canada. He didn't say who the countries were, but when pressed by the interviewer he would not deny myriad unofficial reports that China tops the list.

The director could have said "no comment," during his interview and still not have lied to the Canadian public, but he chose another way to tell the truth. His public candour was refreshing to those who are thankful for the agency fulfilling one of its sworn duties, even if the subject of "agents of influence" has become a tired platitude in the intelligence community. CSIS looked into Chinese economic espionage extensively via Operation Sidewinder back in the 1990s. The project was abruptly shut down, some agents were told to destroy their notes and some parties later publicly discredited its importance and conclusions.

Fadden's remarks came as an apparent shock to some members of Parliament and various other usual suspects, which demanded he appear before a Commons committee and explain why he spoke (seemingly) out of turn. Political critics wanted names and other information made public, which intelligence agencies are not in the business of doing and members of Parliament are not cleared to receive at any rate.

An academic observer even asserted that the director does not understand "the role of CSIS in a democratic society," making comparisons with J. Edgar Hoover and the McCarthy era. He also predicted the director would not last another year in the job. That would be fine for some MPs, who are expected to back a Commons motion requesting his immediate removal for "smearing" the Chinese-Canadian community. "There are thousands of Canadians who feel slighted and humiliated by a senior government official who deliberately cast suspicion on their loyalty," reads the statement. It is well known that some politicians take certain types of hurt feelings very seriously, and the fact that "thousands" are now suffering suggests that this issue might not retire from the national spotlight soon.

At about the same time, the American FBI was rounding up a dozen Russian spies that it believes had been active for at least a decade, four of whom claimed to be Canadians or at least born here. Just like the movies, one agent began a "legend" by assuming the identity of a baby who died in Montreal back in 1962, a practice known as "tombstoning." Moscow claimed all were in fact regular Russian citizens and that the charges were without foundation. The Americans claim they posed as average suburban couples who were really tasked with obtaining positions to provide them with access to confidential political and economic information and certain high technologies. The information was then passed to the Sluzhba Vneshney Razvedki (SVR) Centre in Moscow. Shortly after the case was made public, a diplomatic swap was arranged to settle matters between Moscow and Washington.

Despite today's reduced need for classified communications equipment, SVR agents complemented their off-the-shelf electronic toolkit with invisible inks, coding devices, drop sites with buried supplies, short-burst radiograms, and one-time pads. One operative who went under the name Anna Chapman had quite a few Facebook "friends" and used her red-hot birthday suit to steal secrets. After her game was up, she was featured on the cover of the Russian edition of *Maxim* magazine in her panties — packing a pistol. In today's environment of information warfare, one wonders if this signals a new twist to the standard "de-briefing."

When foreign agents steal defence or state secrets (or perhaps when they look like Anna) the cases tend to receive a lot of media attention and so most are familiar with military and political espionage. But when a country sends its spies to steal our trade secrets, or if a company steals secrets from another one, it seldom makes the radar despite the fact these are everyday occurrences in Canada. Catching and prosecuting offenders is made difficult as companies often bury the crimes to avoid adverse publicity and a potential drop in share values, if the entity is publicly traded.

One company that could not (or would not) bury a case just this year was Dow AgroSciences, a subsidiary of the American chemical giant and the largest biotechnology company in that country. A lead researcher into the genetic engineering of spinosyns (products that attack the central nervous systems of insects, similar agents to nerve gas), Huang Kexue was born in China and worked for Dow in Indiana and was charged with seventeen counts of sending trade secrets to Beijing. This is only the seventh time that such a U.S. criminal charge has been used since its inception in 2001. China was also the destination for information provided by some scientists at DuPont recently, as well as that of Jim Hanjuan, a software engineer for Motorola who was arrested on a plane en route there with a laptop full of data.

Sitting beside me at the Senate committee was Michel Juneau-Katsuya, who is a former senior CSIS officer and one of the country's foremost experts on economic espionage. More than anyone, he should know the score. Here is what he told us:

> In 1995, I was with CSIS as the Chief of Asia-Pacific. I asked one of my analysts at the time to perform an assessment based on fact: How much money are we losing annually because of economic or industrial espionage? We were able to demonstrate that at the time we were losing on average $10 billion to $12 billion per year in Canada. In the U.S. a similar study was conducted. They estimated a loss of $24 billion, which is twice as much. However, their economy is ten times bigger than ours, so per ratio, we were losing five times more than the U.S. A small country like ours cannot afford such a loss. To my knowledge, no other study of that nature, to try to quantify and qualify how much money we are losing, has been produced.
>
> Unfortunately, the U.S. has prepared more studies. The director of the FBI recently revealed that in its estimation, the U.S. currently loses $250 billion per year. They have experienced an exponential increase. We can only speculate that if we double what we lost in 1995, we are probably close to the reality.

The next question is: Why Canada? Why do we have so much? There are myriad reasons. First, there is a lack of discussion around the subject. All governments, one after the other, refuse to talk about it. They practice the policy of speak no evil, see no evil. That goes to the detriment of our industries because companies are not aware that they have been spied upon.

They come to Canada because Canada is a knowledge-based society. We have phenomenal research centres, and we offer a lot of cutting edge technology in many fields, but we do not have a law to protect us. Two short sections were added in an impromptu fashion when we revised the Official Secrets Act, but they have never been used. There is no law so law enforcement does not devote any attention to that perspective and, therefore, there are no resources to investigate.

At the end of the day, the private sector is left to its own devices to try to protect itself, which it is capable of doing. That speaks to the business culture, more than to anything else, which comes from awareness. In my humble estimate, if not for the fact that terrorist acts kill people, foreign espionage would be and should be the most pressing national security issue for Canada.

Kostas Rimsa attended a CSIS briefing on economic espionage given to CEOs back in the 1990s and says even some high technology leaders viewed the issue as anything but pressing. Most were not convinced there was a threat to their firms and others demanded names, dates, and particulars of companies that had approached CSIS for advice on the matters in order to make an evaluation of their own situation. But unfortunately by providing this data, the agency would lose all credibility to attract future sources. Rimsa also says CEOs with government contracts pointed out the lack of law enforcement and this sent a message to them that economic espionage was extremely low-priority.

Today, even basic security checks for military projects can be overlooked. In 2007, the auditor general found twenty-four contracts that went ahead without the required clearances and that included work on NORAD's Above Ground Complex at North Bay, Ontario.

Man of the Year

The Maher Arar file continues to be of interest to taxpaying citizens who can form critical thought patterns, despite the best efforts of the mainstream media and other interested parties to bury the topic. Arar was the subject of a $23 million federal inquiry led by a judge who stated he believed the man was tortured while held in a Syrian prison. He was later awarded over $10 million in compensation by the federal government for alleged damages. That is a record in fact.

But to those of us with an intelligence background, his file felt dirty even back when he was chosen Man of the Year for the Canadian edition of *Time* magazine. Remember that in the intelligence world, nothing really is as it seems, it is cloaked in a type of hard-to-define darkness. Here is an important issue that contributor John Thompson pointed out to the Senate subcommittee:

> One thing that particularly struck me was that we automatically accepted his allegation of torture. He never testified to the committee except by video deposition. Also, everything hinged on the whole point about torture. When was there an independent medical examination? The things he described originally were that in Syria he had been whipped and beaten across the hands with two-inch telephone cables. I have seen the scars from people who are in Iraq who were treated that way under Saddam Hussein's regime. The scars are permanent. The fingers are all broken.
>
> If someone alleges torture and we take it so seriously, should there not have been someone who said: I am a medical doctor, recognized by the court. Can we see the evidence that you were actually tortured?

Most Canadians likely believe he was, as it is still reported by the media as a fact. But it is not a *fact*. It is an *opinion* that was arrived at outside of a court of law — civil or criminal — without even the slightest participation of either the Syrian or American governments.

How many Canadians also mistakenly believe that it was our country that sent the man to Damascus? Michael Ignatieff did, long after his stint as a cosmopolitan intellectual south of the 49th parallel publishing things on the legitimacy of liberal democracies "trafficking in lesser evils." Apparently clarifying his current policy on the subject of torture with respect to his extensive written record, he stated to a British newspaper that after Canada had dispatched Arar to Syria, a court found that he had indeed been tortured, and that he had furnished no intelligence to anyone, ever. "It was a disgrace," he emphasized. When a reporter tried to confirm his errors she was told that his office no longer had a tape of the interview. There are a lot of stories circulating about this case, such as the published — yet so far not discredited — charge that Arar was a covert agent operating on Canadian soil and run by the Americans. This is possible, but other plausible explanations can be found outside the standard narrative the public has been led to believe.

This theatre of the absurd has progressed to a point that would make even Beckett blush. Unfortunately, due to the complexity and conflicting interests of various parties involved, the public will likely never know the truth. But we do know what has been the fallout for Canada. Jihadist sympathizers promote the view that our security services target innocent persons because they are Muslim and send them to third world torture chambers. That is the real disgrace.

The Longest War

About a year before this book originally went to press, Canada had begun deploying combat troops to the notoriously violent Kandahar district in southern Afghanistan and the force would eventually total over 2,200 personnel. They are scheduled to pull out sometime this summer, leaving personnel from Foreign Affairs and CIDA, which will continue to assist in the reconstruction and development efforts of the still extremely fragile country, along with a "behind the wire" training role for a contingent of soldiers far from Kandahar, as there are not enough combat troops ready for another rotation and a large percentage of the army's vital equipment is worn out beyond repair.

Because of American emphasis on the Iraq invasion begun in 2003 and the troop deficit it left, Canadians fought what could best be described as a holding action in what's being termed as a "Forgotten War." In 2009, more U.S. ground troops were committed to the southern region in a so-called surge but in reality, there have never been enough soldiers on the ground to tackle the objective of making the country secure. This has especially been the case in the south, by some estimates another 10,000 troops are required to deny operational territory to terrorists there. To make matters worse, the Obama administration has stated it will begin withdrawing American troops in 2011 as well, throwing a lot of issues into doubt.

The war in Afghanistan has included the longest combat stint in the history of the Canadian Army. Soldiers from nearly all regular and reserve ground units have participated in the conflict — some engaged in its heaviest fighting. As of October 2010, over 2,000 NATO soldiers have died since the invasion began on October 7, 2001. Over 150 have been Canadian in addition to over five hundred wounded in action and another nine hundred injured outside of battle. At times, casualties were higher than usual due to bad equipment in the early years and the fact that the Canadians in Kandahar (like the British in Helmand province) were spread too thin during their deployment. Several accounts of the Canadian Army in Afghanistan punching above its weight have now become widely known due to books such as *Fifteen Days* and *Contact Charlie*.

Throughout the ordeal, public opinion has remained largely unchanged. In late 2010, a poll found that only 21 percent of Canadians see combat operations overseas as an "important role for the military," and would support another rotation of fighting troops there. This is perhaps not surprising, as press coverage has emphasized deaths of individual soldiers and alleged Canadian "war crimes" with respect to Taliban prisoner handovers. This latter issue has maintained domestic political traction due to a civil liberties association, an Ottawa-based university professor, and our media, one outlet of which interviewed thirty Taliban PWs in 2007 who said that they had been tortured.

The challenges for the mission in Afghanistan remain formidable and by most estimates it will take many more years to surmount them. The Afghan culture is divided over the merits of Western influence and the government is incompetent and very corrupt. There are problems with the training, the arming, the equipping, and the paying of the Afghan National Police and the army. Reconstruction efforts depend on security, and as it is lacking in many areas, the country's infrastructure remains primitive. There is a severe shortage of teachers and doctors, vital to any society. Then there is the opium trade. Now with the northwest tribal area of Pakistan entering into the mix, there are new political and military issues with that government.

Western disengagement any time soon is impossible given these dire straits. One thing is for certain: al Qaeda would love to get its hands on Pakistan's nuclear arsenal, and that is one thing the West can never allow to happen. Moreover, if the U.S. is seen as running away from Afghanistan, it will have negative consequences for counter-terrorism efforts around the world.

Rock Star

In just a short time, Omar Khadr will return to Canada due to a plea deal reached in November 2010 that imposed a sentence of eight years for murder and attempted murder "in violation of the laws of war" under the *United States Military Commission Act*. Captured when he was fifteen years old by American forces in Afghanistan in 2002, Khadr had been designated an "unlawful enemy combatant" and has been held prisoner at Guantanamo Bay since then.

Despite the plea deal, a jury of military officers deliberated on the case anyway and recommended a sentence of forty years. The prosecution had asked for just twenty-five. This is the controversial commission's first murder conviction and the plea deal is widely seen as removing a significant political headache for the American government. Upon Khadr's return to Canada he will be eligible for parole almost immediately.

What will likely happen to the man once described as the "Rock Star of Gitmo" when he crosses the border? As a Canadian citizen who fought against NATO troops he could be tried for treason, but most likely he will be released after his first parole hearing. If so, maybe he will go abroad and re-join the Jihad if there is no stipulation to stop him from travelling. Or he could stay here at home and sign book and movie deals, as there are no laws to stop him from profiting, and convicted terrorists have a habit of doing that in Canada. Some feel Omar Khadr regrets what he has done however, so there's a good chance he will donate any proceeds he may derive from his new celebrity status to a charity that assists Canadian veterans who have lost their legs from the mines he used to lay alongside Afghan roads.

PROCEEDINGS OF THE SPECIAL SENATE COMMITTEE ON ANTI-TERRORISM

Issue 3 — Evidence

OTTAWA, Monday, June 14, 2010

The Special Senate Committee on Anti-terrorism met this day at 1 p.m. to examine matters relating to anti-terrorism.

Senator Hugh Segal (Chair) in the chair.

The Chair: Honourable senators, welcome to the fourth meeting of the Special Senate Committee on Anti-terrorism during the Third Session of the Fortieth Parliament. We are continuing our hearings into the dynamics of terrorism, how they have changed, and how our security forces are able to address those changing dynamics. We are fortunate to have three expert witnesses today to help us with our examination of these matters. They have agreed to travel long distances, in some cases, and have provided written statements. Following opening statements of 10 minutes each, I will open the floor to questions by senators.

Our first witness, Mr. Dwight Hamilton, author and former member of Canadian military intelligence, has written extensively on terrorist related issues. He is the principal author and editor of *Inside Canadian Intelligence*, which exposes the new realities of espionage and international terrorism; and a co-author with Kostas Rimsa of *Terror Threat: International and*

Homegrown Terrorists and Their Threat to Canada.

He will be followed by Mr. Michel Juneau-Katsuya, who is a former senior officer of the Royal Canadian Mounted Police and the Canadian Security Intelligence Service. He has been involved as a criminal investigator, intelligence officer and strategic analyst. He was in charge of contingency and emergency planning for CSIS and his knowledge of Asia earned him Directorship of the Strategic Analysis Unit for Asia-Pacific. He is now with the Northgate Group Corp. and offers advice and counsel to both the public and private sectors.

He will be followed by Professor Ronald Crelinsten, who has a PhD in criminology from l'université de Montréal. He is a founding member of the editorial board of Terrorism and Political Violence, the leading academic journal in terrorism studies. He is on the international advisory board of the *International Journal of Conflict and Violence.* He was a professor of criminology at the University of Ottawa from 1982 to 2004, and principal researcher on a research project on gross human rights violations at Leiden University in the Netherlands, and is a senior research member of the Centre for Global Studies at the University of Victoria. We are fortunate that you have made time in your busy careers to help us through some of these issues. Mr. Hamilton, please proceed.

Dwight Hamilton, Author, Terror Threat: International and Home-grown Terrorists and Their Threat to Canada, *as an individual:*

These remarks are intended to provide insight for the subcommittee into the evolving nature of terrorism in Canada, the activities of the security services managing this threat and suggestions on how various stakeholders might improve the effectiveness of a broad-based counterterrorism agenda in Canada.

Due to space and time considerations, I will not cover the activities of the Liberation Tigers of Tamil Eelam, the Babbar Khalsa International, or Canada's involvement in the Afghanistan theatre of military operations.

The primary security threat facing Canada in 2010 is the continuing dilemma of Islamic jihadist homegrown terrorists. The chance of physical harm to Canadian citizens and property is highest from this group. With respect to the organization of individuals who are drawn to this activity, the basic concept of cell structures, support networks and affinity groups, as discussed in detail in chapter 10 of my book written with Kostas Rimsa, still holds. Despite their name, homegrown cells nearly always have links that cross international borders. With Islamic jihaddism possessing a transglobal appeal unlike anything seen since the days of the Comintern, this is a key issue as seen by the case of the Toronto 18. Not only can senior operational advice and leadership come from abroad, but also we see young Canadians from even moderate families venture to overseas conflict zones for a primer in jihad. Upon their return, they could bring invaluable experience to any homegrown operation.

Homegrown cells have become increasingly important to the al Qaeda leadership due to the changing circumstances of the post-9/11 environment. On the international stage, many senior and middle level al Qaeda commanders have been and are being killed and captured by security forces. Most recently, there were the internal and external operations chiefs in December 2009 and the group's number three man Mustfa al-Yazid earlier this month. This has created pressure to gain success via methods that do not necessarily trump the kill count of the 9/11 operation and that do not have the risk associated with their highly trained operatives crossing borders. One leader has stated that many small strikes, including failures, may have the same desired result in keeping up the momentum of the message. Keep in mind that while only three homegrown terrorist attacks have caused mass casualties — Madrid, London and Fort Hood — there have been over two hundred foiled plots around the world since 2001.

Much time has been spent by opinion leaders attempting to ascertain a single root cause that is evident from al Qaeda belief systems that would explain the motivation for jihadist actions. Such simplicity is a fallacy. In chapter 6 of the book, there is a sliding scale of beliefs from conservative to extreme and an overview of broad jihadist motivations can be found in the section entitled "Basic Facilitators." The evolving global situation virtually guarantees jihadists no shortage of ammunition to support their world view. There seems to be nothing on the immediate horizon that would cause them to turn their swords into ploughshares.

With the firebombing this May of an Ottawa bank and the vandalism of Toronto-area banking machines as a result of the upcoming G8 and G20 summits, the question arises whether these acts might be the precursor of something more serious than the socio-political activism and property damage. A group referring to itself as the FFFC claims responsibility for the Ottawa attack.

This event sequence reflects the example of the early days of Direct Action, which was a leftist anarchist group of terrorists active in Canada during the 1980s. Two points are relevant to today's situation. First, Direct Action's attacks became larger and more sophisticated with time. Second, not one person from the direct support arm of about 40 operatives from cells in Vancouver, Winnipeg, Toronto and Montreal was ever charged.

Over two decades have passed since then, but the appeal of multi-cause and anti-establishment adventure has not vanished. It can only be predicted to increase, given the uncertain economic position the Western world now finds itself in. Today, in a society that many of various political stripes feel has lost its vision, we see increasing numbers of technically sophisticated, underemployed youth looking for someone to set an example. Jihadists are not the only ones looking for a mission. There are many to choose from. As recently as two weeks ago, a veteran activist from Victoria, who had been trained as a "human shield" and who had previously undertaken similar missions in hostile environments, was reported missing from the Gaza-bound ship *Challenger II* after it was stormed by Israeli commandos. The press report included a quote from the friend of the human shield: "It is what he does; it is what he believes in." This source was a former convicted Direct Action cell leader who had served seven years in a Canadian prison for the group's activities.

Regarding the readiness and capabilities of security forces to deal with the current emerging threats due to the situation described above, it is my assessment that the Kenny reports coupled with ongoing monitoring by the Auditor General have been excellent in pointing out the shortcomings in the nation's defences. However, if these recommendations are not followed through by government and simply gather dust on the shelf, Canada could be in for an unpleasant surprise someday soon, given the likelihood that groups will employ complex terrorism tactics aided by increasingly sophisticated weapons technology. It is certain that homegrown groups will improve their effectiveness with time. Numerous small strikes can add up to something significant if conducted simultaneously. Remember what 15 mailbox bombs planted around Westmount in 1963 led to.

In my opinion, the most important positive change in the national security landscape since 9/11 has been the development of a task force approach to intelligence and law enforcement by our various agencies.

Institutional siloing has always been the Achilles heel of Western security services, and the Americans are still dealing with their classic divisions in the uproar over the Detroit bomber earlier this year. We should strengthen inter-agency bonds and ideally strive for a seamless approach.

Further strengths include attempting to forge a community-based policing approach at the ground level in response to Islamic jihadism. Security forces must continue to increase recruitment from the Muslim Canadian population yet be especially careful with infiltration in their ranks, since that is a tried and true terrorist tactic. Keep in mind that a member of the Toronto 18 trained in our military.

Immigration levels in Canada will continue to increase in the near and medium terms due to the fact that we do not have enough workers to drive the complex economy Canada has put into place over the last half century. The effect of this demographic trend will include increasing screening duties for CSIS, amongst other things.

I believe it is a platitude among those of us who follow this issue that the security certificate regime must be replaced with a procedure to deport undesirables. Perhaps a third party diplomatic arrangement would work, whereby a host country would accept these people in return for something Canada can offer of equal value. There has been a tremendous waste of taxpayers' money so far in this battle. Government lawyers have had years to come up with a solution, yet we are no further ahead than when the procedure was introduced.

Further trouble is evident in a continuing court drama with persons launching litigation against the government regarding their treatment in international affairs. Already a growth industry, suing the government for its perceived sins within the murky world of international terrorism will soon be an established part of Canadiana. In order to prevent judges from bankrupting the federal treasury with escalating damage awards, perhaps a formal compensation for grievances regime, similar to what was established in the wake of the October crisis, would be pragmatic.

As for our courts prescribing anger management courses for convicted terrorists, with all due respect, not only does this send the worst kind of message to the public, it is wrong. Terrorists are not angry. This is no street fight. Terrorism is a tactic of unconventional war and terrorists and their sympathizers are highly motivated individuals, some of whom would calmly kill us with pleasure, not anger. So the Toronto 18 convict who completed such a course, rather than spending a decade behind bars, which sentencing permits, is now free as a bird; but at least he is not angry. Indeed, his lawyer has said that he is "very happy," and wants to study engineering.

Many experts believe that terrorists cannot be rehabilitated, so if what I have stressed in my earlier writings that an ideas war needs to be won, it is imperative to concentrate on reaching the young before the seed has been planted.

Therefore, it would be wise to develop an anti-terrorism community outreach and public relations infrastructure of some sort. This would not only attempt to destroy the romance of extremism via communication initiatives and dedicated activities but would also include an innovative route that gives conscientious parents the opportunity to receive help if they find their young turning to jihad. It is imperative that this be tied in to the school system.

Very strong leadership in this area is required. Explore ideas like public-private partnerships or tax breaks for corporations that show badly needed vision and throw some serious money at this problem. Turn prominent moderate Muslim Canadian business leaders into anti-jihadist ambassadors. So far, Canada has been lucky to have had less civil strife from jihadist sympathizers than nations such as Great Britain, France and others in Europe, so this is a window of opportunity to keep it that way.

Finally, it could well be argued that the greatest strategic problem Canada faces with terrorism lies in the court of public opinion. It is here that we must look to the media to set an example. Unfortunately, some of its members have been setting a terrible one. In October 2009, CSIS director Richard Fadden spoke publicly of a loose partnership of non-governmental organizations, lawyers and advocacy journalists creating a new hero for our age, a sort of freedom fighting jihadist akin to left-wing undergraduate icon Che Guevara. Here are the director's words:

"It sometimes seems that to be accused of having terrorist connections in Canada has become a status symbol, a badge of courage…. To some members of civil society, there is a certain romance to this."

Nothing would enhance anti-terrorist effectiveness more in our lawful society than the discrediting of this misguided mindset. The Toronto 18 were not a bunch of kids, as a senior television news producer once opined to me. They were wannabe mass murderers. It was not a "hapless winter camping adventure" that took place in Ontario cottage country in 2005, as a columnist for the country's largest newspaper seems to want the Canadian public to believe. It was practice.

Look at it this way. If the "Battle of Toronto" had succeeded, the loss of life on our soil would have exceeded anything in the country's history. It would have made the Dieppe raid seem like a strawberry social. Perhaps today those Canadians who lie beneath that bloody beach in France should be angry.

APPENDIX 11

SECURITY OF INFORMATION ACT

CHAPTER O-5

An Act respecting the security of information

SHORT TITLE

Short title
1. This Act may be cited as the *Security of Information Act.*

R.S., 1985, c. O-5, s. 1; 2001, c. 41, s. 25.

INTERPRETATION

Definitions
2. (1) In this Act,

"Attorney General" means the Attorney General of Canada and includes his or her lawful deputy;

"communicate" includes to make available;

"document" includes part of a document;

"foreign economic entity" means

(a) a foreign state or a group of foreign states, or

(b) an entity that is controlled, in law or in fact, or is substantially owned, by a foreign state or a group of foreign states;

"foreign entity" means

(a) a foreign power,

(b) a group or association of foreign powers, or of one or more foreign powers and one or more terrorist groups, or

(c) a person acting at the direction of, for the benefit of or in association with a foreign power or a group or association referred to in paragraph (b);

"foreign power" means

(a) the government of a foreign state,

(b) an entity exercising or purporting to exercise the functions of a government in relation to a territory outside Canada regardless of whether Canada recognizes the territory as a state or the authority of that entity over the territory, or

(c) a political faction or party operating within a foreign state whose stated purpose is to assume the role of government of a foreign state;

"foreign state" means

(a) a state other than Canada,

(b) a province, state or other political subdivision of a state other than Canada, or

(c) a colony, dependency, possession, protectorate, condominium, trust territory or any territory falling under the jurisdiction of a state other than Canada;

"model" includes design, pattern and specimen;

"munitions of war" means arms, ammunition, implements or munitions of war, military stores or any articles deemed capable of being converted thereinto or made useful in the production thereof;

"offence under this Act" includes any act, omission or other thing that is punishable under this Act;

"office under Her Majesty" includes any office or employment in or under any department or branch of the government of Canada or of any province, and any office or employment in, on or under any board, commission, corporation or other body that is an agent of Her Majesty in right of Canada or any province;

"prohibited place" means

(a) any work of defence belonging to or occupied or used by or on behalf of Her Majesty, including arsenals, armed forces establishments or stations, factories, dockyards, mines, minefields, camps, ships, aircraft, telegraph, telephone, wireless or signal stations or offices, and places used for the purpose of building, repairing, making or storing any munitions of war or any sketches, plans, models or documents relating thereto, or for the purpose of getting any metals, oil or minerals of use in time of war,

(b) any place not belonging to Her Majesty where any munitions of war or any sketches, plans, models or documents relating thereto are being made, repaired, obtained or stored under contract with, or with any person on behalf of, Her Majesty or otherwise on behalf of Her Majesty, and

(c) any place that is for the time being declared by order of the Governor in Council to be a prohibited place on the ground that information with respect thereto or damage thereto would be useful to a foreign power;

"senior police officer" [Repealed, 2001, c. 41, s. 26]

"sketch" includes any mode of representing any place or thing;

"terrorist activity" has the same meaning as in subsection 83.01(1) of the Criminal Code;

"terrorist group" has the same meaning as in subsection 83.01(1) of the Criminal Code.

Her Majesty
(2) In this Act, any reference to Her Majesty means Her Majesty in right of Canada or any province.

Communicating or receiving
(3) In this Act,

(a) expressions referring to communicating or receiving include any communicating or receiving, whether in whole or in part, and whether the sketch, plan, model, article, note, document or information itself or the substance, effect or description thereof only is communicated or received;

(b) expressions referring to obtaining or retaining any sketch, plan, model, article, note or document include the copying of, or causing to be copied, the whole or any part of any sketch, plan, model, article, note or document; and

(c) expressions referring to the communication of any sketch, plan, model, article, note or document include the transfer or transmission of the sketch, plan, model, article, note or document.

Facilitation
(4) For greater certainty, subsection 83.01(2) of the Criminal Code applies for the purposes of the definitions "terrorist activity" and "terrorist group" in subsection (1).

R.S., 1985, c. O-5, s. 2; 2001, c. 41, s. 26.

OFFENCES

Prejudice to the safety or interest of the State

3. (1) For the purposes of this Act, a purpose is prejudicial to the safety or interests of the State if a person

(a) commits, in Canada, an offence against the laws of Canada or a province that is punishable by a maximum term of imprisonment of two years or more in order to advance a political, religious or ideological purpose, objective or cause or to benefit a foreign entity or terrorist group;

(b) commits, inside or outside Canada, a terrorist activity;

(c) causes or aggravates an urgent and critical situation in Canada that

(i) endangers the lives, health or safety of Canadians, or

(ii) threatens the ability of the Government of Canada to preserve the sovereignty, security or territorial integrity of Canada;

(d) interferes with a service, facility, system or computer program, whether public or private, or its operation, in a manner that has significant adverse impact on the health, safety, security or economic or financial well-being of the people of Canada or the functioning of any government in Canada;

(e) endangers, outside Canada, any person by reason of that person's relationship with Canada or a province or the fact that the person is doing business with or on behalf of the Government of Canada or of a province;

(f) damages property outside Canada because a person or entity with an interest in the property or occupying the property has a relationship with Canada or a province or is doing business with or on behalf of the Government of Canada or of a province;

(g) impairs or threatens the military capability of the Canadian Forces, or any part of the Canadian Forces;

(h) interferes with the design, development or production of any weapon or defence equipment of, or intended for, the Canadian Forces, including any hardware, software or system that is part of or associated with any such weapon or defence equipment;

(i) impairs or threatens the capabilities of the Government of Canada in relation to security and intelligence;

(j) adversely affects the stability of the Canadian economy, the financial system or any financial market in Canada without reasonable economic or financial justification;

(k) impairs or threatens the capability of a government in Canada, or of the Bank of Canada, to protect against, or respond to, economic or financial threats or instability;

(l) impairs or threatens the capability of the Government of Canada to conduct diplomatic or consular relations, or conduct and manage international negotiations;

(m) contrary to a treaty to which Canada is a party, develops or uses anything that is intended or has the capability to cause death or serious bodily injury to a significant number of people by means of

(i) toxic or poisonous chemicals or their precursors,

(ii) a microbial or other biological agent, or a toxin, including a disease organism,

(iii) radiation or radioactivity, or

(iv) an explosion; or

(n) does or omits to do anything that is directed towards or in preparation of the undertaking of an activity mentioned in any of paragraphs (a) to (m).

Harm to Canadian interests

(2) For the purposes of this Act, harm is caused to Canadian interests if a foreign entity or terrorist group does anything referred to in any of paragraphs (1)(a) to (n).

R.S., 1985, c. O-5, s. 3; 2001, c. 41, s. 27.

Miscellaneous Offences

Wrongful communication, etc., of information

4. (1) Every person is guilty of an offence under this Act who, having in his possession or control any secret official code word, password, sketch, plan, model, article, note, document or information that relates to or is used in a prohibited place or anything in a prohibited place, or that has been made or obtained in contravention of this Act, or that has been entrusted in confidence to him by any person holding office under Her Majesty, or that he has obtained or to which he has had access while subject to the Code of Service Discipline within the meaning of the National Defence Act or owing to his position as a person who holds or has held office under Her Majesty, or as a person who holds or has held a contract made on behalf of Her Majesty, or a contract the performance of which in whole or in part is carried out in a prohibited place, or as a person who is or has been employed under a person who holds or has held such an office or contract,

(a) communicates the code word, password, sketch, plan, model, article, note, document or information to any person, other than a person to whom he is authorized to communicate with, or a person to whom it is in the interest of the State his duty to communicate it;

(b) uses the information in his possession for the benefit of any foreign power or in any other manner prejudicial to the safety or interests of the State;

(c) retains the sketch, plan, model, article, note, or document in his possession or control when he has no right to retain it or when it is contrary to his duty to retain it or fails to comply with all directions issued by lawful authority with regard to the return or disposal thereof; or

(d) fails to take reasonable care of, or so conducts himself as to endanger the safety of, the secret official code word, password, sketch, plan, model, article, note, document or information.

Communication of sketch, plan, model, etc.
(2) Every person is guilty of an offence under this Act who, having in his possession or control any sketch, plan, model, article, note, document or information that relates to munitions of war, communicates it, directly or indirectly, to any foreign power, or in any other manner prejudicial to the safety or interests of the State.

Receiving code word, sketch, etc.
(3) Every person who receives any secret official code word, password, sketch, plan, model, article, note, document or information, knowing, or having reasonable ground to believe, at the time he receives it, that the code word, password, sketch, plan, model, article, note, document or information is communicated to him in contravention of this Act, is guilty of an offence under this Act, unless he proves that the communication to him of the code word, password, sketch, plan, model, article, note, document or information was contrary to his desire.

Retaining or allowing possession of document, etc.
(4) Every person is guilty of an offence under this Act who

(a) retains for any purpose prejudicial to the safety or interests of the State any official document, whether or not completed or issued for use, when he has no right to retain it, or when it is contrary to his duty to retain it, or fails to comply with any directions issued by any Government department or any person authorized by any Government department with regard to the return or disposal thereof; or

(b) allows any other person to have possession of any official document issued for his use alone, or communicates any secret official code word or password so issued, or, without lawful authority or excuse, has in his possession any official document or secret official code word or password issued for the use of a person other than himself, or on obtaining possession of any official document by finding or otherwise, neglects or fails to restore it to the person or authority by whom or for whose use it was issued, or to a police constable.

R.S., c. O-3, s. 4.

Unauthorized use of uniforms, falsification of reports, forgery, personation and false documents
5. (1) Every person is guilty of an offence under this Act who, for the purpose of gaining admission, or of assisting any other person to gain admission, to a prohibited place, or for any other purpose prejudicial to the safety or interests of the State,

(a) uses or wears, without lawful authority, any military, police or other official uniform or any uniform so nearly resembling such a uniform as to be calculated to deceive, or falsely represents himself to be a person who is or has been entitled to use or wear any such uniform;

(b) orally or in writing in any declaration or application, or in any document signed by him or on his behalf, knowingly makes or connives at the making of any false statement or omission;

(c) forges, alters or tampers with any passport or any military, police or official pass, permit, certificate, licence or other document of a similar character, in this section referred to as an official document, or uses or has in his possession any such forged, altered or irregular official document;

(d) personates or falsely represents himself to be a person holding, or to be in the employment of a person holding, office under Her Majesty, or to be or not to be a person to whom an official document or secret official code word or password has been duly issued or communicated, or with intent to obtain an official document, secret official code word or password, whether for himself or any other person, knowingly makes any false statement; or

(e) uses, or has in his possession or under his control, without the authority of the Government department or the authority concerned, any die, seal or stamp of or belonging to, or used, made or provided by, any Government department, or by any diplomatic or military authority appointed by or acting under the authority of Her Majesty, or any die, seal or stamp so nearly resembling any such die, seal or stamp as to be calculated to deceive, or counterfeits any such die, seal or stamp, or uses, or has in his possession or under his control, any such counterfeited die, seal or stamp.

Unlawful dealing with dies, seals, etc.
(2) Every person who, without lawful authority or excuse, manufactures or sells, or has in his possession for sale, any die, seal or stamp referred to in subsection (1) is guilty of an offence under this Act.

R.S., c. O-3, s. 5.

Approaching, entering, etc., a prohibited place
6. Every person commits an offence who, for any purpose prejudicial to the safety or interests of the State, approaches, inspects, passes over, is in the neighbourhood of or enters a prohibited place at the direction of, for the benefit of or in association with a foreign entity or a terrorist group.

R.S., 1985, c. O-5, s. 6; 2001, c. 41, s. 29.

Interference
7. Every person commits an offence who, in the vicinity of a prohibited place, obstructs, knowingly misleads or otherwise interferes with or impedes a peace officer or a member of Her Majesty's forces engaged on guard, sentry, patrol or other similar duty in relation to the prohibited place.

R.S., 1985, c. O-5, s. 7; 2001, c. 41, s. 29.

Special Operational Information and Persons Permanently Bound to Secrecy

Definitions

8. (1) The following definitions apply in this section and sections 9 to 15.

"department" means a department named in Schedule I to the Financial Administration Act, a division or branch of the public service of Canada set out in column I of Schedule I.1 to that Act and a corporation named in Schedule II to that Act.

"government contractor" means a person who has entered into a contract or arrangement with Her Majesty in right of Canada, a department, board or agency of the Government of Canada or a Crown corporation as defined in subsection 83(1) of the Financial Administration Act, and includes an employee of the person, a subcontractor of the person and an employee of the subcontractor.

"person permanently bound to secrecy" means

(a) a current or former member or employee of a department, division, branch or office of the public service of Canada, or any of its parts, set out in the schedule; or

(b) a person who has been personally served with a notice issued under subsection 10(1) in respect of the person or who has been informed, in accordance with regulations made under subsection 11(2), of the issuance of such a notice in respect of the person.

"special operational information" means information that the Government of Canada is taking measures to safeguard that reveals, or from which may be inferred,

(a) the identity of a person, agency, group, body or entity that was or is intended to be, has been approached to be, or has offered or agreed to be, a confidential source of information, intelligence or assistance to the

Government of Canada;

(b) the nature or content of plans of the Government of Canada for military operations in respect of a potential, imminent or present armed conflict;

(c) the means that the Government of Canada used, uses or intends to use, or is capable of using, to covertly collect or obtain, or to decipher, assess, analyse, process, handle, report, communicate or otherwise deal with information or intelligence, including any vulnerabilities or limitations of those means;

(d) whether a place, person, agency, group, body or entity was, is or is intended to be the object of a covert investigation, or a covert collection of information or intelligence, by the Government of Canada;

(e) the identity of any person who is, has been or is intended to be covertly engaged in an information- or intelligence-collection activity or program of the Government of Canada that is covert in nature;

(f) the means that the Government of Canada used, uses or intends to use, or is capable of using, to protect or exploit any information or intelligence referred to in any of paragraphs (a) to (e), including, but not limited to, encryption and cryptographic systems, and any vulnerabilities or limitations of those means; or

(g) information or intelligence similar in nature to information or intelligence referred to in any of paragraphs (a) to (f) that is in relation to, or received from, a foreign entity or terrorist group.

Deputy head
(2) For the purposes of subsections 10(1) and 15(5), the deputy head is

(a) for an individual employed in or attached or seconded to a department, the deputy head of the department;

(b) for an officer or a non-commissioned member of the Canadian Forces, the Chief of the Defence Staff;

(c) for a person who is a member of the exempt staff of a Minister responsible for a department, the deputy head of the department;

(d) for a government contractor in relation to a contract with

(i) the Department of Public Works and Government Services, the deputy head of that department or any other deputy head authorized for the purpose by the Minister of Public Works and Government Services,

(ii) any other department, the deputy head of that department, and

(iii) a Crown Corporation within the meaning of subsection 83(1) of the Financial Administration Act, the deputy head of the department of the minister responsible for the Crown Corporation; and

(e) for any other person, the Clerk of the Privy Council or a person authorized for the purpose by the Clerk of the Privy Council.

R.S., 1985, c. O-5, s. 8; 2001, c. 41, s. 29; 2004, c. 12, s. 21(E).

Amending schedule
9. The Governor in Council may, by order, amend the schedule by adding or deleting the name of any current or former department, division, branch or office of the public service of Canada, or any of its parts, that, in the opinion of the Governor in Council, has or had a mandate that is primarily related to security and intelligence matters, or by modifying any name set out in the schedule.

R.S., 1985, c. O-5, s. 9; 2001, c. 41, s. 29.

Designation — persons permanently bound to secrecy
10. (1) The deputy head in respect of a person may, by notice in writing, designate the person to be a person permanently bound to secrecy if

the deputy head is of the opinion that, by reason of the person's office, position, duties, contract or arrangement,

(a) the person had, has or will have authorized access to special operational information; and

(b) it is in the interest of national security to designate the person.

Contents
(2) The notice must

(a) specify the name of the person in respect of whom it is issued;

(b) specify the office held, position occupied or duties performed by the person or the contract or arrangement in respect of which the person is a government contractor, as the case may be, that led to the designation; and

(c) state that the person named in the notice is a person permanently bound to secrecy for the purposes of sections 13 and 14.

Exceptions
(3) The following persons may not be designated as persons permanently bound to secrecy, but they continue as such if they were persons permanently bound to secrecy before becoming persons referred to in this subsection:

(a) the Governor General;

(b) the lieutenant governor of a province;

(c) a judge receiving a salary under the Judges Act; and

(d) a military judge within the meaning of subsection 2(1) of the National Defence Act.

R.S., 1985, c. O-5, s. 10; 2001, c. 41, s. 29.

Service

11. (1) Subject to subsection (2), a person in respect of whom a notice is issued under subsection 10(1) is a person permanently bound to secrecy as of the moment the person is personally served with the notice or informed of the notice in accordance with the regulations.

Regulations

(2) The Governor in Council may make regulations respecting the personal service of notices issued under subsection 10(1) and regulations respecting personal notification of the issuance of a notice under that subsection when personal service is not practical.

R.S., 1985, c. O-5, s. 11; 2001, c. 41, s. 29.

Certificate

12. (1) Subject to subsection (2), a certificate purporting to have been issued by or under the authority of a Minister of the Crown in right of Canada stating that a person is a person permanently bound to secrecy shall be received and is admissible in evidence in any proceedings for an offence under section 13 or 14, without proof of the signature or authority of the Minister appearing to have signed it, and, in the absence of evidence to the contrary, is proof of the fact so stated.

Disclosure of certificate

(2) The certificate may be received in evidence only if the party intending to produce it has, before the trial, served on the party against whom it is intended to be produced reasonable notice of that intention, together with a duplicate of the certificate.

R.S., 1985, c. O-5, s. 12; 2001, c. 41, s. 29.

Purported communication

13. (1) Every person permanently bound to secrecy commits an offence who, intentionally and without authority, communicates or confirms information that, if it were true, would be special operational information.

Truthfulness of information

(2) For the purpose of subsection (1), it is not relevant whether the information to which the offence relates is true.

Punishment

(3) Every person who commits an offence under subsection (1) is guilty of an indictable offence and is liable to imprisonment for a term of not more than five years less a day.

R.S., 1985, c. O-5, s. 13; 2001, c. 41, s. 29.

Unauthorized communication of special operational information 14. (1) Every person permanently bound to secrecy commits an offence who, intentionally and without authority, communicates or confirms special operational information.

Punishment

(2) Every person who commits an offence under subsection (1) is guilty of an indictable offence and is liable to imprisonment for a term of not more than 14 years.

R.S., 1985, c. O-5, s. 14; 2001, c. 41, s. 29.

Public interest defence

15. (1) No person is guilty of an offence under section 13 or 14 if the person establishes that he or she acted in the public interest.

Acting in the public interest

(2) Subject to subsection (4), a person acts in the public interest if

(a) the person acts for the purpose of disclosing an offence under an Act of Parliament that he or she reasonably believes has been, is being or is about to be committed by another person in the purported performance of that person's duties and functions for, or on behalf of, the Government of Canada; and

(b) the public interest in the disclosure outweighs the public interest in non-disclosure.

Paragraph (2)(a) to be considered first
(3) In determining whether a person acts in the public interest, a judge or court shall determine whether the condition in paragraph (2)(a) is satisfied before considering paragraph (2)(b).

Factors to be considered
(4) In deciding whether the public interest in the disclosure outweighs the public interest in non-disclosure, a judge or court must consider

(a) whether the extent of the disclosure is no more than is reasonably necessary to disclose the alleged offence or prevent the commission or continuation of the alleged offence, as the case may be;

(b) the seriousness of the alleged offence;

(c) whether the person resorted to other reasonably accessible alternatives before making the disclosure and, in doing so, whether the person complied with any relevant guidelines, policies or laws that applied to the person;

(d) whether the person had reasonable grounds to believe that the disclosure would be in the public interest;

(e) the public interest intended to be served by the disclosure;

(f) the extent of the harm or risk of harm created by the disclosure; and

(g) the existence of exigent circumstances justifying the disclosure.

Prior disclosure to authorities necessary
(5) A judge or court may decide whether the public interest in the disclosure outweighs the public interest in non-disclosure only if the person has complied with the following:

(a) the person has, before communicating or confirming the information, brought his or her concern to, and provided all relevant information in his or her possession to, his or her deputy head or, if not reasonably practical in the circumstances, the Deputy Attorney General of Canada; and

(b) the person has, if he or she has not received a response from the deputy head or the Deputy Attorney General of Canada, as the case may be, within a reasonable time, brought his or her concern to, and provided all relevant information in the person's possession to,

(i) the Security Intelligence Review Committee, if the person's concern relates to an alleged offence that has been, is being or is about to be committed by another person in the purported performance of that person's duties and functions of service for, or on behalf of, the Government of Canada, other than a person who is a member of the Communications Security Establishment, and he or she has not received a response from the Security Intelligence Review Committee within a reasonable time, or

(ii) the Communications Security Establishment Commissioner, if the person's concern relates to an alleged offence that has been, is being or is about to be committed by a member of the Communications Security Establishment, in the purported performance of that person's duties and functions of service for, or on behalf of, the Communications Security Establishment, and he or she has not received a response from the Communications Security Establishment Commissioner within a reasonable time.

Exigent circumstances
(6) Subsection (5) does not apply if the communication or confirmation of the information was necessary to avoid grievous bodily harm or death.

R.S., 1985, c. O-5, s. 15; 1992, c. 47, s. 80; 2001, c. 41, s. 29.

Communications with Foreign Entities or Terrorist Groups

Communicating safeguarded information

16. (1) Every person commits an offence who, without lawful authority, communicates to a foreign entity or to a terrorist group information that the Government of Canada or of a province is taking measures to safeguard if

(a) the person believes, or is reckless as to whether, the information is information that the Government of Canada or of a province is taking measures to safeguard; and

(b) the person intends, by communicating the information, to increase the capacity of a foreign entity or a terrorist group to harm Canadian interests or is reckless as to whether the communication of the information is likely to increase the capacity of a foreign entity or a terrorist group to harm Canadian interests.

Communicating safeguarded information

(2) Every person commits an offence who, intentionally and without lawful authority, communicates to a foreign entity or to a terrorist group information that the Government of Canada or of a province is taking measures to safeguard if

(a) the person believes, or is reckless as to whether, the information is information that the Government of Canada or of a province is taking measures to safeguard; and

(b) harm to Canadian interests results.

Punishment

(3) Every person who commits an offence under subsection (1) or (2) is guilty of an indictable offence and is liable to imprisonment for life.

2001, c. 41, s. 29.

Communicating special operational information

17. (1) Every person commits an offence who, intentionally and without

lawful authority, communicates special operational information to a foreign entity or to a terrorist group if the person believes, or is reckless as to whether, the information is special operational information.

Punishment

(2) Every person who commits an offence under subsection (1) is guilty of an indictable offence and is liable to imprisonment for life.

2001, c. 41, s. 29.

Breach of trust in respect of safeguarded information

18. (1) Every person with a security clearance given by the Government of Canada commits an offence who, intentionally and without lawful authority, communicates, or agrees to communicate, to a foreign entity or to a terrorist group any information that is of a type that the Government of Canada is taking measures to safeguard.

Punishment

(2) Every person who commits an offence under subsection (1) is guilty of an indictable offence and is liable to imprisonment for a term of not more than two years.

2001, c. 41, s. 29.

Economic Espionage

Use of trade secret for the benefit of foreign economic entity

19. (1) Every person commits an offence who, at the direction of, for the benefit of or in association with a foreign economic entity, fraudulently and without colour of right and to the detriment of Canada's economic interests, international relations or national defence or national security

(a) communicates a trade secret to another person, group or organization; or

(b) obtains, retains, alters or destroys a trade secret.

Punishment

(2) Every person who commits an offence under subsection (1) is guilty of an indictable offence and is liable to imprisonment for a term of not more than 10 years.

Defence

(3) A person is not guilty of an offence under subsection (1) if the trade secret was

(a) obtained by independent development or by reason only of reverse engineering; or

(b) acquired in the course of the person's work and is of such a character that its acquisition amounts to no more than an enhancement of that person's personal knowledge, skill or expertise.

Meaning of "trade secret"

(4) For the purpose of this section, "trade secret" means any information, including a formula, pattern, compilation, program, method, technique, process, negotiation position or strategy or any information contained or embodied in a product, device or mechanism that

(a) is or may be used in a trade or business;

(b) is not generally known in that trade or business;

(c) has economic value from not being generally known; and

(d) is the subject of efforts that are reasonable under the circumstances to maintain its secrecy.

2001, c. 41, s. 29.

Foreign-influenced or Terrorist-influenced Threats or Violence

Threats or violence

20. (1) Every person commits an offence who, at the direction of, for the benefit of or in association with a foreign entity or a terrorist group, induces or attempts to induce, by threat, accusation, menace or violence, any person to do anything or to cause anything to be done

(a) that is for the purpose of increasing the capacity of a foreign entity or a terrorist group to harm Canadian interests; or

(b) that is reasonably likely to harm Canadian interests.

Application
(2) A person commits an offence under subsection (1) whether or not the threat, accusation, menace or violence occurred in Canada.

Punishment
(3) Every person who commits an offence under subsection (1) is guilty of an indictable offence and is liable to imprisonment for life.

2001, c. 41, s. 29.

Harbouring or concealing
21. (1) Every person commits an offence who, for the purpose of enabling or facilitating an offence under this Act, knowingly harbours or conceals a person whom he or she knows to be a person who has committed or is likely to commit an offence under this Act.

Punishment
(2) Every person who commits an offence under subsection (1) is guilty of an indictable offence and is liable to imprisonment for a term of not more than 10 years.

2001, c. 41, s. 29.

Preparatory acts
22. (1) Every person commits an offence who, for the purpose of committing an offence under subsection 16(1) or (2), 17(1), 19(1) or

20(1), does anything that is specifically directed towards or specifically done in preparation of the commission of the offence, including

(a) entering Canada at the direction of or for the benefit of a foreign entity, a terrorist group or a foreign economic entity;

(b) obtaining, retaining or gaining access to any information;

(c) knowingly communicating to a foreign entity, a terrorist group or a foreign economic entity the person's willingness to commit the offence;

(d) at the direction of, for the benefit of or in association with a foreign entity, a terrorist group or a foreign economic entity, asking a person to commit the offence; and

(e) possessing any device, apparatus or software useful for concealing the content of information or for surreptitiously communicating, obtaining or retaining information.

Punishment
(2) Every person who commits an offence under subsection (1) is guilty of an indictable offence and is liable to imprisonment for a term of not more than two years.

2001, c. 41, s. 29.

Conspiracy, attempts, etc.
23. Every person commits an offence who conspires or attempts to commit, is an accessory after the fact in relation to or counsels in relation to an offence under this Act and is liable to the same punishment and to be proceeded against in the same manner as if he or she had committed the offence.

2001, c. 41, s. 29.

GENERAL

Attorney General's consent
24. No prosecution shall be commenced for an offence against this Act without the consent of the Attorney General.

2001, c. 41, s. 29.

Jurisdiction
25. An offence against this Act may be tried, in any place in Canada, regardless of where in Canada the offence was committed.

2001, c. 41, s. 29.

Extraterritorial application
26. (1) A person who commits an act or omission outside Canada that would be an offence against this Act if it were committed in Canada is deemed to have committed it in Canada if the person is

(a) a Canadian citizen;

(b) a person who owes allegiance to Her Majesty in right of Canada;

(c) a person who is locally engaged and who performs his or her functions in a Canadian mission outside Canada; or

(d) a person who, after the time the offence is alleged to have been committed, is present in Canada.

Jurisdiction
(2) If a person is deemed to have committed an act or omission in Canada, proceedings in respect of the offence may, whether or not the person is in Canada, be commenced in any territorial division in Canada, and the person may be tried and punished in respect of the offence in the same manner as if the offence had been committed in that territorial division.

Appearance of accused at trial
(3) For greater certainty, the provisions of the Criminal Code relating to

requirements that a person appear at and be present during proceedings and the exceptions to those requirements apply in respect of proceedings commenced in a territorial division under subsection (2).

Person previously tried outside Canada

(4) If a person is alleged to have committed an act or omission that is an offence by virtue of this section and the person has been tried and dealt with outside Canada in respect of the offence in a manner such that, if the person had been tried and dealt with in Canada, the person would be able to plead autrefois acquit, autrefois convict or pardon, the person shall be deemed to have been so tried and dealt with in Canada.

2001, c. 41, s. 29.

Punishment

27. Unless this Act provides otherwise, a person who commits an offence under this Act is guilty of

(a) an indictable offence and liable to imprisonment for a term of not more than 14 years; or

(b) an offence punishable on summary conviction and liable to imprisonment for a term of not more than 12 months or to a fine of not more than $2,000, or to both.

2001, c. 41, s. 29.

28. [Repealed, 2001, c. 41, s. 130]

SCHEDULE

(Subsection 8(1) and section 9)

Canadian Security Intelligence Service
Commission of Inquiry into the Actions of Canadian Officials in Relation to Maher Arar

Communications Branch of the National Research Council
Communications Security Establishment
Criminal Intelligence Program of the R.C.M.P.
Office of the Communications Security Establishment Commissioner
Office of the Inspector General of the Canadian Security Intelligence Service
Protective Operations Program of the R.C.M.P.
R.C.M.P. Security Service
Security Intelligence Review Committee
Technical Operations Program of the R.C.M.P.

2001, c. 41, s. 30; SOR/2004-20.

AMENDMENT NOT IN FORCE

— 2003, c. 22, para. 224(z.76):

Replacement of "public service of Canada"
224. The expression "public service of Canada" is replaced by the expression "federal public administration" wherever it occurs in the English version of the following provisions:

(z.76) the definition "department" in subsection 8(1), paragraph (a) of the definition "person permanently bound to secrecy" in subsection 8(1) and section 9 of the *Security of Information Act*;

(Source: Department of Justice. This is not the official version.)

PART II.1 OF THE CANADIAN CRIMINAL CODE (TERRORISM)

PART II.1

TERRORISM

Interpretation

Definitions

83.01 (1) The following definitions apply in this Part.

"Canadian" means a Canadian citizen, a permanent resident within the meaning of subsection 2(1) of the Immigration and Refugee Protection Act or a body corporate incorporated and continued under the laws of Canada or a province.

"entity" means a person, group, trust, partnership or fund or an unincorporated association or organization.

"listed entity" means an entity on a list established by the Governor in Council under section 83.05.

"terrorist activity" means

(a) an act or omission that is committed in or outside Canada and that, if committed in Canada, is one of the following offences:

(i) the offences referred to in subsection 7(2) that implement the Convention for the Suppression of Unlawful Seizure of Aircraft, signed at The Hague on December 16, 1970,

(ii) the offences referred to in subsection 7(2) that implement the Convention for the Suppression of Unlawful Acts against the Safety of Civil Aviation, signed at Montreal on September 23, 1971,

(iii) the offences referred to in subsection 7(3) that implement the Convention on the Prevention and Punishment of Crimes against Internationally Protected Persons, including Diplomatic Agents, adopted by the General Assembly of the United Nations on December 14, 1973,

(iv) the offences referred to in subsection 7(3.1) that implement the International Convention against the Taking of Hostages, adopted by the General Assembly of the United Nations on December 17, 1979,

(v) the offences referred to in subsection 7(3.4) or (3.6) that implement the Convention on the Physical Protection of Nuclear Material, done at Vienna and New York on March 3, 1980,

(vi) the offences referred to in subsection 7(2) that implement the Protocol for the Suppression of Unlawful Acts of Violence at Airports Serving International Civil Aviation, supplementary to the Convention for the Suppression of Unlawful Acts against the Safety of Civil Aviation, signed at Montreal on February 24, 1988,

(vii) the offences referred to in subsection 7(2.1) that implement the Convention for the Suppression of Unlawful Acts against the Safety of Maritime Navigation, done at Rome on March 10, 1988,

(viii) the offences referred to in subsection 7(2.1) or (2.2) that implement the Protocol for the Suppression of Unlawful Acts against the Safety of Fixed Platforms Located on the Continental Shelf, done at Rome on March 10, 1988,

(ix) the offences referred to in subsection 7(3.72) that implement the International Convention for the Suppression of Terrorist Bombings, adopted by the General Assembly of the United Nations on December 15, 1997, and

(x) the offences referred to in subsection 7(3.73) that implement the International Convention for the Suppression of the Financing of Terrorism, adopted by the General Assembly of the United Nations on December 9, 1999, or

(b) an act or omission, in or outside Canada,

(i) that is committed

(A) in whole or in part for a political, religious or ideological purpose, objective or cause, and

(B) in whole or in part with the intention of intimidating the public, or a segment of the public, with regard to its security, including its economic security, or compelling a person, a government or a domestic or an international organization to do or to refrain from doing any act, whether the public or the person, government or organization is inside or outside Canada, and

(ii) that intentionally

(A) causes death or serious bodily harm to a person by the use of violence,

(B) endangers a person's life,

(C) causes a serious risk to the health or safety of the public or any segment of the public,

(D) causes substantial property damage, whether to public or private property, if causing such damage is likely to result in the conduct or harm referred to in any of clauses (A) to (C), or

(E) causes serious interference with or serious disruption of an essential service, facility or system, whether public or private, other than as a result of advocacy, protest, dissent or stoppage of work that is not intended to result in the conduct or harm referred to in any of clauses (A) to (C),

and includes a conspiracy, attempt or threat to commit any such act or omission, or being an accessory after the fact or counselling in relation to any such act or omission, but, for greater certainty, does not include an act or omission that is committed during an armed conflict and that, at the time and in the place of its commission, is in accordance with customary international law or conventional international law applicable to the conflict, or the activities undertaken by military forces of a state in the exercise of their official duties, to the extent that those activities are governed by other rules of international law.

"terrorist group" means

(a) an entity that has as one of its purposes or activities facilitating or carrying out any terrorist activity, or

(b) a listed entity,

and includes an association of such entities.

For greater certainty
(1.1) For greater certainty, the expression of a political, religious or ideological thought, belief or opinion does not come within paragraph (b) of the definition

"terrorist activity" in subsection (1) unless it constitutes an act or omission that satisfies the criteria of that paragraph.

Facilitation
(2) For the purposes of this Part, facilitation shall be construed in accordance with subsection 83.19(2).

2001, c. 41, ss. 4, 126.

Financing of Terrorism

Providing or collecting property for certain activities
83.02 Every one who, directly or indirectly, wilfully and without lawful justification or excuse, provides or collects property intending that it be used or knowing that it will be used, in whole or in part, in order to carry out

(a) an act or omission that constitutes an offence referred to in subparagraphs (a)(i) to (ix) of the definition of "terrorist activity" in subsection 83.01(1), or

(b) any other act or omission intended to cause death or serious bodily harm to a civilian or to any other person not taking an active part in the hostilities in a situation of armed conflict, if the purpose of that act or omission, by its nature or context, is to intimidate the public, or to compel a government or an international organization to do or refrain from doing any act,

is guilty of an indictable offence and is liable to imprisonment for a term of not more than 10 years.

2001, c. 41, s. 4.

Providing, making available, etc., property or services for terrorist purposes 83.03 Every one who, directly or indirectly, collects property, provides or invites a person to provide, or makes available property or financial or other related services

(a) intending that they be used, or knowing that they will be used, in whole or in part, for the purpose of facilitating or carrying out any terrorist activity, or for the purpose of benefiting any person who is facilitating or carrying out such an activity, or

(b) knowing that, in whole or part, they will be used by or will benefit a terrorist group,

is guilty of an indictable offence and is liable to imprisonment for a term of not more than 10 years.

2001, c. 41, s. 4.

Using or possessing property for terrorist purposes
83.04 Every one who

(a) uses property, directly or indirectly, in whole or in part, for the purpose of facilitating or carrying out a terrorist activity, or

(b) possesses property intending that it be used or knowing that it will be used, directly or indirectly, in whole or in part, for the purpose of facilitating or carrying out a terrorist activity,

is guilty of an indictable offence and is liable to imprisonment for a term of not more than 10 years.

2001, c. 41, s. 4.

List of Entities

Establishment of list
83.05 (1) The Governor in Council may, by regulation, establish a list on which the Governor in Council may place any entity if, on the recommendation of the Solicitor General of Canada, the Governor in Council is satisfied that there are reasonable grounds to believe that

(a) the entity has knowingly carried out, attempted to carry out, participated in or facilitated a terrorist activity; or

(b) the entity is knowingly acting on behalf of, at the direction of or in association with an entity referred to in paragraph (a).

Recommendation
(1.1) The Solicitor General may make a recommendation referred to in subsection (1) only if the Solicitor General has reasonable grounds to believe that the entity to which the recommendation relates is an entity referred to in paragraph (1)(a) or (b).

Application to Solicitor General
(2) On application in writing by a listed entity, the Solicitor General shall decide whether there are reasonable grounds to recommend to the Governor in Council that the applicant no longer be a listed entity.

Deeming
(3) If the Solicitor General does not make a decision on the application referred to in subsection (2) within 60 days after receipt of the application, the Solicitor General is deemed to have decided to recommend that the applicant remain a listed entity.

Notice of the decision to the applicant
(4) The Solicitor General must give notice without delay to the applicant of any decision taken or deemed to have been taken respecting the application referred to in subsection (2).

Judicial review
(5) Within 60 days after the receipt of the notice of the decision referred to in subsection (4), the applicant may apply to a judge for judicial review of the decision.

Reference
(6) When an application is made under subsection (5), the judge shall, without delay

(a) examine, in private, any security or criminal intelligence reports considered in listing the applicant and hear any other evidence or information that may be presented by or on behalf of the Solicitor General and may, at the request of the Solicitor General, hear all or part of that evidence or information in the absence of the applicant and any counsel representing the applicant, if the judge is of the opinion that the disclosure of the information would injure national security or endanger the safety of any person;

(b) provide the applicant with a statement summarizing the information available to the judge so as to enable the applicant to be reasonably informed of the reasons for the decision, without disclosing any information the disclosure of which would, in the judge's opinion, injure national security or endanger the safety of any person;

(c) provide the applicant with a reasonable opportunity to be heard; and

(d) determine whether the decision is reasonable on the basis of the information available to the judge and, if found not to be reasonable, order that the applicant no longer be a listed entity.

Evidence
(6.1) The judge may receive into evidence anything that, in the opinion of the judge, is reliable and appropriate, even if it would not otherwise be admissible under Canadian law, and may base his or her decision on that evidence.

Publication
(7) The Solicitor General shall cause to be published, without delay, in the Canada Gazette notice of a final order of a court that the applicant no longer be a listed entity.

New application
(8) A listed entity may not make another application under subsection (2), except if there has been a material change in its circumstances since the time when the entity made its last application or if the Solicitor General has completed the review under subsection (9).

Review of list
(9) Two years after the establishment of the list referred to in subsection (1), and every two years after that, the Solicitor General shall review

the list to determine whether there are still reasonable grounds, as set out in subsection (1), for an entity to be a listed entity and make a recommendation to the Governor in Council as to whether the entity should remain a listed entity. The review does not affect the validity of the list.

Completion of review

(10) The Solicitor General shall complete the review as soon as possible and in any event, no later than 120 days after its commencement. After completing the review, the Solicitor General shall cause to be published, without delay, in the Canada Gazette notice that the review has been completed.

Definition of "judge"

(11) In this section, "judge" means the Chief Justice of the Federal Court or a judge of that Court designated by the Chief Justice.

2001, c. 41, ss. 4, 143.

Admission of foreign information obtained in confidence

83.06 (1) For the purposes of subsection 83.05(6), in private and in the absence of the applicant or any counsel representing it,

(a) the Solicitor General of Canada may make an application to the judge for the admission of information obtained in confidence from a government, an institution or an agency of a foreign state, from an international organization of states or from an institution or an agency of an international organization of states; and

(b) the judge shall examine the information and provide counsel representing the Solicitor General with a reasonable opportunity to be heard as to whether the information is relevant but should not be disclosed to the applicant or any counsel representing it because the disclosure would injure national security or endanger the safety of any person.

Return of information

(2) The information shall be returned to counsel representing the Solicitor General and shall not be considered by the judge in making the determination under paragraph 83.05(6)(d), if

(a) the judge determines that the information is not relevant;

(b) the judge determines that the information is relevant but should be summarized
in the statement to be provided under paragraph 83.05(6)(b); or

(c) the Solicitor General withdraws the application.

Use of information

(3) If the judge decides that the information is relevant but that its disclosure would injure national security or endanger the safety of persons, the information shall not be disclosed in the statement mentioned in paragraph 83.05(6)(b), but the judge may base the determination under paragraph 83.05(6)(d) on it.

2001, c. 41, s. 4.

Mistaken identity

83.07 (1) An entity claiming not to be a listed entity may apply to the Solicitor General of Canada for a certificate stating that it is not a listed entity.

Issuance of certificate

(2) The Solicitor General shall, within 15 days after receiving the application, issue a certificate if satisfied that the applicant is not a listed entity.

2001, c. 41, s. 4.

Freezing of Property

83.08 (1) No person in Canada and no Canadian outside Canada shall knowingly

(a) deal directly or indirectly in any property that is owned or controlled by or on behalf of a terrorist group;

(b) enter into or facilitate, directly or indirectly, any transaction in respect of property referred to in paragraph (a); or

(c) provide any financial or other related services in respect of property referred to in paragraph (a) to, for the benefit of or at the direction of a terrorist group.

No civil liability
(2) A person who acts reasonably in taking, or omitting to take, measures to comply with subsection (1) shall not be liable in any civil action arising from having taken or omitted to take the measures, if the person took all reasonable steps to satisfy themself that the relevant property was owned or controlled by or on behalf of a terrorist group.

2001, c. 41, s. 4.

Exemptions
83.09 (1) The Solicitor General of Canada or a person designated by the Solicitor General may authorize any person in Canada or any Canadian outside Canada to carry out a specified activity or transaction that is prohibited by section 83.08, or a class of such activities or transactions.

Ministerial authorization
(2) The Solicitor General or a person designated by the Solicitor General may make the authorization subject to any terms and conditions that are required in their opinion, and may amend, suspend, revoke or reinstate it.

Existing equities maintained
(3) All secured and unsecured rights and interests in the frozen property that are held by persons, other than terrorist groups or their agents, are

entitled to the same ranking that they would have been entitled to had the property not been frozen.

Third party involvement

(4) If a person has obtained an authorization under subsection (1), any other person involved in carrying out the activity or transaction, or class of activities or transactions, to which the authorization relates is not subject to sections 83.08, 83.1 and 83.11 if the terms or conditions of the authorization that are imposed under subsection (2), if any, are met.

2001, c. 41, s. 4.

Disclosure

83.1 (1) Every person in Canada and every Canadian outside Canada shall disclose forthwith to the Commissioner of the Royal Canadian Mounted Police and to the Director of the Canadian Security Intelligence Service

(a) the existence of property in their possession or control that they know is owned or controlled by or on behalf of a terrorist group; and

(b) information about a transaction or proposed transaction in respect of property referred to in paragraph (a).

Immunity

(2) No criminal or civil proceedings lie against a person for disclosure made in good faith under subsection (1).

2001, c. 41, s. 4.

Audit

83.11 (1) The following entities must determine on a continuing basis whether they are in possession or control of property owned or controlled by or on behalf of a listed entity:

(a) authorized foreign banks within the meaning of section 2 of the Bank Act in respect of their business in Canada, or banks to which that Act applies;

(b) cooperative credit societies, savings and credit unions and caisses populaires regulated by a provincial Act and associations regulated by the Cooperative Credit Associations Act;

(c) foreign companies within the meaning of subsection 2(1) of the Insurance Companies Act in respect of their insurance business in Canada;

(c.1) companies, provincial companies and societies within the meaning of subsection 2(1) of the Insurance Companies Act;

(c.2) fraternal benefit societies regulated by a provincial Act in respect of their insurance activities, and insurance companies and other entities engaged in the business of insuring risks that are regulated by a provincial Act;

(d) companies to which the Trust and Loan Companies Act applies;

(e) trust companies regulated by a provincial Act;

(f) loan companies regulated by a provincial Act; and

(g) entities authorized under provincial legislation to engage in the business of dealing in securities, or to provide portfolio management or investment counselling services.

Monthly report
(2) Subject to the regulations, every entity referred to in paragraphs (1) (a) to (g) must report, within the period specified by regulation or, if no period is specified, monthly, to the principal agency or body that supervises or regulates it under federal or provincial law either

(a) that it is not in possession or control of any property referred to in subsection (1), or

(b) that it is in possession or control of such property, in which case it must also report the number of persons, contracts or accounts involved and the total value of the property.

Immunity
(3) No criminal or civil proceedings lie against a person for making a report in good faith under subsection (2).

Regulations
(4) The Governor in Council may make regulations

(a) excluding any entity or class of entities from the requirement to make a report referred to in subsection (2), and specifying the conditions of exclusion; and

(b) specifying a period for the purposes of subsection (2).

2001, c. 41, s. 4.

Offences — freezing of property, disclosure or audit
83.12 (1) Every one who contravenes any of sections 83.08, 83.1 and 83.11 is guilty of an offence and liable

(a) on summary conviction, to a fine of not more than $100,000 or to imprisonment for a term of not more than one year, or to both; or

(b) on conviction on indictment, to imprisonment for a term of not more than 10 years.

No contravention
(2) No person contravenes section 83.1 if they make the disclosure referred to in that section only to the Commissioner of the Royal Canadian Mounted Police or the Director of the Canadian Security Intelligence Service.

2001, c. 41, s. 4.

Seizure and Restraint of Property

Seizure and restraint of assets

83.13 (1) Where a judge of the Federal Court, on an ex parte application by the Attorney General, after examining the application in private, is satisfied that there are reasonable grounds to believe that there is in any building, receptacle or place any property in respect of which an order of forfeiture may be made under subsection 83.14(5), the judge may issue

(a) if the property is situated in Canada, a warrant authorizing a person named therein or a peace officer to search the building, receptacle or place for that property and to seize that property and any other property in respect of which that person or peace officer believes, on reasonable grounds, that an order of forfeiture may be made under that subsection; or

(b) if the property is situated in or outside Canada, a restraint order prohibiting any person from disposing of, or otherwise dealing with any interest in, that property other than as may be specified in the order.

Contents of application

(1.1) An affidavit in support of an application under subsection (1) may be sworn on information and belief, and, notwithstanding the Federal Court Rules, 1998, no adverse inference shall be drawn from a failure to provide evidence of persons having personal knowledge of material facts.

Appointment of manager

(2) On an application under subsection (1), at the request of the Attorney General, if a judge is of the opinion that the circumstances so require, the judge may

(a) appoint a person to take control of, and to manage or otherwise deal with, all or part of the property in accordance with the directions of the judge; and

(b) require any person having possession of that property to give possession of the property to the person appointed under paragraph (a).

Appointment of Minister of Public Works and Government Services
(3) When the Attorney General of Canada so requests, a judge appointing a person under subsection (2) shall appoint the Minister of Public Works and Government Services.

Power to manage
(4) The power to manage or otherwise deal with property under subsection (2) includes

(a) in the case of perishable or rapidly depreciating property, the power to sell that property; and

(b) in the case of property that has little or no value, the power to destroy that property.

Application for destruction order
(5) Before a person appointed under subsection (2) destroys property referred to in paragraph (4)(b), he or she shall apply to a judge of the Federal Court for a destruction order.

Notice
(6) Before making a destruction order in relation to any property, a judge shall require notice in accordance with subsection (7) to be given to, and may hear, any person who, in the opinion of the judge, appears to have a valid interest in the property.

Manner of giving notice
(7) A notice under subsection (6) shall be given in the manner that the judge directs or as provided in the rules of the Federal Court.

Order
(8) A judge may order that property be destroyed if he or she is satisfied that the property has little or no financial or other value.

When management order ceases to have effect
(9) A management order ceases to have effect when the property that is the subject of the management order is returned to an applicant in accordance with the law or forfeited to Her Majesty.

Application to vary
(10) The Attorney General may at any time apply to a judge of the Federal Court to cancel or vary an order or warrant made under this section, other than an appointment made under subsection (3).

Procedure
(11) Subsections 462.32(4) and (6), sections 462.34 to 462.35 and 462.4, subsections 487(3) and (4) and section 488 apply, with such modifications as the circumstances require, to a warrant issued under paragraph (1)(a).

Procedure
(12) Subsections 462.33(4) and (6) to (11) and sections 462.34 to 462.35 and 462.4 apply, with such modifications as the circumstances require, to an order issued under paragraph (1)(b).

2001, c. 41, s. 4.

Forfeiture of Property

Application for order of forfeiture
83.14 (1) The Attorney General may make an application to a judge of the Federal Court for an order of forfeiture in respect of

(a) property owned or controlled by or on behalf of a terrorist group; or

(b) property that has been or will be used, in whole or in part, to facilitate or carry out a terrorist activity.

Contents of application
(2) An affidavit in support of an application by the Attorney General under subsection (1) may be sworn on information and belief, and,

notwithstanding the Federal Court Rules, 1998, no adverse inference shall be drawn from a failure to provide evidence of persons having personal knowledge of material facts.

Respondents

(3) The Attorney General is required to name as a respondent to an application under subsection (1) only those persons who are known to own or control the property that is the subject of the application.

Notice

(4) The Attorney General shall give notice of an application under subsection (1) to named respondents in such a manner as the judge directs or as provided in the rules of the Federal Court.

Granting of forfeiture order

(5) If a judge is satisfied on a balance of probabilities that property is property referred to in paragraph (1)(a) or (b), the judge shall order that the property be forfeited to Her Majesty to be disposed of as the Attorney General directs or otherwise dealt with in accordance with the law.

Use of proceeds

(5.1) Any proceeds that arise from the disposal of property under subsection (5) may be used to compensate victims of terrorist activities and to fund antiterrorist initiatives in accordance with any regulations made by the Governor in Council under subsection (5.2).

Regulations

(5.2) The Governor in Council may make regulations for the purposes of specifying how the proceeds referred to in subsection (5.1) are to be distributed.

Order refusing forfeiture

(6) Where a judge refuses an application under subsection (1) in respect of any property, the judge shall make an order that describes the property and declares that it is not property referred to in that subsection.

Notice

(7) On an application under subsection (1), a judge may require notice to be given to any person who, in the opinion of the Court, appears to have an interest in the property, and any such person shall be entitled to be added as a respondent to the application.

Third party interests

(8) If a judge is satisfied that a person referred to in subsection (7) has an interest in property that is subject to an application, has exercised reasonable care to ensure that the property would not be used to facilitate or carry out a terrorist activity, and is not a member of a terrorist group, the judge shall order that the interest is not affected by the forfeiture. Such an order shall declare the nature and extent of the interest in question.

Dwelling-house

(9) Where all or part of property that is the subject of an application under subsection (1) is a dwelling-house, the judge shall also consider

(a) the impact of an order of forfeiture on any member of the immediate family of the person who owns or controls the dwelling-house, if the dwelling-house was the member's principal residence at the time the dwelling-house was ordered restrained or at the time the forfeiture application was made and continues to be the member's principal residence; and

(b) whether the member appears innocent of any complicity or collusion in the terrorist activity.

Motion to vary or set aside

(10) A person who claims an interest in property that was forfeited and who did not receive notice under subsection (7) may bring a motion to the Federal Court to vary or set aside an order made under subsection (5) not later than 60 days after the day on which the forfeiture order was made.

No extension of time

(11) The Court may not extend the period set out in subsection (10).

2001, c. 41, s. 4.

Disposition of property
83.15 Subsection 462.42(6) and sections 462.43 and 462.46 apply, with such modifications as the circumstances require, to property subject to a warrant or restraint order issued under subsection 83.13(1) or ordered forfeited under subsection 83.14(5).

2001, c. 41, s. 4.

Interim preservation rights
83.16 (1) Pending any appeal of an order made under section 83.14, property restrained under an order issued under section 83.13 shall continue to be restrained, property seized under a warrant issued under that section shall continue to be detained, and any person appointed to manage, control or otherwise deal with that property under that section shall continue in that capacity.

Appeal of refusal to grant order
(2) Section 462.34 applies, with such modifications as the circumstances require, to an appeal taken in respect of a refusal to grant an order under subsection 83.14(5).

2001, c. 41, s. 4.

Other forfeiture provisions unaffected
83.17 (1) This Part does not affect the operation of any other provision of this or any other Act of Parliament respecting the forfeiture of property.

Priority for restitution to victims of crime
(2) Property is subject to forfeiture under subsection 83.14(5) only to the extent that it is not required to satisfy the operation of any other provision of this or any other Act of Parliament respecting restitution to, or compensation of, persons affected by the commission of offences.

2001, c. 41, s. 4.
Participating, Facilitating, Instructing and Harbouring

Participation in activity of terrorist group
83.18 (1) Every one who knowingly participates in or contributes to, directly or indirectly, any activity of a terrorist group for the purpose of enhancing the ability of any terrorist group to facilitate or carry out a terrorist activity is guilty of an indictable offence and liable to imprisonment for a term not exceeding ten years.

Prosecution

(2) An offence may be committed under subsection (1) whether or not

(a) a terrorist group actually facilitates or carries out a terrorist activity;

(b) the participation or contribution of the accused actually enhances the ability of a terrorist group to facilitate or carry out a terrorist activity; or

(c) the accused knows the specific nature of any terrorist activity that may be facilitated or carried out by a terrorist group.

Meaning of participating or contributing
(3) Participating in or contributing to an activity of a terrorist group includes

(a) providing, receiving or recruiting a person to receive training;

(b) providing or offering to provide a skill or an expertise for the benefit of, at the direction of or in association with a terrorist group;

(c) recruiting a person in order to facilitate or commit

(i) a terrorism offence, or

(ii) an act or omission outside Canada that, if committed in Canada, would be a terrorism offence;

(d) entering or remaining in any country for the benefit of, at the direction of or in association with a terrorist group; and

(e) making oneself, in response to instructions from any of the persons who constitute a terrorist group, available to facilitate or commit

(i) a terrorism offence, or

(ii) an act or omission outside Canada that, if committed in Canada, would be a terrorism offence.

Factors
(4) In determining whether an accused participates in or contributes to any activity of a terrorist group, the court may consider, among other factors, whether the accused

(a) uses a name, word, symbol or other representation that identifies, or is associated with, the terrorist group;

(b) frequently associates with any of the persons who constitute the terrorist group;

(c) receives any benefit from the terrorist group; or

(d) repeatedly engages in activities at the instruction of any of the persons who constitute the terrorist group.

2001, c. 41, s. 4.

Facilitating terrorist activity
83.19 (1) Every one who knowingly facilitates a terrorist activity is guilty of an indictable offence and liable to imprisonment for a term not exceeding fourteen years.

Facilitation

(2) For the purposes of this Part, a terrorist activity is facilitated whether or not

(a) the facilitator knows that a particular terrorist activity is facilitated;

(b) any particular terrorist activity was foreseen or planned at the time it was facilitated; or

(c) any terrorist activity was actually carried out.

2001, c. 41, s. 4.

Commission of offence for terrorist group

83.2 Every one who commits an indictable offence under this or any other Act of Parliament for the benefit of, at the direction of or in association with a terrorist group is guilty of an indictable offence and liable to imprisonment for life.

2001, c. 41, s. 4.

Instructing to carry out activity for terrorist group

83.21 (1) Every person who knowingly instructs, directly or indirectly, any person to carry out any activity for the benefit of, at the direction of or in association with a terrorist group, for the purpose of enhancing the ability of any terrorist group to facilitate or carry out a terrorist activity, is guilty of an indictable offence and liable to imprisonment for life.

Prosecution

(2) An offence may be committed under subsection (1) whether or not

(a) the activity that the accused instructs to be carried out is actually carried out;

(b) the accused instructs a particular person to carry out the activity referred to in paragraph (a);

(c) the accused knows the identity of the person whom the accused instructs to carry out the activity referred to in paragraph (a);

(d) the person whom the accused instructs to carry out the activity referred to in paragraph (a) knows that it is to be carried out for the benefit of, at the direction of or in association with a terrorist group;

(e) a terrorist group actually facilitates or carries out a terrorist activity;

(f) the activity referred to in paragraph (a) actually enhances the ability of a terrorist group to facilitate or carry out a terrorist activity; or

(g) the accused knows the specific nature of any terrorist activity that may be facilitated or carried out by a terrorist group.

2001, c. 41, s. 4.

Instructing to carry out terrorist activity
83.22 (1) Every person who knowingly instructs, directly or indirectly, any person to carry out a terrorist activity is guilty of an indictable offence and liable to imprisonment for life.

Prosecution
(2) An offence may be committed under subsection (1) whether or not

(a) the terrorist activity is actually carried out;

(b) the accused instructs a particular person to carry out the terrorist activity;

(c) the accused knows the identity of the person whom the accused instructs to carry out the terrorist activity; or

(d) the person whom the accused instructs to carry out the terrorist activity knows that it is a terrorist activity.

2001, c. 41, s. 4.

Harbouring or concealing

83.23 Every one who knowingly harbours or conceals any person whom he or she knows to be a person who has carried out or is likely to carry out a terrorist activity, for the purpose of enabling the person to facilitate or carry out any terrorist activity, is guilty of an indictable offence and liable to imprisonment for a term not exceeding ten years.

2001, c. 41, s. 4.

Proceedings and Aggravated Punishment

Attorney General's consent

83.24 Proceedings in respect of a terrorism offence or an offence under section 83.12 shall not be commenced without the consent of the Attorney General.

2001, c. 41, s. 4.

Jurisdiction

83.25 (1) Where a person is alleged to have committed a terrorism offence or an offence under section 83.12, proceedings in respect of that offence may, whether or not that person is in Canada, be commenced at the instance of the Government of Canada and conducted by the Attorney General of Canada or counsel acting on his or her behalf in any territorial division in Canada, if the offence is alleged to have occurred outside the province in which the proceedings are commenced, whether or not proceedings have previously been commenced elsewhere in Canada.

Trial and punishment

(2) An accused may be tried and punished in respect of an offence referred to in subsection (1) in the same manner as if the offence had been committed in the territorial division where the proceeding is conducted.

2001, c. 41, s. 4.

Sentences to be served consecutively
83.26 A sentence, other than one of life imprisonment, imposed on a person for an offence under any of sections 83.02 to 83.04 and 83.18 to 83.23 shall be served consecutively to

(a) any other punishment imposed on the person, other than a sentence of life imprisonment, for an offence arising out of the same event or series of events; and

(b) any other sentence, other than one of life imprisonment, to which the person is subject at the time the sentence is imposed on the person for an offence under any of those sections.

2001, c. 41, s. 4.

Punishment for terrorist activity
83.27 (1) Notwithstanding anything in this Act, a person convicted of an indictable offence, other than an offence for which a sentence of imprisonment for life is imposed as a minimum punishment, where the act or omission constituting the offence also constitutes a terrorist activity, is liable to imprisonment for life.

Offender must be notified
(2) Subsection (1) does not apply unless the prosecutor satisfies the court that the offender, before making a plea, was notified that the application of that subsection would be sought.

2001, c. 41, s. 4.

Investigative Hearing

Definition of "judge"
83.28 (1) In this section and section 83.29, "judge" means a provincial court judge or a judge of a superior court of criminal jurisdiction.

Order for gathering evidence
(2) Subject to subsection (3), a peace officer may, for the purposes of an investigation of a terrorism offence, apply ex parte to a judge for an order for the gathering of information.

Attorney General's consent
(3) A peace officer may make an application under subsection (2) only if the prior consent of the Attorney General was obtained.

Making of order
(4) A judge to whom an application is made under subsection (2) may make an order for the gathering of information if the judge is satisfied that the consent of the Attorney General was obtained as required by subsection (3) and

(a) that there are reasonable grounds to believe that

(i) a terrorism offence has been committed, and

(ii) information concerning the offence, or information that may reveal the whereabouts of a person suspected by the peace officer of having committed the offence, is likely to be obtained as a result of the order; or

(b) that

(i) there are reasonable grounds to believe that a terrorism offence will be committed,

(ii) there are reasonable grounds to believe that a person has direct and material information that relates to a terrorism offence referred to in subparagraph (i), or that may reveal the whereabouts of an individual who the peace officer suspects may commit a terrorism offence referred to in that subparagraph, and

(iii) reasonable attempts have been made to obtain the information referred to in subparagraph (ii) from the person referred to in that subparagraph.

Contents of order

(5) An order made under subsection (4) may

(a) order the examination, on oath or not, of a person named in the order;

(b) order the person to attend at the place fixed by the judge, or by the judge designated under paragraph (d), as the case may be, for the examination and to remain in attendance until excused by the presiding judge;

(c) order the person to bring to the examination any thing in their possession or control, and produce it to the presiding judge;

(d) designate another judge as the judge before whom the examination is to take place; and

(e) include any other terms or conditions that the judge considers desirable, including terms or conditions for the protection of the interests of the person named in the order and of third parties or for the protection of any ongoing investigation.

Execution of order

(6) An order made under subsection (4) may be executed anywhere in Canada.

Variation of order

(7) The judge who made the order under subsection (4), or another judge of the same court, may vary its terms and conditions.

Obligation to answer questions and produce things

(8) A person named in an order made under subsection (4) shall answer questions put to the person by the Attorney General or the Attorney General's agent, and shall produce to the presiding judge things that the person was ordered to bring, but may refuse if answering a question or producing a thing would disclose information that is protected by any law relating to non-disclosure of information or to privilege.

Judge to rule
(9) The presiding judge shall rule on any objection or other issue relating to a refusal to answer a question or to produce a thing.

No person excused from complying with subsection (8)
(10) No person shall be excused from answering a question or producing a thing under subsection (8) on the ground that the answer or thing may tend to incriminate the person or subject the person to any proceeding or penalty, but

(a) no answer given or thing produced under subsection (8) shall be used or received against the person in any criminal proceedings against that person, other than a prosecution under section 132 or 136; and

(b) no evidence derived from the evidence obtained from the person shall be used or received against the person in any criminal proceedings against that person, other than a prosecution under section 132 or 136.

Right to counsel
(11) A person has the right to retain and instruct counsel at any stage of the proceedings.

Order for custody of thing
(12) The presiding judge, if satisfied that any thing produced during the course of the examination will likely be relevant to the investigation of any terrorism offence, shall order that the thing be given into the custody of the peace officer or someone acting on the peace officer's behalf.

2001, c. 41, s. 4.

Arrest warrant
83.29 (1) The judge who made the order under subsection 83.28(4), or another judge of the same court, may issue a warrant for the arrest of the person named in the order if the judge is satisfied, on an information in writing and under oath, that the person

(a) is evading service of the order;

(b) is about to abscond; or

(c) did not attend the examination, or did not remain in attendance, as required by the order.

Execution of warrant
(2) A warrant issued under subsection (1) may be executed at any place in Canada by any peace officer having jurisdiction in that place.

Person to be brought before judge
(3) A peace officer who arrests a person in the execution of a warrant issued under subsection (1) shall, without delay, bring the person, or cause the person to be brought, before the judge who issued the warrant or another judge of the same court. The judge in question may, to ensure compliance with the order, order that the person be detained in custody or released on recognizance, with or without sureties.

2001, c. 41, s. 4.

Recognizance with Conditions

Attorney General's consent required to lay information
83.3 (1) The consent of the Attorney General is required before a peace officer may lay an information under subsection (2).

Terrorist activity
(2) Subject to subsection (1), a peace officer may lay an information before a provincial court judge if the peace officer

(a) believes on reasonable grounds that a terrorist activity will be carried out; and

(b) suspects on reasonable grounds that the imposition of a recognizance with conditions on a person, or the arrest of a person, is necessary to prevent the carrying out of the terrorist activity.

Appearance
(3) A provincial court judge who receives an information under subsection (2) may cause the person to appear before the provincial court judge.

Arrest without warrant
(4) Notwithstanding subsections (2) and (3), if

(a) either

(i) the grounds for laying an information referred to in paragraphs (2) (a) and (b) exist but, by reason of exigent circumstances, it would be impracticable to lay an information under subsection (2), or

(ii) an information has been laid under subsection (2) and a summons has been issued, and

(b) the peace officer suspects on reasonable grounds that the detention of the person in custody is necessary in order to prevent a terrorist activity,

the peace officer may arrest the person without warrant and cause the person to be detained in custody, to be taken before a provincial court judge in accordance with subsection (6).

Duty of peace officer
(5) If a peace officer arrests a person without warrant in the circumstance described in subparagraph (4)(a)(i), the peace officer shall, within the time prescribed by paragraph (6)(a) or (b),

(a) lay an information in accordance with subsection (2); or

(b) release the person.

When person to be taken before judge
(6) A person detained in custody shall be taken before a provincial court judge in accordance with the following rules:

(a) if a provincial court judge is available within a period of twenty-four hours after the person has been arrested, the person shall be taken before a provincial court judge without unreasonable delay and in any event within that period, and

(b) if a provincial court judge is not available within a period of twenty-four hours after the person has been arrested, the person shall be taken before a provincial court judge as soon as possible,

unless, at any time before the expiry of the time prescribed in paragraph (a) or (b) for taking the person before a provincial court judge, the peace officer, or an officer in charge within the meaning of Part XV, is satisfied that the person should be released from custody unconditionally, and so releases the person.

How person dealt with
(7) When a person is taken before a provincial court judge under subsection (6),

(a) if an information has not been laid under subsection (2), the judge shall order that the person be released; or

(b) if an information has been laid under subsection (2),

(i) the judge shall order that the person be released unless the peace officer who laid the information shows cause why the detention of the person in custody is justified on one or more of the following grounds:

(A) the detention is necessary to ensure the person's appearance before a provincial court judge in order to be dealt with in accordance with subsection (8),

(B) the detention is necessary for the protection or safety of the public, including any witness, having regard to all the circumstances including

(I) the likelihood that, if the person is released from custody, a terrorist activity will be carried out, and

(II) any substantial likelihood that the person will, if released from custody, interfere with the administration of justice, and

(C) any other just cause and, without limiting the generality of the foregoing, that the detention is necessary in order to maintain confidence in the administration of justice, having regard to all the circumstances, including the apparent strength of the peace officer's grounds under subsection (2), and the gravity of any terrorist activity that may be carried out, and

(ii) the judge may adjourn the matter for a hearing under subsection (8) but, if the person is not released under subparagraph (i), the adjournment may not exceed forty-eight hours.

Hearing before judge
(8) The provincial court judge before whom the person appears pursuant to subsection (3)

(a) may, if satisfied by the evidence adduced that the peace officer has reasonable grounds for the suspicion, order that the person enter into a recognizance to keep the peace and be of good behaviour for any period that does not exceed twelve months and to comply with any other reasonable conditions prescribed in the recognizance, including the conditions set out in subsection (10), that the provincial court judge considers desirable for preventing the carrying out of a terrorist activity; and

(b) if the person was not released under subparagraph (7)(b)(i), shall order that the person be released, subject to the recognizance, if any, ordered under paragraph (a).

Refusal to enter into recognizance

(9) The provincial court judge may commit the person to prison for a term not exceeding twelve months if the person fails or refuses to enter into the recognizance.

Conditions — firearms

(10) Before making an order under paragraph (8)(a), the provincial court judge shall consider whether it is desirable, in the interests of the safety of the person or of any other person, to include as a condition of the recognizance that the person be prohibited from possessing any firearm, cross-bow, prohibited weapon, restricted weapon, prohibited device, ammunition, prohibited ammunition or explosive substance, or all of those things, for any period specified in the recognizance, and where the provincial court judge decides that it is so desirable, the provincial court judge shall add such a condition to the recognizance.

Surrender, etc.

(11) If the provincial court judge adds a condition described in subsection (10) to a recognizance, the provincial court judge shall specify in the recognizance the manner and method by which

(a) the things referred to in that subsection that are in the possession of the person shall be surrendered, disposed of, detained, stored or dealt with; and

(b) the authorizations, licences and registration certificates held by the person shall be surrendered.

Reasons

(12) If the provincial court judge does not add a condition described in sub-section (10) to a recognizance, the provincial court judge shall include in the record a statement of the reasons for not adding the condition.

Variance of conditions

(13) The provincial court judge may, on application of the peace

officer, the Attorney General or the person, vary the conditions fixed in the recognizance.

Other provisions to apply
(14) Subsections 810(4) and (5) apply, with any modifications that the circumstances require, to proceedings under this section.

2001, c. 41, s. 4.

Annual report (sections 83.28 and 83.29)
83.31 (1) The Attorney General of Canada shall prepare and cause to be laid before Parliament and the Attorney General of every province shall publish or otherwise make available to the public an annual report for the previous year on the operation of sections 83.28 and 83.29 that includes

(a) the number of consents to make an application that were sought, and the number that were obtained, by virtue of subsections 83.28(2) and (3);

(b) the number of orders for the gathering of information that were made under subsection 83.28(4); and

(c) the number of arrests that were made with a warrant issued under section 83.29.

Annual report (section 83.3)
(2) The Attorney General of Canada shall prepare and cause to be laid before Parliament and the Attorney General of every province shall publish or otherwise make available to the public an annual report for the previous year on the operation of section 83.3 that includes

(a) the number of consents to lay an information that were sought, and the number that were obtained, by virtue of subsections 83.3(1) and (2);

(b) the number of cases in which a summons or a warrant of arrest was issued for the purposes of subsection 83.3(3);

(c) the number of cases where a person was not released under subsection 83.3(7) pending a hearing;

(d) the number of cases in which an order to enter into a recognizance was made under paragraph 83.3(8)(a), and the types of conditions that were imposed;

(e) the number of times that a person failed or refused to enter into a recognizance, and the term of imprisonment imposed under subsection 83.3(9) in each case; and

(f) the number of cases in which the conditions fixed in a recognizance were varied under subsection 83.3(13).

Annual report (section 83.3)
(3) The Solicitor General of Canada shall prepare and cause to be laid before Parliament and the Minister responsible for policing in every province shall publish or otherwise make available to the public an annual report for the previous year on the operation of section 83.3 that includes

(a) the number of arrests without warrant that were made under subsection 83.3(4) and the period of the arrested person's detention in custody in each case; and

(b) the number of cases in which a person was arrested without warrant under subsection 83.3(4) and was released

(i) by a peace officer under paragraph 83.3(5)(b), or

(ii) by a judge under paragraph 83.3(7)(a).

Limitation
(4) The annual report shall not contain any information the disclosure of which would

(a) compromise or hinder an ongoing investigation of an offence under an Act of Parliament;

(b) endanger the life or safety of any person;

(c) prejudice a legal proceeding; or

(d) otherwise be contrary to the public interest.

2001, c. 41, s. 4.

Sunset provision
83.32 (1) Sections 83.28, 83.29 and 83.3 cease to apply at the end of the fifteenth sitting day of Parliament after December 31, 2006 unless, before the end of that day, the application of those sections is extended by a resolution — the text of which is established under subsection (2) — passed by both Houses of Parliament in accordance with the rules set out in subsection (3).

Order in Council
(2) The Governor General in Council may, by order, establish the text of a resolution providing for the extension of the application of sections 83.28, 83.29 and 83.3 and specifying the period of the extension, which may not exceed five years from the first day on which the resolution has been passed by both Houses of Parliament.

Rules
(3) A motion for the adoption of the resolution may be debated in both Houses of Parliament but may not be amended. At the conclusion of the debate, the Speaker of the House of Parliament shall immediately put every question necessary to determine whether or not the motion is concurred in.

Subsequent extensions
(4) The application of sections 83.28, 83.29 and 83.3 may be further extended in accordance with the procedure set out in this section,with

the words "December 31, 2006" in subsection (1) read as "the expiration of the most recent extension under this section".

Definition of "sitting day of Parliament"
(5) In subsection (1), "sitting day of Parliament" means a day on which both Houses of Parliament sit.

2001, c. 41, s. 4.

Transitional provision
83.33 (1) In the event that sections 83.28 and 83.29 cease to apply pursuant to section 83.32, proceedings commenced under those sections shall be completed if the hearing before the judge of the application made under subsection 83.28(2) began before those sections ceased to apply.

Transitional provision
(2) In the event that section 83.3 ceases to apply pursuant to section 83.32, a person detained in custody under section 83.3 shall be released when that section ceases to apply, except that subsections 83.3(7) to (14) continue to apply to a person who was taken before a judge under subsection 83.3(6) before section 83.3 ceased to apply.

2001, c. 41, s. 4.

(Source: Department of Justice. This is not the official version)

APPENDIX IV

BILL C-409

BILL C-409
An Act to establish the Canadian Foreign Intelligence Agency
First reading, March 17, 2003

Summary

This enactment provides for the establishment of the Canadian Foreign Intelligence Agency.

2nd Session, 37th Parliament,

51-52 Elizabeth II, 2002-2003

House of Commons of Canada

Bill C-409

51-52 Elizabeth II, 2002-2003

An Act to establish the Canadian Foreign Intelligence Agency

Short title
1. This Act may be cited as the *Canadian Foreign Intelligence Agency Act.*

interpretation

Definitions

2. The definitions in this section apply in this Act.

"Agency" means the Canadian Foreign Intelligence Agency established by subsection 3(1).

"department," in relation to the Government of Canada or of a province, includes

(a) any portion of a department of the Government of Canada or of the province; and

(b) any Ministry of State, institution or other body of the Government of Canada or of the province or any portion thereof.

"Director" means the Director of the Agency.

"employee" means a person who is appointed as an employee of the Agency pursuant to subsection 7(1) and includes a person who is attached or seconded to the Agency as an employee.

"foreign state" means any state other than Canada.

"Minister" means the Solicitor General of Canada.

"Review Committee" means the Foreign Intelligence Review Committee established by subsection 24(1).

Part 1

Canadian foreign intelligence agency

Establishment of Agency

Establishment of Agency
3. (1) The Canadian Foreign Intelligence Agency is hereby established, consisting of the Director and employees of the Agency.

Principal office
(2) The principal office of the Agency shall be in the National Capital Region described in the schedule to the *National Capital Act.*

Director

Appointment
4. (1) The Governor in Council shall appoint the Director of the Agency.

Nomination

Term of office
(2) The Director shall be appointed to hold office during pleasure for a term not exceeding five years.

Re-appointment
(3) Subject to subsection (4), the Director is eligible, on the expiration of a first or any subsequent term of office, to be re-appointed for a further term not exceeding five years.

Limitation
(4) No person shall hold office as Director for terms exceeding ten years in the aggregate.

Absence or incapacity
(5) In the event of the absence or incapacity of the Director, or if the office of Director is vacant, the Governor in Council may appoint another person to hold office instead of the Director for a term not exceeding six months, and that person shall, while holding that office, have all of the powers, duties and functions of the Director under this Act or any other Act of Parliament and be paid such salary or other remuneration and expenses as may be fixed by the Governor in Council.

Salary and expenses
5. (1) The Director is entitled to be paid a salary to be fixed by the Governor in Council and shall be paid reasonable travel and living expenses incurred by the Director in the performance of duties and functions under this Act.

Pension benefits
(2) The provisions of the *Public Service Superannuation Act,* other than those relating to tenure of office, apply to the Director, except that a person appointed as Director from outside the Public Service, as defined in the *Public Service Superannuation Act,* may, by notice in writing given to the President of the Treasury Board not more than sixty days after the date of appointment, elect to participate in the pension plan provided by the *Diplomatic Service (Special) Superannuation Act,* in which case the provisions of that Act, other than those relating to tenure of office, apply to the Director from the date of appointment and the provisions of the *Public Service Superannuation Act* do not apply.

Management of Agency

Role of Director
6. (1) The Director, under the direction of the Minister, has the control and management of the Agency and all matters connected therewith.

Minister may issue directions
(2) In providing the direction referred to in subsection (1), the Minister may issue to the Director written directions with respect to the Agency and a copy of any such direction shall, forthwith after it is issued, be given to the Review Committee.

Directions deemed not to be statutory instruments
(3) Directions issued by the Minister under subsection (2) shall be deemed not to be statutory instruments for the purposes of the *Statutory Instruments Act.*

Powers and duties of Director

7. (1) Notwithstanding the Financial Administration Act and the *Public Service Employment Act,* the Director has exclusive authority to appoint employees and, in relation to the personnel management of employees, other than persons attached or seconded to the Agency as employees,

(a) to provide for the terms and conditions of their employment; and

(b) subject to the regulations,

(i) to exercise the powers and perform the duties and functions of the Treasury Board relating to personnel management under the *Financial Administration Act,* and

(ii) to exercise the powers and perform the duties and functions assigned to the Public Service Commission by or pursuant to the *Public Agency Employment Act.*

Discipline and grievances of employees

(2) Notwithstanding the *Public Service Staff Relations Act* but subject to subsection (3) and the regulations, the Director may establish procedures respecting the conduct and discipline of, and the presentation, consideration and adjudication of grievances in relation to, employees, other than persons attached or seconded to the Agency as employees.

Adjudication of employee grievances

(3) When a grievance is referred to adjudication, the adjudication shall not be heard or determined by any person, other than a full-time member of the Public Service Staff Relations Board established under section 11 of the *Public Service Staff Relations Act.*

Regulations

(4) The Governor in Council may make regulations

(a) governing the exercise of the powers and the performance of the duties and functions of the Director referred to in subsection (1); and

(b) in relation to employees to whom subsection (2) applies, governing their conduct and discipline and the presentation, consideration and adjudication of grievances.

Process for resolution of disputes of support staff
8. (1) Notwithstanding the *Public Service Staff Relations Act,*

(a) the process for resolution of a dispute applicable to employees of the Agency in a bargaining unit determined for the purposes of that Act is by the referral of the dispute to arbitration; and

(b) the process for resolution of a dispute referred to in paragraph (a) shall not be altered pursuant to that Act.

Public Service Superannuation Act
(2) Employees of the Agency shall be deemed to be employed in the Public Service for the purposes of the *Public Service Superannuation Act.*

No suspension of arbitration
9. (1) Notwithstanding section 62 of the *Public Service Staff Relations Act* but subject to subsection (2), the operation of sections 64 to 75.1 of that Act is not suspended in respect of the resolution of any dispute applicable to employees of the Agency.

Limit on maximum rate of increase
(2) During the period referred to in paragraph 62(1)(b) of the *Public Service Staff Relations Act,* an arbitration board, as defined in subsection 2(1) of that Act, shall, in rendering an arbitral award, limit the aggregate amount of any increase in pay and other benefits in respect of any dispute applicable to employees of the Agency to that concluded through collective bargaining or otherwise by a comparable bargaining unit in the Public Service, within the meaning of that Act, after the compensation plan applicable to that bargaining unit ceased to be continued by virtue of the *Public Sector Compensation Act.*

Oaths

10. The Director and every employee shall, before commencing the duties of office, take an oath of allegiance and the oaths set out in the schedule.

Certificate

11. A certificate purporting to be issued by or under the authority of the Director and stating that the person to whom it is issued is an employee is evidence of that fact and is admissible in evidence without proof of the signature or official character of the person purporting to have issued it.

Duties and Functions of Agency

Functions of Agency

12. (1) Subject to subsection (2), the Agency shall carry out the following functions:

(a) those functions assigned to the Agency by the Governor in Council pursuant to subsection (3);

(b) to obtain and analyze, in accordance with any functions assigned under subsection (3), intelligence about the capabilities, intentions or activities of people or organizations outside Canada;

(c) to communicate, in accordance with section 17 and any functions assigned under subsection (3), the intelligence referred to in paragraph (b);

(d) to conduct counter-intelligence activities;

(e) to liaise with the security or intelligence services, or other authorities, of other countries; and

(f) to undertake such other activities as the Minister directs relating to the capabilities, intentions or activities of people or organizations outside Canada.

Limitations on functions

(2) The functions of the Agency are to be performed only to safeguard

the interest of Canada's sovereignty, security, democratic integrity, international relations or economic well-being and only to the extent that those matters are affected by the capabilities, intentions or activities of people or organizations outside Canada. They do not include policing or law-enforcement responsibilities but this does not prevent the Agency from obtaining intelligence under paragraph (1)(b) and communicating any such intelligence relating to serious crime to the appropriate law enforcement authorities. The Agency shall not be involved, directly or indirectly, in the assassination of any person or in the replacement, by violent means, of any government.

Assignment of functions

(3) The Governor in Council may assign to the Agency whatever functions it determines to be necessary in order to further the interest of Canada's sovereignty, security, democratic integrity international relations or economic well being.

Advice to Ministers

13. The Agency may

(a) advise any minister of the Crown on matters relating to any matter assigned to the Agency pursuant to subsection 12(3), or

(b) provide any minister of the Crown with information relating to security or foreign intelligence matters or criminal activities,

that is relevant to the exercise of any power or the performance of any duty or function by that Minister under the *Citizenship Act* or the *Immigration and Refugee Protection Act.*

Investigations

14. The Agency may conduct such investigations as are required for the purpose of providing advice pursuant to section 13.

Cooperation

15. (1) For the purpose of performing its duties and functions under this Act, the Agency may,

(a) with the approval of the Minister, enter into an arrangement or otherwise cooperate with

(i) any department of the Government of Canada or the government of a province or any department thereof, or

(ii) any police force in a province, with the approval of the Minister responsible for policing in the province; or

(b) with the approval of the Minister after consultation by the Minister with the Minister of Foreign Affairs, enter into an arrangement or otherwise cooperate with the government of a foreign state or an institution thereof or an international organization of states or an institution thereof.

Copies of arrangements to Review Committee
(2) Where a written arrangement is entered into pursuant to subsection (1), a copy thereof shall be given forthwith to the Review Committee.

Offence to disclose identity
16. (1) Subject to subsection (2), no person shall disclose any information that the person obtained or to which the person had access in the course of the performance by that person of duties and functions under this Act or the participation by that person in the administration or enforcement of this Act and from which the identity of

(a) any other person who is or was a confidential source of information or assistance to the Agency, or

(b) any person who is or was an employee engaged in covert operational activities of the Agency can be inferred.

Exceptions
(2) A person may disclose information referred to in subsection (1) for the purposes of the performance of duties and functions under this Act or any other Act of Parliament or the administration or enforcement of this Act or as required by any other law or in the circumstances described

in any of paragraphs 17(2)(a) to (d).

Offence
(3) Every one who contravenes subsection (1)

(a) is guilty of an indictable offence and liable to imprisonment for a term not exceeding five years; or

(b) is guilty of an offence punishable on summary conviction.

Unauthorized disclosure of information prohibited
17. (1) Information obtained in the performance of the duties and functions of the Agency under this Act shall not be disclosed by the Agency except in accordance with this section.

Authorized disclosure of information
(2) The Agency may disclose information referred to in subsection (1) for the purposes of the performance of its duties and functions under this Act or the administration or enforcement of this Act or as required by any other law and may also disclose such information,

(a) where the information may be used in the investigation or prosecution of an alleged contravention of any law of Canada or a province, to a peace officer having jurisdiction to investigate the alleged contravention and to the Attorney General of Canada and the Attorney General of the province in which proceedings in respect of the alleged contravention may be taken;

(b) where the information relates to the conduct of the international affairs of Canada, to the Minister of Foreign Affairs or a person designated by the Minister of Foreign Affairs for the purpose;

(c) where the information is relevant to the defence of Canada, to the Minister of National Defence or a person designated by the Minister of National Defence for the purpose; or

(d) where, in the opinion of the Minister, disclosure of the information to any minister of the Crown or person in the public service of Canada is essential in the public interest and that interest clearly outweighs any invasion of privacy that could result from the disclosure, to that minister or person.

Report to Review Committee
(3) The Director shall, as soon as practicable after a disclosure referred to in paragraph (2)(d) is made, submit a report to the Review Committee with respect to the disclosure.

Protection of employees
18. (1) The Director and employees have, in performing the duties and functions of the Agency under this Act, the same protection under the law as peace officers have in performing their duties and functions as peace officers.

Unlawful conduct
(2) If the Director is of the opinion that an employee may, on a particular occasion, have acted unlawfully in Canada in the purported performance of the duties and functions of the Agency under this Act, the Director shall cause to be submitted a report in respect thereof to the Minister.

Report and comments to Attorney General of Canada
(3) The Minister shall cause to be given to the Attorney General of Canada a copy of any report that he receives pursuant to subsection (2), together with any comment that he considers appropriate in the circumstances.

Copies to Review Committee
(4) A copy of anything given to the Attorney General of Canada pursuant to subsection (3) shall be given forthwith to the Review Committee.

Part 2

Review

Interpretation

Definitions

19. The definitions in this section apply in this Part.

"Commissioner" means the Commissioner of Foreign Intelligence Review.

"deputy head" means, in relation to

(a) a department named in Schedule I to the Financial Administration Act, the deputy minister thereof;

(b) the Canadian Forces, the Chief of the Defence Staff;

(c) the Royal Canadian Mounted Police, the Commissioner;

(d) the Agency, the Director; and

(e) any other portion of the public service of Canada, the person designated by order in council pursuant to this paragraph and for the purposes of this Part to be the deputy head of that portion of the public service of Canada.

Commissioner of Foreign Intelligence Review
20. (1) The Governor in Council shall appoint an officer to be known as the Commissioner of Foreign Intelligence Review,who is responsible to the Minister.

Functions of Commissioner
(2) The functions of the Commissioner are

(a) to monitor the compliance by the Agency with its operational policies;

(b) to review the operational activities of the Agency; and

(c) to submit certificates pursuant to subsection 23(2).

Access to information

21. (1) Notwithstanding any other Act of Parliament but subject to subsection (2), the Commissioner is entitled to have access to any information under the control of the Agency that relates to the performance of the duties and functions of the Commissioner and is also entitled to receive from the Director and employees such information, reports and explanations as the Commissioner deems necessary for the performance of those duties and functions.

Compelling production of information

(2) No information described in subsection (1), other than a confidence of the Queen's Privy Council for Canada in respect of which subsection 39(1) of the *Canada Evidence Act* applies, may be withheld from the Commissioner of on any grounds.

Compliance with security requirements

22. The Commissioner shall comply with all security requirements applicable by or under this Act to an employee and shall take the oath of secrecy set out in the schedule.

Periodic reports by Director

23. (1) The Director shall, in relation to every period of twelve months or such lesser period as is specified by the Minister, submit to the Minister, at such times as the Minister specifies, reports with respect to the operational activities of the Agency during that period, and shall cause the Commissioner to be given a copy of each such report.

Certificates of Commissioner

(2) As soon as practicable after receiving a copy of a report referred to in subsection (1), the Commissioner shall submit to the Minister a certificate stating the extent to which the Commissioner is satisfied with the report and whether any act or thing done by the Agency in the course of its operational activities during the period to which the report relates is, in the opinion of the Commissioner,

(a) not authorized by or under this Act or contravenes any directions issued by the Minister under subsection 6(2); or

(b) involves an unreasonable or unnecessary exercise by the Agency of any of its powers.

Transmission to Review Committee
(3) As soon as practicable after receiving a report referred to in subsection (1) and a certificate referred to in subsection (2), the Minister shall cause the report and certificate to be transmitted to the Review Committee.

Foreign Intelligence Review Committee
24. (1) There is hereby established a committee, to be known as the Foreign Intelligence Review Committee, consisting of a Chairman and not less than two and not more than four other members, all of whom shall be appointed by the Governor in Council from among members of the Queen's Privy Council for Canada who are not members of the Senate or the House of Commons, after consultation by the Prime Minister of Canada with the Leader of the Opposition in the House of Commons and the leader in the House of Commons of each party having at least twelve members in that House.

Term of office
(2) Each member of the Review Committee shall be appointed to hold office during good behaviour for a term not exceeding five years.

Re-appointment
(3) A member of the Review Committee is eligible to be re-appointed for a term not exceeding five years.

Expenses
(4) Each member of the Review Committee is entitled to be paid, for each day that the member performs duties and functions under this Act, such remuneration as is fixed by the Governor in Council and shall be paid reasonable travel and living expenses incurred by the member in the performance of those duties and functions.

Chairman of the Review Committee

25. (1) The Chairman of the Review Committee is the chief executive officer of the Committee.

Acting Chairman of the Review Committee

(2) The Chairman of the Review Committee may designate another member of the Committee to act as the Chairman in the event of the absence or incapacity of the Chairman and, if no such designation is in force or the office of Chairman is vacant, the Minister may designate a member of the Committee to act as the Chairman.

Staff of Review Committee

26. The Review Committee may, with the approval of the Treasury Board,

(a) engage a secretary and such other staff as it requires; and

(b) fix and pay the remuneration and expenses of persons engaged pursuant to paragraph (a).

Compliance with security requirements

27. Every member of the Review Committee and every person engaged by it shall comply with all security requirements applicable by or under this Act to an employee and shall take the oath of secrecy set out in the schedule.

Functions of Review Committee

28. The functions of the Review Committee are

(a) to review generally the performance by the Agency of its duties and functions and, in connection therewith,

(i) to review the reports of the Director and certificates of the Commissioner transmitted to it pursuant to subsection 23(3),

(ii) to review directions issued by the Minister under subsection 6(2),

(iii) to review arrangements entered into by the Agency pursuant to subsection 15(1) and to monitor the provision of information and intelligence pursuant to those arrangements,

(iv) to review any report or comment given to it pursuant to subsection 18(4), and

(v) to compile and analyse statistics on the operational activities of the Agency;

(b) to arrange for reviews to be conducted, or to conduct reviews, pursuant to section 30; and

(c) to conduct investigations in relation to complaints made to the Review Committee under section 31.

Committee procedures
29. (1) Subject to this Act, the Review Committee may determine the procedure to be followed in the performance of any of its duties or functions.

Access to information
(2) Notwithstanding any other Act of Parliament or any privilege under the law of evidence, but subject to subsection (3), the Review Committee is entitled

(a) to have access to any information under the control of the Agency or of the Commissioner that relates to the performance of the duties and functions of the Committee and to receive from the Commissioner, Director and employees such information, reports and explanations as the Committee deems necessary for the performance of its duties and functions; and

(b) during any investigation referred to in paragraph 28(c), to have access to any information under the control of the deputy head concerned that is relevant to the investigation.

Idem
(3) No information described in subsection (2), other than a confidence of the Queen's Privy Council for Canada in respect of which subsection 39(1) of the *Canada Evidence Act* applies, may be withheld from the Review Committee on any grounds.

Idem

Review
30. For the purpose of ensuring that the activities of the Agency are carried out in accordance with this Act, the regulations and directions issued by the Minister under subsection 6(2) and that the activities do not involve any unreasonable or unnecessary exercise by the Agency of any of its powers, the Review Committee may

(a) direct the Agency or Commissioner to conduct a review of specific activities of the Agency and provide the Committee with a report of the review; or

(b) where it considers that a review by the Agency or the Commissioner would be inappropriate, conduct such a review itself.

Complaints
31. (1) Any Canadian citizen or permanent resident may make a complaint to the Review Committee with respect to any act or thing done by the Agency and the Committee shall, subject to subsection (2), investigate the complaint if

(a) the complainant has made a complaint to the Director with respect to that act or thing and the complainant has not received a response within such period of time as the Committee considers reasonable or is dissatisfied with the response given; and

(b) the Committee is satisfied that the complaint is not trivial, frivolous, vexatious or made in bad faith.

Other redress available
(2) The Review Committee shall not investigate a complaint in respect of which the complainant is entitled to seek redress by means of a grievance procedure established pursuant to this Act or the *Public Service Staff Relations Act.*

Member of Review Committee authorized to act alone
32. A member of the Review Committee may exercise any of the powers or perform any of the duties or functions of the Committee under this Part in relation to complaints.

Complaints submitted on behalf of complainants
33.Nothing in this Act precludes the Review Committee from receiving and investigating complaints described in section 31 that are submitted by a person authorized by the complainant to act on behalf of the complainant, and a reference to a complainant in any other section includes a reference to a person so authorized.

Written complaint
34. A complaint under this Part shall be made to the Review Committee in writing unless the Committee authorizes otherwise.

Investigations

Investigations in private
35. (1) Every investigation of a complaint under this Part by the Review Committee shall be conducted in private.

Right to make representations
(2) In the course of an investigation of a complaint under this Part by the Review Committee, the complainant and the Director shall be given an opportunity to make representations to the Review Committee, to present evidence and to be heard personally or by counsel, but no one is entitled as of right to be present during, to have access to or to comment on representations made to the Review Committee by any other person.

Canadian Human Rights Commission may comment

36. In the course of an investigation of a complaint under this Part, the Review Committee shall, where appropriate, ask the Canadian Human Rights Commission for its opinion or comments with respect to the complaint.

Powers of Review Committee

37. The Review Committee has, in relation to the investigation of any complaint under this Part, power

(a) to summon and enforce the appearance of persons before the Committee and to compel them to give oral or written evidence on oath and to produce such documents and things as the Committee deems requisite to the full investigation and consideration of the complaint in the same manner and to the same extent as a superior court of record;

(b) to administer oaths; and

(c) to receive and accept such evidence and other information, whether on oath or by affidavit or otherwise, as the Committee sees fit, whether or not that evidence or information is or would be admissible in a court of law.

Evidence in other proceedings

38. Except in a prosecution of a person for an offence under section 132 of the Criminal Code (perjury) in respect of a statement made under this Act, evidence given by a person in proceedings under this Part and evidence of the existence of the proceedings are inadmissible against that person in a court or in any other proceedings.

Report of findings

39. The Review Committee shall,

(a) on completion of an investigation in relation to a complaint under section 31, provide the Minister and the Director with a report containing the findings of the investigation and any recommendations that the Committee considers appropriate; and

(b) at the same time as or after a report is provided pursuant to paragraph (a), report the findings of the investigation to the complainant and may, if it thinks fit, report to the complainant any recommendations referred to in that paragraph.

Reports
Annual reports
40. The Review Committee shall, not later than September 30 in each fiscal year, submit to the Minister a report of the activities of the Review Committee during the preceding fiscal year and the Minister shall cause the report to be laid before each House of Parliament on any of the first fifteen days on which that House is sitting after the day the Minister receives it.

Special reports
41. The Review Committee may, on request by the Minister or at any other time, furnish the Minister with a special report concerning any matter that relates to the performance of its duties and functions.

Protection of confidential information
42. The Review Committee shall consult with the Director in order to ensure compliance with section 27 in preparing a report under paragraph 39(b) or section 40.

Part 3

Review by Parliament

Review of Act after five years
43. (1) Five years after this Act comes into force, a comprehensive review of the provisions and operation of the Act shall be undertaken by such committee of the House of Commons or of both Houses of Parliament as may be designated or established by Parliament for that purpose.

Report to Parliament
(2) The committee referred to in subsection (1) shall, within a year after a review is undertaken pursuant to that subsection or within such further time

as Parliament may authorize, submit a report on the review to Parliament including a statement of any changes the committee recommends.

Schedule
(Section 10)

Oath of Office

I, _____, swear that I will faithfully and impartially to the best of my abilities perform the duties required of me as (the Director, an employee) of the Canadian Foreign Intelligence Agency. So help me God.

Oath of Secrecy

I, _____, swear that I will not, without due authority, disclose or make known to any person any information acquired by me by reason of the duties performed by me on behalf of or under the direction of the Canadian Foreign Intelligence Agency or by reason of any office or employment held by me pursuant to the Canadian Foreign Intelligence Agency Act. So help me God. (Source: Government of Canada)

(This is not the official version.)

ABOUT THE AUTHORS

Dwight Hamilton is a former member of Canadian military intelligence. He worked at *Influence* and *Toronto Life* magazines before beginning to write for the *Toronto Sun* and the *Financial Post Magazine*. He has been a staff editor at two of Canada's largest professional journals, has served on the board of directors of the Canadian Society of Magazine Editors, and his work has appeared in over a dozen publications in the last twenty years. He is a graduate of Trinity College School, OCAD University, the University of Toronto (international relations), and Ryerson University (journalism).

Kostas Rimsa served for many years as an officer in Canadian military intelligence and once instructed a program on international terrorism at Humber College in Toronto. He is a graduate of Ottawa's Ashbury College as well as the University of Toronto. He worked in a variety of roles in the former Soviet Union for over a decade, teaching crisis management and assisting in the formation of Lithuania's new secret service.

John Thompson is president of the Mackenzie Institute, a think-tank that researches political instability and terrorism. He was in the Canadian military from 1977 to 1990. During his military career, he once served a three-year appointment as an intelligence officer. Thompson has testified to committees of both the U.S. Congress and Canadian Parliament on national security.

Robert Matas is a national correspondent with the *Globe and Mail*. He has been a bureau chief, political writer, investigative reporter, columnist, and beat reporter for the paper since 1980. Based in Vancouver, he is the only journalist to have reported on the Air India trials of both Inderjit Reyat in 1990–91 and Bagri and Malik in 2003–05.

INDEX

INDEX

ALSO FROM DWIGHT HAMILTON AND KOSTAS RIMSA

Terror Threat
International and Homegrown Terrorists and Their Threat to Canada
978-1550027365 / $35.00, £17.50

The discovery of a suspected homegrown Islamic terrorist cell in our own backyard last year shocked most Canadians. The question arose: Is this country the next on al Qaeda's hit list? But although terrorism in Canada did not begin with al Qaeda, its fundamental dynamics are as unfamiliar to most of the public as the minutiae of quantum physics.

How could such shocking developments happen in a nation of "peacekeepers" that opposed the American intervention in Iraq? The majority of Canadians have no idea why soldiers are presently sacrificing their lives in Afghanistan. *Terror Threat* provides an examination of every key facet of current terrorist operation affecting this country — and it does so in a way that shows how serious the danger really is. Who are these people? How do they operate? And why in the world are they trying to kill us?

Available at your favourite bookseller.

 **DUNDURN**
www.dundurn.com

What did you think of this book?
Visit www.dundurn.com for reviews, videos, updates, and more!